T0330146

Fact and Fantasy about Leadership

NEW HORIZONS IN LEADERSHIP STUDIES

Series Editor: Joanne B. Ciulla, *Professor and Coston Family Chair in Leadership and Ethics, Jepson School of Leadership Studies, University of Richmond, USA*

This important series is designed to make a significant contribution to the development of leadership studies. This field has expanded dramatically in recent years and the series provides an invaluable forum for the publication of high quality works of scholarship and shows the diversity of leadership issues and practices around the world.

The main emphasis of the series is on the development and application of new and original ideas in leadership studies. It pays particular attention to leadership in business, economics and public policy and incorporates the wide range of disciplines that are now part of the field. Global in its approach, it includes some of the best theoretical and empirical work with contributions to fundamental principles, rigorous evaluations of existing concepts and competing theories, historical surveys and future visions.

Titles in the series include:

Fact and Fantasy about Leadership

Micha Popper
University of Haifa, Israel

NEW HORIZONS IN LEADERSHIP STUDIES

Edward Elgar
Cheltenham, UK • Northampton, MA, USA

Published by
Edward Elgar Publishing Limited
The Lypiatts
15 Lansdown Road
Cheltenham
Glos GL50 2JA
UK

Edward Elgar Publishing, Inc.
William Pratt House
9 Dewey Court
Northampton
Massachusetts 01060
USA

A catalogue record for this book
is available from the British Library

Library of Congress Control Number: 2011942550

ISBN 978 0 85793 614 1 (cased)

Typeset by Cambrian Typesetters, Frimley, Surrey
Printed and bound by MPG Books Group, UK

To the children in my family: Guy, Leor, Eitan, Itamar, Yahli, Roi, Gali

May you take pleasure in magic and fantasy, but learn to distinguish between fantasy and falsehood

Contents

Acknowledgements

Writing a book is not the kind of work that ends at a certain time of the day. As the writer becomes more involved in the subjects of his (or her) book they become more like companions to him. Thus, at least in my experience (and as testified by other authors) the writer may find himself 'talking with his topics' while driving, eating, watching TV and even while conversing with other people. Briefly he may easily become intolerable to those around him. Therefore I want first of all to thank my family for being so patient with me while I was totally absorbed in writing.

I also wish to thank wholeheartedly the people who read complete or partial drafts of the manuscript or subjected themselves to interrogation concerning parts of the book. Thanks are due to my sister Naomi for separating the wheat from the chaff, and to my close friends Buzzy and Gingie, Gali Raz, Karin Amit, Gadi Amir, Eliav Zakai, Elly Hilman and Noa Viener – all of them friends and partners in various leadership projects.

I am grateful to some 'normal members of society' who are neither leadership scholars nor are they involved in the subject in any way, yet they patiently suffered my annoying behaviour while I was writing the book (abroad on a sabbatical) and volunteered – out of interest or politeness – to read drafts of the manuscript. At all events their remarks, based on personal experience of leadership or on common sense, were extremely helpful. Thank you, Dan Gelbart, Geoffrey Druker, Amichai Gilad and Yakov Shteif.

Naturally I was influenced not only by the people I spoke with but also by the ideas and research of other writers, as indicated by the many references in the book to various sources. But there are some writers who had more impact on the basic approach, on the core ideas, and I feel the need to thank these writers separately. Barry Schwartz's books on Lincoln and Washington opened my eyes to the centrality of psychosociological processes in constructing leadership concepts. Reading Schwartz's book on Lincoln was in fact the first stimulus that led me to jot down ideas that reached fruition some years later. Ian Kershaw's books on Hitler and James MacGregor Burns's book on leadership helped to deepen my understanding of the psychology of followers – the cornerstone of this book. Anita Shapira's works on identity helped me a great deal in clarifying starting positions from which to address this complex subject with its abundant psychological literature. In particular I was impressed by the works of the social psychologists Boas Shamir, Hazel Markus and Steve Heine, and the sociologists Emile Durkheim, Charles Lindholm and Herbert Blumer. In addition, I was profoundly impressed by the work of Manfred Kets de Vries and Vamik Volkan, dealing with unconscious processes that are relevant to followers' attraction to leaders.

Focusing on the psychology of followers, the book features some well-known historical examples to illustrate various theories and arguments. However, it is not restricted to famous cases but also deals with leadership in everyday life – in organizations, in communities, in daily social contexts. Here I found the conceptualizations of Henry Mintzberg and Karl Weick most helpful. In the sphere of leadership in organizations, one cannot but be influenced by the monumental work of Bernard Bass and his diligent and prolific student Bruce Avolio. To all of these I am eternally grateful.

And finally, special thanks to Hazel Arieli, the editor and translator of all my books and a large part of my other academic works. Hazel has worked with me for many years and the phrase 'my right hand' is an understatement. I can't imagine what it would be like to work without her. Thank you.

Introduction

> The difficulty lies not so much in developing new ideas as in escaping
> from old ones.
> (John Maynard Keynes)

Like the memory of most first experiences, I remember clearly the first conference I attended at the beginning of my academic career. Scholars from all over
the world attended the conference but what made it special for me was my
meeting with a person who was affectionately called by the participants 'the
wise chief'. He was indeed the oldest of the participants and worthy of the
title. It is hard to describe how all the people (usually a highly critical and
disputatious audience) hung on his every word. Every time he opened his
mouth to speak the room fell silent and there was a rare feeling that his words
were not mere displays of erudition but expressed insights beyond what is
found in scholarly journals. 'Words of truth are recognized', to quote ancient
sources.

As we were standing together in line to receive our conference folders, he
suggested that we have lunch together. During the meal we discovered several
converging lines in our family histories. And on this background of shared
associations we found ourselves, an 80-year-old man 15 years after his retirement from the highest peaks of an academic career, and one who was just
beginning his academic career, strolling together daily along the beautiful
wooded paths and talking for hours like father and son, like mentor and
student. This man was a success story in the academic world. His books were
considered mandatory reading in his field and his articles were quoted extensively. But the most interesting point in this story, the memory of which came
back to me a few years ago, was the fact of what happened after his retirement.
A few years after retiring he published a series of articles and lectures attacking the foundations of his own work. 'How is it that you didn't see these things
for so many years?' I asked him wonderingly. He spent hours explaining to me
that he had been locked in a paradigm, that he lacked reflective ability, adding
similar expressions of self-criticism that seemed to me at the time inexplicable and exaggerated. Lacking experience, I could not fathom the meaning that
he gave to the process: 'I was so busy achieving tenure [based on publications]
and then on establishing my career, and later defending the theories that had

made me famous, that I was unable to deviate from my chosen path. You simply excel in what you know how to do,' he said.

It was only years after his retirement, when he was free of the 'rules of the game' as he called it, and had begun to read other literature than the kind he had read for scores of years and started 'to listen, not just to hear', especially to listen to people from other disciplines, that he arrived at different conclusions, of which he said, 'I never meant to reach them.'

I cite this story at the beginning of my book because it is only in the last few years that I have begun to comprehend the process that that man underwent and to understand fully the meaning of the expression 'locked in a paradigm'. Many years after those talks we had I now truly understand his words and the feelings that he spoke about.

This book, too, is the outcome of personal maturation, not just at the level of knowledge but mainly growth of the ability, both emotional and intellectual, to diverge from the research path that I have followed for many years. I have published numerous studies and written some books on leadership. Anyone who has read my works will see that in this book I diverge from some of the arguments I have proposed in previous works, but now, in light of the above anecdote, I understand how that can happen.

Leadership is a phenomenon that fascinates many people. Anyone who reads the abundant material written on leadership in various disciplines will easily identify the fundamental issue that was so aptly phrased by Warren Bennis (1997) who has been researching leadership for many years: the question as to 'whether leaders are larger-than-life figures – heroes…, or embodiments of forces greater than themselves' (p. 22).[1] Indeed the question as to the place and weight of personality versus the weight of circumstances is everpresent. A review of the relevant literature indicates that most writers focus on the leader and his or her influence,[2] a bias that is already found in the Old Testament with its numerous stories of leaders, as well as in the writings of ancient philosophers who attempted to examine the leadership phenomenon more systematically.[3] Beyond the specific questions posed by these philosophers, questions such as who is worthy to be a leader, the question that most occupied them was why and how leaders influence people. Over the years I have reached the insight that this is not the cardinal question.

In my recent books I argued that the leadership phenomenon cannot be understood by focusing only on leaders and their personality. On the other hand, focusing on the circumstances while ignoring the leaders themselves, as reflected in the works of philosophers and sociologists like Karl Marx, is no less misleading. Instead of a dichotomous solution, I argued, we can visualize leadership as fire – a metaphor borrowed from the researchers Katherine Klein and Robert House,[4] fire that is fed by three components: fuel (the followers), oxygen (the environmental context) and the spark (the leader). The combination of these three components can explain the leadership pattern. I am still convinced of this. But like most scholars, I used to begin the analysis with the spark – the leader. In this sense I was locked in the biases typical of most people, including leadership scholars – the bias of exaggerating the weight of the leader's influence, particularly in the case of political leaders. Although all the components of leadership were included in the analysis (leader, followers and circumstances), the angle of vision created a different composition of the scenery, just as a valley viewed from the top of a cliff and the same cliff viewed from deep inside the valley create two different landscapes although the area is exactly the same. What became clear to me in the course of time was the recognition that the analysis should begin with the followers (especially when it comes to political leadership). In other words, many of the questions that I address in this book and have dealt with in the past appear to be similar and yield similar answers. I even cite a few examples of leaders whom I have discussed in previous books, but the analysis is different. In this sense I return more emphatically to the point of departure of the German sociologist Max Weber, who claimed that charisma is not a trait possessed by a leader but a characteristic perceived by the viewer.[5] Accordingly, as will be widely discussed in Chapters 2 and 3, a leader may be charismatic to one group of people and totally lacking in charisma to another group. He or she can be admired at a certain point in time and later on be forgotten.[6]

Weber's statement is important in that it illustrates a major social phenomenon, but he did not address the psychological question as to why people wrap a certain person in the robe of charisma and why they divest him or her of it. We can point to such examples, but the psychological laws underlying these questions have yet to be probed in depth.

These questions are addressed in the book, which is both a psychological and a historical work in the sense that it identifies (in the first part) myths concerning political leaders and analyses the process of their mythicization. The basic assumption is that myths do not appear by chance; there is a psychological law underlying their creation.[7] This book seeks to identify the psychological laws concerning a specific type of myth – leadership myths. In this context the book deals with aspects that were not examined by Max Weber and his followers, namely characterization and analysis of the psychological processes by which leadership myths are created.

Almost every discussion on leaders involves expressions like charisma, vision, trust, hope, faith, values and commitment, keywords that are often voiced at graduation ceremonies of officers' courses, leadership courses in schools of management, and also in descriptions of historical leaders. On the face of it we may infer that 'leadership is leadership is leadership'. Its characteristics are universal and are not confined to situational, cultural or task-related contexts. Political leadership and leadership in everyday life, in commercial, military and social organizations, sports teams and social groups, all are similar in essence. Is this really so? Can the admired commander of a military unit be the successful leader of a nation? Can a person who attains political leadership through elections also succeed in the task of political leader? Will a political leader who has proven successful in the test of history necessarily be perceived as charismatic? These questions are clouded by the bias of focusing on leaders (the psychological source of which will be discussed later), but the fact is that we use similar adjectives to describe leaders in all contexts. Looking at these issues from the followers' angle of vision may sharpen the distinction between leadership emergence (e.g., success in elections) and the leader's successful functioning in this role, and also highlight the differences between political leadership and leadership in everyday life – in organizations and communities. In these senses an understanding of the psychology of the followers may lead to clearer insights than those yielded by theories and research on leaders.

Furthermore, analysis of leadership from the point of departure of the followers is more promising in terms of research. With regard to quantitative studies this claim requires no explanation. Samples of followers are always larger than samples of leaders; hence the ability to generalize is greater. But studies of a more qualitative character can also be more firmly grounded. There are, indeed, many definitions of leadership, but as the famous leadership scholar Bernard Bass[8] remarked, there is no disputing the fact that a leader is a person who has followers. Therefore, it is only natural to seek to identify the psychological characteristics of a certain population that is influenced exclusively by one particular leader, or to ask why communities are influenced by a specific leader during a certain period and reject that same leader during a different period. The cardinal question, then, is not why leaders influence people but why followers are influenced by them.

A universal characteristic that often serves as a psychological explanation for the attraction to leaders who are perceived as strong and giving a sense of security, particularly in crisis situations,[9] is the craving for security. But beyond this, the psychology of followers in respect to choice of leaders and compliance with leaders in quiet times when there is no urgent sense of existential crisis is culturally biased.[10] That is a major assumption underlying this book, but it is not a simple assumption. It calls for explanation because *culture*, and particularly *intercultural differences*, is among the most discussed and researched subject in all the social sciences.[11] Global conflicts are explained by the 'clash of civilizations'.[12] International corporations attempt to decipher the psychological meanings involved in multicultural management.[13] Failure in wars or military campaigns such as the war in Vietnam are analysed in terms of (in)ability to understand the local culture.[14] The same issue occupies captains and field commanders patrolling towns and villages in countries that are culturally alien to them.

Dealing with the psychology of leadership, this book cannot avoid addressing the cultural aspect, particularly when elaborating on the leadership phenomenon from the viewpoint of the followers. The American culture scholar Harry Triandis cites an example in which an American manager serving in a managerial role in a branch of his company in Greece asks a Greek employee how long he thinks it will take to complete a task that he has been assigned. The employee wonders at the question. 'He's the boss. Why doesn't he tell me how long I have to perform the task?'[15] In fact, many intercultural comparative studies have shown that without understanding of the cultural context, namely the mentality of the followers in a certain culture, it is impossible to understand the leaders' influence. There is abundant evidence of this in the sphere of leadership in organizations. Comparative studies dealing with the connection between leadership, job satisfaction and worker productivity showed that French employees were more satisfied and more productive when they perceived their manager as a paternalistic, authoritarian leader who gave clear instructions. On the other hand, British and German employees were at their best when their superiors' approach was democratic and consultative. Indian employees were at their best with a manager who was a kind of 'big brother', while Peruvian employees preferred managers who closely followed every detail.[16]

A simple proof of the existence of culture-bound leadership concepts was presented by the Swedish scholar Ingrid Tollgerdt-Andersson, who analysed 1400 job offers of leadership roles advertised in newspapers. She found that the requirements – ability to cooperate, social skills and interpersonal abilities – appeared in 80 per cent of the advertisements in Sweden, Denmark and Norway, while these requirements were mentioned much less (less than 50 per cent) in Italy and Spain.[17] As the Dutch scholar Geert Hofstede remarked:

> Beliefs regarding leaders represent a dominant cultural part of a society or a given country. Asking people's opinions regarding the qualities of good leaders is like describing their culture. The leader is a culture hero in the sense that he constitutes a role model.[18]

The reader of such comparative studies may indeed wonder whether there are universal elements in leadership. It appears that culture is a kind of genetic code that is universally recognized as important but it lacks the substantiality that permits biologists, for example, to study it.

The result of this is a confusing variety of definitions, methods, articles and studies on culture. I was aware of the danger that I might 'succeed' in adding some more interesting questions and perhaps even a new classification, but that, I felt, would be just 'more of the same'.

Generally speaking, returning later to questions that one addressed when younger, now more equipped with academic knowledge and experience, and especially with less defensive criticism and more integrative ability, may do more than improve one's analytic ability. It also provides a better prospect of minimizing the danger referred to by the British philosopher Isaiah Berlin, the sometimes-obsessive tendency of academics to want above all to say things that are interesting in themselves. It seems to me that experience can help to moderate the sometimes hasty tendency to familiarize oneself only with the patterns and regularity of phenomena. No less important, in my opinion, is clarity – a criterion that is not always in the forefront of academic writing and therefore tends to be discussed in closed clubs of academics who specialize in very narrow and specific corners of a phenomenon, when in fact a broader view is vital for understanding its nature.

I hope that my analyses will stimulate interest and thought among broad circles (and not because they are provocative). Therefore it is important to me at this early stage to explain the rationale and the boundaries of concepts such as culture and identity, which I use in some parts of the book. Despite the extensive literature on these concepts it seems to me that there is still a need for conceptual 'cleaning'. This is important for our purposes here because these concepts are essential for the discussion of what lies at the heart of this book – the psychology of leadership.

Here I should add a few words in connection with my reference to the issues of culture and identity: my entrance into the cultural arena was determined after I had dived deeply into the literature on intercultural research and arrived at the conclusion that the important questions were formulated by the pioneers in this field. The thousands of articles and research reports written in their wake show how we cannot see the forest for the trees. For example, the American scholar Florence Kluckhohn[19] claimed that the basic questions concerning the evolvement of certain cultures concern people's attitudes to each other, to nature, to the supernatural, to activity and to time. Such questions, phrased somewhat differently, were posed by the giants in whose footsteps, to repeat a famous cliché, followed many dwarfs.

I return to this point of departure in order to clarify that the book deals mainly with leadership as a psychological phenomenon and therefore the discussion in it addresses a specific component within the broad discourse on culture. This component is people's relations with others, and more specifically, how they relate to the person who represents authority. Leadership is a certain kind of authority but, as I will show, perceptions of authority are also grounded in cultural patterns; some of these are visible and some are concealed and have to be scrutinized and revealed.[20] In this respect any curious and explorative tourist is a 'naive anthropologist' in the sense that he or she can identify external manifestations of cultural phenomena. This does not mean that they always fully understand the sources of the various ways of relating to aspects of life such as work, time, manner of speech and performance of rituals. But if they are observant and spend enough time in a certain place they can comprehend the law underlying people's behavioural and symbolic expressions in spheres with which they come into contact.

The tension between the view that ascribes universality to human nature and human development (e.g., psychoanalytic thinking), and the more contextual culture-bound view has occupied many prominent researchers.[21] According to my experience and observations there is no simple solution to this tension, and when it comes to analysing specific cultural phenomena a process of elimination and well-grounded choice of variables is required. How is this elimination achieved and by what methodology?

In a book that I wrote a few years ago[22] I presented a simulation developed by a colleague of mine and used in the IDF (Israel Defense Forces) Staff and Command College. The simulation demonstrated aspects that affect evaluation of decisions.[23] The subjects, officers participating in a course at the level of major and lieutenant colonel, were given a written description of an incident, beginning as follows: 'You are a battalion commander in the area of the border fence in the north of the country. In a briefing with the brigade commander you were told not to move from your post or deploy forces in case of any incident without the permission of the brigade commander.' This was the background. Then the incident was described, along with four different possible decisions, which the officers were asked to evaluate:

1. You received an alert from the border fence that the fence had been breached and a terrorist cell had apparently infiltrated. You tried to contact the brigade commander but could not find him, so you decided to take the soldiers and you went out with them to the border fence. You did not encounter any terrorists. After a few hours you returned to the outpost and nothing happened.

2. You received an alert from the border fence that the fence had been breached and a terrorist cell had apparently infiltrated. You called the brigade commander but could not find him, so you decided in these circumstances to search for the terrorists, and you went out, taking some of the soldiers with you. During your absence a terrorist cell attacked the outpost and some soldiers were wounded.

3. You received an alert from the border fence that the fence had been breached and a terrorist cell had apparently infiltrated. You called the brigade commander, could not find him, and decided to look for the terrorists with some of the soldiers. After a while you encountered the terrorists and killed them.

4. You received an alert from the border fence that the fence had been breached and a terrorist cell had apparently infiltrated. You called the brigade commander and could not find him. You decided to stay in the outpost, according to the instructions of the commander.

The participants were instructed to act as a committee that had to rate each of the four decisions in the circumstances described. The highest score was given to decision 3, where the commander left the outpost, contravening his superior's orders, but succeeded in killing the terrorists. The lowest score was given to decision 2, where the commander went out to search for the terrorists, but while he was away the terrorists attacked the outpost.

The analysis of the simulation demonstrated some important principles; the main one is known in army slang as *either a medal or corporal* (meaning [not literally] commendation or demotion). In other words, the final result determines the quality of the decision. The 'best' decision, the one that received the highest score, was the decision to go out and kill the terrorists. It was the best because it succeeded. The 'worst' decision was to leave the outpost, which was then attacked and soldiers were wounded. But it was exactly *the same decision*. The only difference between the two was the result, success or failure. And in this case, success or failure was almost certainly a matter of luck, nothing else. The main points that arose in the discussion concerned different aspects of judgement and evaluation of decisions, the tendency to ignore inputs and processes, the halo effect of the 'bottom line', and other implications relevant to processes of inference and learning.

The interesting and important point for the present discussion, the point that led me to repeat this story here, arose by chance at a conference in the USA attended by American army officers. In one of the sessions I told this story. To my surprise, the officers, highly intelligent and serious people, completely failed to understand the outpost commander's dilemma. 'Why did he hesitate?', they wondered. 'What, don't you see that there is a serious operational dilemma here?', I asked. 'No,' said the officers decisively. 'The officer received an order not to leave the post. Orders are orders, none of us would hesitate.'

This incident demonstrated two points to me: (1) that intercultural differences are manifested in relation to specific subjects. The attitude to authority is one of the features that most clearly reflect intercultural differences (as supported by research findings),[24] and (2) that situations of dilemma have great focusing power. They accentuate salient dimensions of people's identity.

Identity is a term widely used by anthropologists, psychologists, historians and social scientists. All of them understand that it is important and essential but, as Erik Erikson, a psychologist who is strongly associated with the study of identities, remarked, this concept is all-pervasive.[25] In situations that call for decision-making it is necessary for people to determine priorities in their hierarchy of identities. In this way identity becomes a concept that is more dynamic and at the same time more operative, and even provides an empirical response to the tension between the universal and the context-bound. The American anthropologist Melford Spiro, who has dealt extensively with these subjects, demonstrates in a series of articles and studies how it is possible to give a conceptual and empirical response to this theoretical tension.[26] In a study that he conducted among Israeli kibbutz children in the 1950s[27] he investigated the tension between what he considered to be universal human tendencies such as achievement orientation, and cultural influences based on the kibbutz ideology, such as the welfare of the collective as a primary concern, cooperation and sharing. Success in internalizing these values can, of course, counteract the tendencies that Spiro referred to as universal, and can also reveal the dominant weight of the cultural environment in shaping identities. However, even at the point in time when the research was conducted, during a period when the ideology of partnership was politically correct, Spiro did not find great success in their internalization of cooperative values. Nevertheless he balanced the tension with the argument that although children tend to be competitive and possessive, kibbutz children, whose socialization includes internalization of cooperative values, when faced with conflicting choices will decide in favour of the values they have absorbed from their culture. Self-concept and self-worth are concepts used by social psychologists for predicting people's decisions in such situations. After all, some will argue, people want to see themselves in a positive light, and this positive light is influenced by the sociocultural environment.[28] Therefore the approach that I have adopted here is conceptually clear and also has methodological advantages, the approach according to which identity has a *hierarchy of salience.*[29]

Samuel Huntington, a historian from Harvard, in the introduction to his book on identities,[30] demonstrates this simply with the story of Rachel Newman, which was published in *Newsweek* after the collapse of the Twin Towers on 11 September 2001. She reported:

> When I was 19 I moved to New York City. If you asked me to describe myself then, I would have told you I was a musician, a poet, an artist, and, on some political level, a woman, a lesbian, and a Jew. Being an American wouldn't have made my list. In my college class my girlfriend and I were so frustrated by inequality in America that we discussed moving to another country. On September 11 all that changed. I realized that I had been taking the freedom I have here for granted. Now I have an American flag on my backpack, I cheer at the fighter jets as they pass overhead and I am calling myself a patriot.[31]

This example shows how a dramatic event brought to the surface a certain identity and made it most salient in the hierarchy of identities. This is also what certain leaders, most noticeably political leaders, can do to followers. But the example points to a latent aspect; there is no creation here of a new identity. The elements that connect socialization, culture and values – the prototypical schemas – are the concepts that lie concealed in a 'heap'. Dramatic events, dilemmas or leaders are the catalysts that can raise to the surface and accentuate identities from the heap. Analysis from the followers' angle of vision may pinpoint not only these raw materials but also the psychological processes occurring in the followers when such catalyzation is created. Only from the followers' angle of vision is it possible to analyse questions such as how it came about that Abraham Lincoln, who barely won the presidential election and was a source of contention and disliked by wide circles during his presidency, became the most revered president in American history, or why Winston Churchill, Britain's great leader during World War II, was not elected prime minister after the war. How is it that Andrew Jackson, who was seen as the embodiment of charisma, became in the course of years relatively marginal in the collective memory? These are examples of the questions that will be discussed and analysed on the theoretical level relating to the psychological processes that are more relevant to the choice of political leaders. But is the psychology of followers that is relevant to the choice of political leaders equally relevant or similar to the followers' response to military or business leaders, or to leaders in social organizations? Does meteoric success in managing an industrial corporation increase the probability of success in political leadership, or is there perhaps no connection between the different types of demands? There have been many cases when leaders who moved to politics from various organizations were less than successful due to their internalization of operational norms, which obstructed their ability to see ideological visions and abstract aspects that require a philosophical and historical view. And vice versa, perhaps for this reason Winston Churchill's military leadership is held in question, especially his functioning as a regimental commander in the interval between his political roles, while his leadership as a statesman is revered.[32] Or could it be that different predispositions and a different psychological profile distinguish between managers and leaders? These are some of the questions that will be addressed in this book, questions that have not hitherto been examined in depth from the point of view of the followers.

The title of the book was chosen after some reflection. The phrase 'fact and fantasy' carries a hint of elusiveness, a characteristic that is mentioned in many articles and books on leadership. Charles Lindholm likened leadership to love – two phenomena much observed and discussed although we do not succeed in understanding them fully.[33] 'Leadership is one of the most observed and least understood phenomena on earth,' wrote James MacGregor Burns.[34] As for me, I would not have spent days and nights in the attempt to write a book that arrived at the same familiar conclusion, first because it has been said many times before, and second because it is worthwhile trying to advance our understanding of this important phenomenon. The attempt to characterize fact and fantasy with regard to leadership, and to analyse this from the followers' point of view at different angles can help to lessen the elusiveness of the phenomenon. True, the need (and the potential) for analysing followership was already highlighted more than 30 years ago by James MacGregor Burns, one of the most influential leadership scholars, who wrote that 'one of the most serious failures in the study of leadership has been the bifurcation between the literature on leadership and the literature on followership'.[35] Since then, some work has been done on followership,[36] but most writings have discussed followership either as an independent subject, such as studies on obedience,[37] or as a subject to be explored in organizational settings. These works have dealt with aspects such as 'followership styles' or 'effective followership',[38] rather than with conceptual and psychological issues relating followership to leadership. In that respect, this book is a delayed attempt to address the imperative raised by Burns 30 years ago.

In this context, I want to make it clear that the word fantasy here is not used in the sense of illusion, but rather in the sense of imaginative conceptualization. I originally considered using the word myth in the title, but that word appears frequently in the context of shattering myths, and this book is not concerned with shattering myths about leadership. On the contrary, the basic assumption is that myths, and certainly myths about leadership, do not spring from nowhere. In this book I attempt to deal with what the myths scholar Robert Segal defined as the most important questions to be asked regarding myths, stories and fantasies: how they are created, why they survive and how they survive.[39]

Moreover some myths, fantasies and stories survive and some disappear. Some survive for generations and fill a need that is more fundamental or more powerful. This is an interesting point with regard to leaders, a point that can only be examined in terms of collective memory. Such an analysis naturally deflects the discussion from the leaders themselves to those who remember them directly – generational memory. But, as we know, there are leaders who become myths for generations; they become objects of intergenerational memory. So which myths survive beyond one generation and which are forgotten, and why?

The notions of fantasy and myth are quite closely related, but fantasy emphasizes the story element more. Leadership is discussed in this book from various psychological angles, one of which is the view of the leader as a story. The story may be entirely true, or partly true, but in the end it acquires a life of its own and becomes what the French sociologist Emile Durkheim called a 'social fact',[40] meaning knowledge that influences the manner of thinking and modes of behaviour of many people.

Looking at leadership as a story emphasizes the sociopsychological aspect, because a story by its very nature is either narrated in social settings or written for wider audiences. In this respect the book also deals with the more specific question: are there leadership stories that are unique to a certain public (namely, a public with shared characteristics such as ethnic groups or nations)?

Is Ataturk a leadership story that speaks only to the Turkish nation? Is John Kennedy a typical American story? Is Lee Kuan Yew the story of Singapore? And if so, is it important to understand why? Clearly, this arouses further speculation. Are there leadership stories that cross borders (and generations)? If there are, what distinguishes them from 'local stories'? The book includes examples of leaders who are perceived as distinctly local stories and of leaders who are universal stories, while attempting to clarify in psychological terms what distinguishes between the two types.

Fantasies are not created in a vacuum but emerge from diverse psychological sources. In the case of direct leaders in the workplace, in military units or in social systems, where the followers can see and meet the leader, they can form impressions of him or her directly, leaving less scope for the imagination to create fantasies. In many cases however, certainly in cases of political leadership, the leader is a person whom one hears about from others or reads about in newspapers or books, or sees on television, mostly in predetermined or selective settings. This is a process of *mediation*. The different kinds of 'storytellers' about leaders include journalists, historians, researchers, educators, teachers or publicity agents in various social networks (including electronic networks). Thus many people may be involved in the creation of fantasies, all of them with their own biases, agendas, beliefs and perhaps interests to promote.

The book touches on this aspect of the creation of a fantasy, using examples of outstanding images of leaders created by prominent scholars, journalists and shapers of public opinion. The foundations and characteristics of this process are also analysed in the book. However, I want to emphasize that despite the extension of the analysis in these directions, it is not a postmodern analysis of the kind that assumes, to put it simplistically, that there is no truth and everything is relative. The discussion and analysis of leaders, contexts and fantasies is followed by an attempt to understand the 'big picture', which might be likened to a map. The book ventures to provide what is metaphorically needed for identification of the coordination lines that can help to understand the map and navigate by it. In this specific area – the psychology of followership – such reading is of the utmost importance, because followers are those who choose the leader, followers can decide how far to comply with the leader. Followers in many cases also determine the success of the leader. In fact, as previously mentioned, the most basic definition of leadership is that a leader is someone who has followers. The theoretical meaning of this is that the real leadership theory is simply followership theory. As a believer in Kurt Lewin's well-known saying[41] that nothing is more practical than a good theory, I believe that development of a good theory on followership can bring about the improvement of leadership in the basic sense of improving the ability to make more educated decisions in the space between choice of leaders and obedience to them. Thus, beyond the deep-seated desire shared by most researchers to arouse interest and thought, my motivation for writing this book was spurred by the wish to create a type of knowledge that is also meaningful for decision-making and action. I would also like to think that understanding the psychology of followership may help to reduce our tendency to overlook the power of ourselves as followers.

NOTES

1. Bennis, Warren (1997), *Managing People is Like Herding Cats*, Provo, UT: Executive Excellence Publishing.
2. Bass, Bernard M. (2008), *The Bass Handbook of Leadership* (4th edition), New York: Free Press. Bass's book is considered the most comprehensive encyclopaedic survey of leadership research, particularly of psychological studies on leadership.
3. See, for example, basic issues concerning the personality, role and training of leaders in the works of Plato. See also Thomas Carlyle's influential work on hero worship; Plato (1973), *The Collected Dialogues of Plato*, Princeton, NJ: Princeton University Press; Carlyle, Thomas ([1841] 1907), *On Heroes, Hero-Worship, and the Heroic in History*, Boston: Houghton-Mifflin.
4. Klein, Katherine and Robert House (1995), 'On fire: Charismatic leadership and levels of analysis', *Leadership Quarterly*, **6** (2), 183–98.
5. Weber, Max ([1924] 1947), *The Theory of Social and Economic Organization* (trans. T. Parsons), New York: Free Press.
6. For illustrative examples see Shapira, Anita (1997a), *Yehudim Hadashim, Yehudim Yeshanim* [*New Jews, Old Jews*], Tel Aviv: Sifriat Ofakim and Am Oved Publications [Hebrew], p. 294.
7. Segal, Robert (2004), *Myth, A Very Short Introduction*, Oxford: Oxford University Press.
8. Bass, Bernard M. (1985), *Leadership and Performance Beyond Expectations*, New York: Free Press.
9. Pillai, Rajnandini (1996), 'Crisis and the emergence of charismatic leadership in groups: An experimental investigation', *Journal of Applied Social Psychology*, **26** (6), 543–62.
10. Popper, Micha (2001), *Hypnotic Leadership: Leaders, Followers and the Loss of Self*, Westport, CT: Praeger.
11. Den Hartog, Deanne N., R.J. House, P.J. Hanges, S.A. Ruiz-Quintanilla and P.W. Dorfman (1999), 'Culture specific and cross-culturally generalizable implicit leadership theories: Are alternatives of charismatic/transformational leadership universally endorsed?', *Leadership Quarterly*, **10** (2), 219–57; Dorfman, Peter W. (1996), 'International and cross-cultural leadership research', in Betty J. Punnett and O. Shenkar (eds), *Handbook for International Management Research*, Oxford: Blackwell, pp. 267–349.
12. Huntington, Samuel P. (1998), *The Clash of Civilizations and the Remaking of World Order*, New York: Simon & Schuster.
13. Hofstede, Geert and Jan Hofstede (2005), *Culture and Organizations: The Software of the Mind*, New York: McGraw-Hill.
14. Tuchman, Barbara (1984), *The March of Folly: From Troy to Vietnam*, New York: Knopf.
15. Triandis, Harry C. (1973), 'Culture training, cognitive complexity, and interpersonal attitudes', in D.S. Hoopes (ed.), *Readings in Intercultural Communication*, Pittsburgh, PA: Regional Council for International Education, pp. 55–68.
16. Hofstede, Geert (2001), *Culture's Consequences: Comparing Values, Behaviors, Institutions, and Organizations Across Nations*, Thousand Oaks, CA: Sage Publications.
17. Tollgerdt-Andersson, Ingrid (1996), 'Attitudes, values and demands on leadership. A cultural comparison among some European countries', in P. Joynt and M. Warner (eds), *Managing across Cultures: Issues and Perspectives*, London: Thomson, pp. 166–78.

14   *Fact and fantasy about leadership*

18. Hofstede and Hofstede (2005, p. 268)
19. Kluckhohn, Florence (1950), 'Dominant and substitute profiles of cultural orientations. Their significance for the analysis of social stratification', *Social Forces*, **28** (4), 376–93.
20. Schein, Edgar (1985), *Organizational Culture and Leadership*, San Francisco, CA: Jossey-Bass.
21. Kilborne, Benjamin and L.L. Langness (1987), *Culture and Human Nature: Theoretical Papers of Melford E. Spiro*, Chicago: University of Chicago Press.
22. Popper, Micha (1994), *Al Menahalim Kemanhigim [On Managers as Leaders]*, Tel Aviv: Ramot Publishing House, Tel Aviv University [Hebrew].
23. Lipshitz, Raanan (1991), '"Either a medal or a corporal". The effects of success and failure on the evaluation of decision making and decision makers', *Organizational Behavior and Human Decision Processes*, **44** (3), 380–95.
24. Hofstede and Hofstede (2005).
25. Erikson, Eric (1959), *Identity and the Life Cycle*, Bloomington, IN: Indiana University Press.
26. Spiro, Melford E. (1954), 'Is the family universal?', *American Anthropologist*, **56** (5), 839–46.
27. Spiro, Melford E. (1956), *Kibbutz: Venture in Utopia*, Cambridge, MA: Harvard University Press.
28. Markus, Hazel and Elissa Wurf (1987), 'The dynamic self-concept: A social-psychological perspective', *Annual Review of Psychology*, **38**, 299–337.
29. Shamir, Boas, Robert J. House and Michael B. Arthur (1993), 'The motivational effects of charismatic leadership: A self-concept-based theory', *Organizational Science*, **4** (4), 577–93.
30. Huntington, Samuel P. (2004), *Who Are We? The Challenge to America's National Identity*, New York: Simon & Schuster, p. 4.
31. Newman, Rachel (2001), 'The day the world changed, I did too', *Newsweek*, 1 October, 9.
32. Best, Geoffrey (2001), *Churchill: A Study in Greatness*, London and New York: Hambledon & London.
33. Lindholm, Charles (1988), 'Lovers and leaders', *Social Science Information*, **16**, 227–46.
34. Burns, James MacGregor (1978), *Leadership*, New York: Harper & Row, p. 4.
35. Cited from Riggio, Ronald E., Ira Chaleff and Jean Lipman-Blumen (2008), *The Art of Followership*, San Francisco, CA: Jossey-Bass, p. xii.
36. Kelley, Robert. E. (1992), *The Power of Followership*, New York: Currency/Doubleday. See also Riggio et al. (2008).
37. Milgram, Stanley (1974), *Obedience to Authority: An Experimental Approach*, New York: Harper & Row.
38. Riggio et al. (2008).
39. Segal (2004).
40. Durkheim, Emile (1973), 'The dualism of human nature and its social conditions', in Robert N. Bellah (ed.), *Emile Durkheim on Morality and Society*, Chicago: University of Chicago Press.
41. Lewin, Kurt (1947), 'Frontiers in group dynamics: Concept, method, and reality in social science', *Human Relations*, **1** (4), 5–42.

1. Another book about leadership?

Whither a man wishes to go, there he is led.
(Rashi)

On 24 July 1945 General Carl Spaatz, head of the US Air Force Strategic Command, received an order to use the atomic bomb against Japan, thus fulfilling the recommendation of the Special Committee (comprising the Secretary of State, Defense Secretary, two representatives of universities, two delegates from the Navy and the State Department, and Robert Oppenheimer, director of the Los Alamos National Laboratory) to activate the bomb without warning. On that day President Truman himself, without putting the issue to vote, made one of the cruellest decisions in human history. Yet the term cruel is not associated with Truman's leadership. In retrospect this decision was one of the building blocks in the construction of the myth of Truman as a leader who occupied a place of honour in the pantheon of world leaders.

A look at the life stories of people like Ataturk, David Ben-Gurion, Winston Churchill and George Washington – who were among the most outstanding leaders in history – reveals similar themes; although called by different names such as determination, foresight, decisiveness and ability to convey clear messages, the implied meaning (and it is always implied) is unmistakable. It is the ability to take harsh decisions.

This introduction of the subject may seem provocative to many people, but the bare facts (without the interpretations and their origins, which will be discussed later) are unequivocal. For example, George Washington, one of the few leaders identified as the Fathers of the Nation, described to a British officer how he had dealt with problems of drunkenness, wanton behaviour and soldiers going AWOL when he served as commander of the Virginia Regiment. 'I gave orders to construct a gallows almost 40 feet high and hang two or three of the men as an example to others.' According to the report he slept well on the nights after confirming the execution order even when the condemned man submitted a special appeal to alleviate his punishment on the grounds of courage in battle. Washington set clear limits and nobody who overstepped them was forgiven.[1]

Another founding father, David Ben-Gurion, decided during Israel's War of Independence to launch the Battle of Latrun in order to open the road to Jerusalem, which was under siege. His determination (perhaps his ability to make harsh decisions) was manifested just before the attack on the night of 23–24 May 1948. Senior military personnel pleaded with him not to launch the attack, both because they thought it more important to prepare for battles in other areas and because they estimated (rightly, as it turned out) that the regiment was not ready for battle. It was inadequately equipped and was manned largely by Holocaust survivors who had just arrived in boatloads from the inferno of World War II, lacking all military skills. But Ben-Gurion was adamant. On 25 May the regiment launched an attack that many people later described as slaughter. The accounts of soldiers who had survived the Nazi death camps only to fall in a futile battle without proper training were horrifying.[2] Nevertheless, in the course of time the bitter fiasco of Latrun became a constitutive myth, a fundamental event in the development of the nation. It emphasized the centrality of Jerusalem as a national ethos and symbol, and also glorified Ben-Gurion as a farsighted leader who thought in historical and strategic terms. The military fiasco of Latrun became, as one historian wrote, 'a great heroic epiphany such as occurs during the birth of nations or the historical breakthrough of national liberation movements'.[3]

That is how the national memory worked in the case of George Washington's repeated failures in his wars against the Indians and the French. Not only did these failures not detract from his image as a leader, in some way (which will be discussed later) they also enhanced and constructed his image as a national leader in anticipation of the confrontation with the British.[4]

As mentioned in the introduction to this book, these examples are not cited here for the purpose of myth shattering; they are cited in the psychological context that seeks to understand why certain aspects of leadership are consistently omitted from the leadership story or, to put it differently, why certain aspects of leaders are systematically emphasized by different researchers and writers. The discussion, then, is on the psychology of leadership, namely, the psychology of leaders, of followers, of the relations between followers and leaders and, equally important, the psychology of scholars and writers on leadership, who to a large extent shape the leaders' image in the public eye. Although it is clear for all to see that the perceptions of people who write on leaders are deeply influenced not only by their emotional attitude toward the leaders whom they investigate but also by the cultural codes and symbols of the period, this very important aspect and its implications for research and discussion on leadership are largely neglected.

LEADERS AND RULERS

To illustrate this point, let us take the aspect that I referred to as the ability to take cruel decisions. This ability is described (and even emphasized) in many works relating to two types of leader: (1) leaders from early periods: kings, emperors or military leaders. The literature is full of descriptions of the cruelty of Genghis Khan, Ivan the Terrible, the insane caprices of Roman emperors like Nero and Julius Caesar and the murderous behaviour of kings like Herod, Chinese emperors and kings of England and France, whose grandiose urges led them to erect monuments constructed with the utmost cruelty; and (2) leaders in modern times, such as Stalin, Pol Pot or Saddam Hussein, who were in fact rulers rather than leaders. The people they governed did not elect them and their rule was based on power that intimidated the followers and forced them to obey. The distinction between rulers and leaders has been described by various writers.[5] The German sociologist Max Weber formulated a model that distinguished between the rational-legal authority of an official role bearer (e.g., a general), traditional hereditary authority like that of a royal line, and the charismatic authority of a person whose followers are enchanted by them (charisma means divine gift in Greek) and yearn for them.[6] Most of the psychological discourse and research on leadership focuses on individuals whose followers are amenable to influence, hence the discussion on leadership in modern times concerns the dynamics of amenable *influence* and its sources.[7] In Weber's terms too, it is easy to see the similarity between kings and emperors of earlier periods and figures like Stalin – all of them were rulers. Thus, we may assume that it is easier to attribute cruelty to rulers than to leaders to whom we are drawn in a way similar to romantic love, as described by the American anthropologist Charles Lindholm.[8] It is hard to believe that the objects of one's love are capable of cruel acts. Moreover, in many senses exaggeration of the rulers' cruelty makes it easier to explain the followers' obedience. Perhaps we see here a kind of primitive defence mechanism in the form of a split in which the leader is 'the only bad one in the story' and 'he is so cruel that it is impossible not to obey him' – an argument that was voiced in referring to the inexplicable obedience to Stalin, Hitler or Pol Pot. Evil and cruelty are thus imputed either to an earlier period when other norms prevailed and there were different sources of authority based mainly on rulership, or to certain individuals in modern times who are 'not really leaders' but rulers. Some support for this bias can be found in early writings on leadership. For example, the works of Machiavelli[9] (1469–1527), John Locke (1632–1704)[10] and Jean-Jacques Rousseau (1712–78)[11] deal extensively with the dark side of what was then seen as leadership. Even the writers of the *Federalist Papers* started from the point of view that ascribed considerable weight to the wicked exploitative side of authority, and suggested checks and balances to contain it.[12]

This distinction between leadership and rulership is not only substantive in distinguishing between kings, directors and elected leaders, but also in more mundane senses. Obeying the commander of a military unit for fear of punishment in no way resembles readiness to follow the commander out of trust, identification and admiration. Obedience in the latter case is not motivated by fear of punishment but by the readiness to act in a way that the American leadership scholar Bernard Bass defined as above and beyond the call of duty.[13] The space between obedience that is imposed or 'worthwhile' and willingness for action that is above and beyond is a behavioural distinction that defines the fundamental difference between the influence of rulers and of leaders. Thus managers, officers, instructors or parents may be similar in their authoritarian powers (in Weber's terms) but different in their influence. The sociologist Amitai Etzioni[14] proposed distinctions relevant to this discussion. Obedience relations are those in which compliance is based on fear (in jail, for example). Utilitarian relations are those in which compliance is based on assessment of worthwhileness – give and take relations, such as exist in many business organizations. Normative relations are relations that contain an element of commitment to a value, an idea, a perception or a person. People who are committed to something will invest and act in the area of their involvement although it may require special effort or sacrifice, or even a price that does not seem worthwhile in conventional terms (such as risking one's life). The argument here is that the more the compliance to the leader is based on commitment, the more 'leaderly' the relationship.

A psychological study on leadership dating back a hundred years[15] indicates that the followers play a considerable part in determining the outlines of the leader's character and influence. This argument (which was discussed briefly in the Introduction) may help to clarify why, psychologically speaking, the idea of a cruel leader is a dissonance that is hard to accept. Indeed, the psychological research on leadership reveals a bias – which some people regard as optimistic verging on childishness – in evaluating leaders and following them blindly. Scholars like the psychologist Daniel Goleman[16] see this as a universal bias. According to him, existential need creates an intrinsic tendency to deny undesirable aspects. 'The emotional and physical existence is based partly on denial and illusion. In other words, optimism serves our aims. It acts in the service of the existential interest of the self' (p. 191).

Beyond this general bias, a look at the encyclopaedic surveys (known as handbooks) on leadership shows that most of the psychological research on leadership is American.[17] This fact in itself corresponds to the general trend and also strengthens positive and optimistic descriptions of the leadership phenomenon.

The American sociologist Talcott Parsons, in a comprehensive discussion on the American conception of authority and power, stated that American thinking is characterized largely by utopianism.[18] Barbara Kellerman,[19] a leadership scholar from Harvard, clearly identified this bias, pointing out that the most profoundly internalized and quoted speeches of venerated leaders in

American history do not emphasize expressions like Churchill's 'blood, sweat and tears', but prefer texts that enhance the optimistic, creative and moral aspects in the character of free people in general and Americans in particular. Martin Luther King's most famous speech repeatedly emphasized the power of the dream, which was always optimistic and full of belief in justice and in the human ability to implement it. George Washington in his historical farewell address referred several times to the 'natural' human ability to be guided by justice and generosity.[20] And Barack Obama, in his victorious election campaign of 2008, which was undoubtedly a landmark in American history, emphasized messages of change and hope, and especially the ability to be much better and more socially conscious. His success in the elections will undoubtedly be analysed by experts in the course of time, but even now it is clear that he repeated the motifs that were articulated by his most revered leaders, such as Lincoln and Martin Luther King, messages that emphasize the good and the positive that men and women can find in themselves. Are people really like that? This has been a topic of debate in philosophical writings from biblical times. History is replete with examples reflecting both good and evil. This is not the place to reach a conclusion on the matter (if it is possible at all), but an analysis of the rhetoric of leaders and election campaigns in the democratic world, perhaps especially in the American culture, reveals the tendency that was identified by Kellerman and substantiated by research in social psychology,[21] namely the desire of people to see themselves (and be seen by significant others) as good and kind. If this self-concept is so important to them why would they try to choose a leader whom they perceive as cruel? I venture to suggest that, except in extreme situations of crisis or danger, most people will not choose a person who tries to persuade the public that he or she has 'cruel capabilities'. Yet the truth is that some of those who are considered great leaders did indeed demonstrate such capabilities and their leadership was even lauded for it. This fact demonstrates only one specific aspect in a long list of paradoxes and contradictions connected with political leaders in the democratic world, namely the gap between leaders' rhetoric (which usually reaches its peak during election campaigns) and the decisions that they may, and often do, take (and of course the personality traits related to this gap). The difference between electoral success and leadership in practice has been described by writers who were familiar with leaders and their actions. Sometimes the discrepancy is so great that it causes people to doubt whether there is any connection between election to a leadership role and actually functioning as a leader. This was aptly described by Harry Truman, who wondered 'where Moses would have ended up if he had held a referendum before the exodus from Egypt'.[22] Human history contains numerous examples of leaders' decisions that contradicted the rhetoric that had helped them to achieve their roles. To see the gap between resolute speech during elections and totally antithetical statements when leaders face the necessity to make vital decisions, it is enough to recall the liberation of Algeria by Charles de Gaulle, or Menachem Begin's decision to return the whole of Sinai to Egypt. The interesting point is that these very decisions (which almost certainly would have prevented the leader's election) turned some of the leaders into highly esteemed historic figures.[23]

There are numerous reports on the gap between leaders' appearance, behaviours and life stories – which are covered extensively by the modern media – and their actual leadership behaviour. The Serbian leader Radovan Karadzic was a psychiatrist who acquired part of his education in New York. His professional life was dedicated to helping the needy, particularly those suffering from depression (he worked in a Sarajevo hospital as a specialist on depression). He was also known as a poet – an occupation associated with sensitivity and even sentimentality. His occupations, his education and his writing create an image of humanity, even a stereotypical impression of delicacy. Yet this sensitive man became a murderous leader who was identified with the terrible strategy of creating a 'Greater Serbia', partly through ethnic cleansing including among other things, systematic use of rape (there were special rape rooms in the camps).[24] The transformation was so extreme that he seemed to be a Jekyll and Hyde character. Robert Lifton, who investigated this kind of duality regarding the behaviour of doctors in Auschwitz, described two psychological entities existing in such people. He defined one entity as 'the prior self' and the other as 'the Auschwitz-self'.[25] The fact that such phenomena exist makes it yet more difficult to identify the gap between semblance and manifestations of leadership in practice.

The reader may argue, and rightly so, that examples like those of Karadzic or Hitler who wreaked horrendous damage and destruction are not representative examples, at least statistically. Nevertheless, even the analysis of leaders who are generally respected for their positive contribution to their people brings us back to the fundamental issue of the gap between semblance and the leader's actual behaviours. Ataturk, the hallowed Turkish leader, the father of the modern Turkish nation, the man who is identified more than anyone else with the reforms that transformed Turkey into the most Westernized state in the Islamic world, who fought for women's rights, censured their abuse and insisted on removing the veil, this same man in his private life did not reveal such exemplary behaviour towards women. Not only was he unfaithful to the numerous women in his life, he also expressed an attitude contrary to his public actions. When asked what he most appreciated in women he answered without hesitation – their availability.[26]

This gap between semblance and reality is reflected even in Internet quizzes. In one quiz the readers are asked to identify some well-known leaders on the basis of certain behaviours: the first was a heavy drinker, the second had extra-marital affairs and the third was a vegetarian who loved animals and didn't drink alcohol. And here are the correct answers. The first leader was Winston Churchill, the second was Franklin Roosevelt and the third was Adolf Hitler. If we look closely at the behaviours of many leaders we see that even leaders whose daily behaviour is Machiavellian can advance Platonic ideas, as one scholar, Avihu Ronen, wrote.[27] Moreover there are countless examples (especially in the military sphere) of officers who displayed outstanding leadership behaviours, personal examples, trustworthiness and courage, but were not outstanding or influential as political leaders.[28] Apparently, qualities such as setting an example and other kinds of flawless behaviour that are studied and internalized in schools of command and leadership do not always guarantee leadership in other contexts, and certainly not the leadership of many of those who appear in history books as paragons of leadership.

With reference to Napoleon's request for lucky generals, meaning those who brought victories (and nothing else mattered), many people may argue that the end result is the only important thing and everything else is secondary. This was expressed succinctly by Richard Reeves, who conducted research on some American presidents: 'We don't pay the president of the USA to work hard, at the end of the day we pay him [the leader] for (three, four) decisions that he is expected to make'.[29] However, even from this point of view a closer look exposes discrepancies that are hard to reconcile with the facts. In Joseph Ellis's biography of George Washington he remarks that as a combat officer Washington played a crucial role in four battles in which he took mistaken decisions. One of these was slaughter performed under his command, the second was a massacre from which he escaped by the skin of his teeth, the third was a humiliating defeat and the fourth was a hollow victory.[30] In fact, says Ellis in reviewing Washington's military leadership, 'he was not a military genius by any standard and he lost more battles than he won. As a matter of fact he lost more battles than any decorated hero in modern times'.[31] According to Ellis, Washington was not chosen as a leader (during the preparation for battle against the British) by virtue of his military victories; he was chosen first of all because he came from Virginia, and the appointment of a Virginian was politically necessary in order to ensure that the richest and most highly populated province would rally to the cause. Furthermore, and we see here the importance of external appearance even in those days, Adams used to say that Washington was always chosen as leader by discerning bodies, whatever the purpose, because he was always the tallest man in the room.[32] And as Ellis comments, Adams's joking remark contained an element of truth, as expressed by many of his contemporaries. Washington was favoured with a regal appearance, as described by Benjamin Rush, a prestigious Philadelphian doctor and one of the founding fathers: 'All his actions speak of military honour so great that you would single him out as a commander and soldier among ten thousand people'.[33] Thus, even before the era of electronic communication, outward appearance was often more important than actions. Perhaps, as the British historian Ian Kershaw stated in analysing Hitler's influence, the media do not necessarily diminish the effect of outward appearance; rather, they can intensify it with the appropriate manipulation.[34]

LEADERSHIP = VISION?

One of the recurrent themes in the literature and rhetoric on leaders is vision, a keyword that seems to be indispensable for describing leadership.[35] However, a closer examination of leaders does not necessarily support this claim. Franklin Delano Roosevelt did not seek election on the basis of the ideas and the social order that retrospectively associated him with vision and even 'greatness'. Some historians argue that Roosevelt was above all a shrewd pragmatist.[36] The New Deal and other initiatives that expanded the social responsibility of government and appear to be expressions of ideology and social vision were simply practical solutions for dealing with the economic and social crises that American society was undergoing in the 1930s. Roosevelt, an adept in the art of practical politics, was quick to identify the political opportunities that were presented to him and create ad hoc solutions.

Yitzhak Rabin's image in the public consciousness today barely recalls the bashful man who commanded the Israeli army in the Six Day War. His image now is that of 'Rabin's heritage', summarized as his vision of peace. During his lifetime he was criticized mainly for lacking vision, he was seen as a practical man who disliked big words and sentimentality, yet the qualities attributed to him today are vision and foresight. The ability to foresee future events is largely a question of responding to circumstances created by others. Like Roosevelt in his time, Rabin was persuaded by others that an opportunity had arisen and should be seized – pure pragmatism.[37] Vision is deemed so important that it has come to be seen as the quality that distinguishes between leaders and managers. As John Kotter, a leadership scholar from Harvard, argued, 'Managers deal with routine ongoing administration, leaders are those responsible for vision, for change, for direction'.[38]

This distinction between the how (management) and the what (vision and leadership) features as a major theme in many bestselling books citing examples of leaders of organizations such as Jack Welsh of General Electric, Lee Iacocca, former president of Chrysler, Bill Gates of Microsoft, or Steve Jobs of Apple,[39] leaders who serve as role models in workshops run by schools of management. However, a deeper examination of the theoretical and practical significance of these examples inevitably leads to the conclusion that vision as described by most leadership writers is mainly the concern of heads of systems, founders of organizations, founding fathers – leaders at the top of the pyramid.[40] Hence the very expectation for leadership at junior levels is, to say the least, puzzling. By definition, these lower ranks in the hierarchy of a system are supposed to implement the vision, but in practice the expectation transmitted to them by verbal messages, training, workshops and counselling, is that they themselves will create the vision. In point of fact, organizations in the USA alone invest billions of dollars every year in the attempt to turn managers into leaders at all levels.[41]

An action study examining the relationship between thinking and acting among junior officers[42] shows just how much the importance attributed in the literature to creation of vision needs to be critically examined. In the research simulation, officers were asked to respond to a situation in which a recruit in a combat unit forgot to fill a water bottle to the top before going out on a night training exercise. All of the officers responded in the same way to this situation: the soldier should be punished by having a water container strung on his back (in addition to the regular equipment he carried). When questioned about the reasoning for this choice of punishment, the officers replied that the punishment was appropriate because it clearly suited the misdemeanour. The soldier who had forgotten to fill up the water bottle carried an extra weight of water on his back and this would ensure that such negligent behaviour would not occur again. The officers perceived the punishment as educational and not arbitrary. To the question, how is it that everyone chose exactly the same punishment, the officers replied, that's how our officers treated us. This answer apparently expresses a basic tenet according to which we often behave (consciously or otherwise) towards our children, our subordinates and our students, just as authority figures in our lives – our parents, teachers and so forth – behaved towards us. The point to be stressed in this context is the powerful effect of automatic reaction. A somewhat deeper examination of the process shows that a misdemeanour has operational significance. A bottle that is not completely empty makes a noise at night (therefore, in training exercises every three soldiers are supposed to drink one bottle until it is empty). None of the officers spoke of this. Here we see a clear case of understanding a component within a *given vision* – preparation of the military unit for action. That is the essence of the vision that is supposed to be understood and internalized by a combat officer of every rank. Despite the clarity of the vision, in the officer's awareness the connection between their everyday activities and the operational vision is often vague or even non-existent. What is more dominant in their awareness is custom and tradition. The example cited here may arouse surprise that is relevant to many cases of leadership, surprise that most leaders in all systems are, in fact, not responsible for developing vision; it is simply not their role. Their role, first of all (and perhaps above all), is to know and understand the vision, to internalize it and express it in their daily behaviour (e.g., by reward and punishment). This enigma presents a serious challenge to much of the leadership literature, particularly literature on leadership in organizations.

Perhaps the fundamental bias is the great weight ascribed to leaders by all those concerned – leaders with regard to themselves and their influence, followers with regard to authority figures in general and, of course, writers and researchers on leadership. In a comprehensive book analysing George Washington's transformation into a symbol of leadership, the American sociologist Barry Schwartz writes bluntly: 'Considering the extent of George Washington's shortcomings, it is hard to regard the reverence for him as stemming from his personal qualities alone'.[43] If the reverence for Washington did not stem from deep admiration of his personality, what then were the sources of this reverence?

The American leadership scholar James Meindl pointed to a phenomenon that he called 'the romanticization of leadership' – an innate tendency of followers to magnify and sometimes even deify the figure of many leaders.[44] This interpretation naturally raises the question as to how it happens that certain leaders, like George Washington, who were controversial during their lifetime, became symbols of leadership; while others, such as Lenin, who were idolized during their lifetime and personified the concept of charisma, were forgotten years after their death. And the reverse situation is equally perplexing – leaders who were perceived as pale anti-charismatic figures when they held leadership roles were perceived years after their death as outstanding leaders. When Harry Truman resigned from the presidency in 1953, only 33 per cent of the public thought that he was a good president. In an opinion poll conducted in 2000, historians were asked to evaluate the leadership of American presidents. Harry Truman was ranked as one of the greatest presidents of the USA, after Lincoln, Franklin Delano Roosevelt, Washington and Theodore Roosevelt.[45]

The tendency to exaggerate in describing leaders' personalities is reflected in the status of biographies in literature, especially in the context of historical writing. It is a well-known fact that biography writing is an inferior genre among historians,[46] yet precisely the most inferior genre in historical research – detailed descriptions of leaders and their lives – is the one that breaks through to the general public. This may be explained in various ways: love of the simple human story, voyeurism, the ability to identify with a certain figure and so forth. These possible explanations will be examined later in a broader psychological context, but statistically speaking the facts are clear – people are much less interested in an educated and detailed analysis of complex processes. Most people are interested in leaders as characters; that is, how they like to read about them, get to know them and vote for them in elections. The number of people who view televised political debates between presidential candidates is incomparably greater than the number of those who read the party platform.

The tendency to emphasize leaders' personal success stories is dominant in the popular literature on leadership in organizations. Many such books glorify leaders of organizations and present them as role models, but even supposedly conservative academic journals treating issues such as management and organizations prominently feature studies on correlations between variables related to leadership styles and criteria of success in organizations. Thousands of studies seek to find the 'success factor' in leadership through the use of statistical formulae.[47] Naturally this bias highlights the large number of studies in business organizations,[48] thus strengthening the cumulative effect of the bias in leadership discourse, namely the almost blind belief that leadership is the most important factor for success. And this in turn generates countless attempts to understand the secret of success. A classic example of this bias is a book by Tom Peters and Robert Waterman,[49] which is one of the greatest bestsellers in the history of books on organizations. CEOs bought the book in batches, distributed it among their managers and discussed it as part of their leadership development programme. This example illustrates the type of bias that I refer to. Not only did the book provide food for thought and imitation in management workshops, presented as research containing statistical data (making it seem more scientific) among its reports, the book also became a source of inspiration for further studies on the relationship between leadership and success – which fascinated many. Some scholars detected this bias,[50] but no deep and methodical discussion of the sources and the rules governing it has so far identified specific variables.

The question arises: the tendency to glorify leaders and relate in depth only to certain aspects while ignoring the totality, especially the link between the various aspects – is this tendency a pattern imprinted in the followers and also in leadership scholars? Is the tendency to mythologize leaders simply a result of the cognitive and affective complexity involved in the understanding of the phenomenon? These questions are the core of this book. In order to discuss them we need first to be familiar with the language – the psychological concepts and models required for analysing these subjects.

NOTES

1. Ellis, Joseph J. (2004), *His Excellency George Washington*, New York: Random House, p. 37.
2. Shapira, Anita (1997b), 'Historiography and memory: The case of Latrun in 1948', in *Yehudim Hadashim, Yehudim Yeshanim* [*New Jews, Old Jews*], Tel Aviv: Sifriat Ofakim and Am Oved Publications, pp. 46–87 [Hebrew].
3. Yisrael Ber, in Anita Shapira (1997a), *Yehudim Hadashim, Yehudim Yeshanim* [*New Jews, Old Jews*], Tel Aviv: Sifriat Ofakim and Am Oved [Hebrew], p. 56.
4. Ellis (2004).
5. On the distinction between leaders and rulers see the opening chapter of James MacGregor Burns's book: Burns, James MacGregor (1978), *Leadership*, New York: Harper and Row.

6. Weber, Max ([1924] 1947), *The Theory of Social and Economic Organization* [trans. T. Parsons], New York: Free Press.
7. Willner, Ann R. (1984), *The Spellbinders: Charismatic Political Leadership*, New Haven, CT: Yale University Press.
8. Lindholm, Charles (1988), 'Lovers and leaders', *Social Science Information*, **16**, 227–46.
9. Machiavelli, Nicolo (1985), *The Prince*, Chicago: University of Chicago Press.
10. Locke, John ([1690] 1952), *Second Treatise of Government*, Indianapolis: Bolls-Merrill.
11. Rousseau, Jean-Jacques ([1762] 1968), *The Social Contract* [trans. by Maurice Cranston], Middlesex, UK: Penguin.
12. Rossiter, Clinton (1961), *Introduction to the Federalist Papers*, New York: Mentor, p. xiv.
13. Bass, Bernard M. (1985), *Leadership and Performance Beyond Expectations*, New York: Free Press.
14. Etzioni, Amitai (1975), *A Comparative Analysis of Complex Organizations*, New York: Free Press.
15. Lewis Madison Terman's study is generally referred to as the first research attempt of psychology as a discipline to study leadership, meaning to study this phenomenon using statistical concepts and tools developed by psychologists. See: Terman, Lewis Madison ([1904] 1974), 'A preliminary study of the psychology of leadership', in Ralph M. Stogdill, *Handbook of Leadership Research: A Survey of Theory and Research*, Riverside, NJ: Free Press.
16. Goleman, Daniel J. (1989), 'What is negative about positive illusions? When benefits for the individual harm the collective', *Journal of Social and Clinical Psychology*, **8**, 191.
17. Bass, Bernard M. (2008), *The Bass Handbook of Leadership*, 4th edition, New York: Free Press.
18. Parsons, Talcott (1947), *The Theory of Social and Economic Organizations by Max Weber*, New York: Free Press.
19. Kellerman, Barbara (2004), *Bad Leadership: What it Is, How it Happens, Why it Matters*, Boston: Harvard Business School Press.
20. George Washington, *Farewell Address*, 17 September 1796.
21. Jones, Stephen C. (1973), 'Self and interpersonal evaluations: Esteem theories versus consistency theories', *Psychological Bulletin*, **79** (3), 185–99. See also: Beauregard, Keith and David Dunning (1998), 'Turning up the contrast: Self-enhancement motives prompt egocentric contrast effects in social judgments', *Journal of Personality and Social Psychology*, **74** (3), 606–21.
22. McCullough, David (1995), 'Harry Truman 1945–1953', in R.A. Wilson (ed.), *Character Above All: Ten Presidents from FDR to George Bush*, New York: Simon & Schuster, p. 39.
23. Lippmann, Walter (1913), *A Preface to Politics*, New York: Mitchell Kennerly.
24. Kellerman (2004).
25. Lifton, Robert Jay (1986), *Medical Killing and the Psychology of Genocide*, New York: Basic Books.
26. Volkan, Vamik D. and Norman Itzkowitz (1984), *The Immortal Ataturk – A Psychobiography*, Chicago: University of Chicago Press, p. xviii.
27. Ronen, Avihu (1992), 'Hamanhig Vihakhevra' (Leader and society), in Micha Popper and Avihu Ronen (eds), *Al Hamanhigut [On Leadership]*, Tel Aviv: Ministry of Defense Publications, p. 38 [Hebrew].
28. Popper, Micha (2005), *Leaders Who Transform Society: What Drives Them and Why We Are Attracted*, Westport, CT: Praeger.
29. Reeves, Richard (1995), 'John F. Kennedy', in R.A. Wilson (ed.), *Character Above All: Ten Presidents from FDR to George Bush*, p. 100.
30. Ellis (2004, p. 28).
31. Ellis (2004, p. 29).
32. Ellis (2004, p. 30).
33. Ellis (2004, p. 31).
34. Kershaw, I. (1998), *Hitler, 1889–1936 Hubris*, New York: W.W. Norton.
35. Bennis, Warren and Burt Nanus (1985), *Leaders: The Strategies for Taking Charge*, New York: HarperCollins.

36. Goodwin, Doris K. (1995), 'Franklin Roosevelt 1933–1945', in R.A. Wilson, *Character Above All: Ten Presidents from FDR to George Bush*, New York: Simon & Schuster. See also: Burns, James MacGregor ([1956] 2002), *Roosevelt: The Lion and the Fox*, New York: Mariner.
37. Goldstein, Yosef (2007), *Rabin – Biographiya [Rabin – A Biography]*, Tel Aviv: Schocken Publishing [Hebrew].
38. Kotter, John P. (1988), *The Leadership Factor*, New York: Free Press. See also: Kotter, John P. (1990), 'What leaders really do', *Harvard Business Review*, **68** (3), 103–11.
39. Bennis and Nanus (1985).
40. Schein, Edgar (1985), *Organizational Culture and Leadership*, San Francisco, CA: Jossey-Bass.
41. Morgan McCall et al. remark in their book of 1988 that American corporations invest an estimated yearly sum of 40 billion dollars in what is called manager development. See: McCall, Morgan W., Jr., Michael M. Lombardo and Ann Morrison (1988), *The Lessons of Experience*, Lexington, MA: Lexington Books.
42. Popper, Micha (1994), *Al Menahalim Kemanhigim [On Managers as Leaders]*, Tel Aviv University: Ramot Publishing House [Hebrew].
43. Schwartz, Barry (1987), *George Washington: The Making of an American Symbol*, New York: Free Press, Collier Macmillan.
44. Meindl, James R. (1995), 'The romance of leadership as a follower-centric theory: A social constructionist approach', *Leadership Quarterly*, **6** (3), 329–41.
45. Presidential Rankings (2000), Poll from C-SPAN. Survey of Historians, CNN, 21 February.
46. Shapira, Anita (1997c), 'The mysteries of biography', in *Yehudim Hadashim, Yehudim Yeshanim [New Hews, Old Jews]*, Tel Aviv: Sifriat Ofakim and Am Oved [Hebrew].
47. Kotter (1988).
48. Bass (2008).
49. Peters, Tom and Robert Waterman (1982), *In Search of Excellence: Lessons from America's Best-Run Companies*, New York: Harper Business.
50. Goleman (1989).

2. Leadership as a psychological phenomenon

Towards the end of 2008 a search in Google yielded 288 million mentions of the word leader, 159 million mentions of leadership and 10 million of followership. A careful scrutiny of the contents of these items can serve as a database for some fascinating research on the way in which these subjects are presented in popular literature, academic publications, conferences – in fact every means of communication. However, a cursory glance at the major categories reveals the nature of the interest in these subjects. The main topic of interest is the leader – their personality, characteristics, behaviours and what they say. Under the heading 'leadership' there are journals, research foundations and institutes that are mainly occupied with questions such as who is a leader, how one becomes a leader or how leadership can be improved.

The psychological research on leadership also reflects the tendency to focus on the leader. This began over a hundred years ago, when an American scholar named Terman attempted to identify what characteristics distinguish between leaders and others.[1] Terman sought these characteristics through observation in schools and reports of teachers and students. His research findings indicated that the results of his observations were congruent with the reports of friends and teachers. According to the findings the leaders were taller, better dressed and more fluent in speech and reading than their friends.

Terman's choice of research method and variables can only be understood if we are familiar with the context in which the research was conducted. First, the psychological knowledge that existed at the beginning of the twentieth century was limited. Psychology was still in its early stages, prior to the wide circulation of great discoveries such as those of Sigmund Freud and his followers, which paved the way for insights concerning the internal world of humans. Some of these contributions only reached the stage when they were ripe for research in the middle of the twentieth century.[2] Second, in the early days of psychology as an academic discipline the researchers aspired to make it a science like the natural sciences. In fact they envisaged it as 'the mathematics and physics of human behaviour'. For example, a glance at the writings of Kurt Lewin,[3] one of the leading psychologists in the first half of the twentieth century, reveals that some important models that he developed were formulated in terms of magnetic fields.

So much for aspirations concerning research methods. With regard to the contents that were formulated as research questions, it is easy to see that research on the psychology of leadership was influenced at first by philosophers who saw the leader's personality as the heart of the matter. This was aptly expressed by the Scottish philosopher Thomas Carlyle in a sentence that is frequently quoted in various surveys of leadership: 'History is merely the biography of leaders.'[4] Carlyle and other philosophers who studied leadership were occupied mainly with questions that had already been raised by Plato: Who is worthy of being a leader? What motivates people to be leaders? How can people be trained for leadership?[5] The psychologists posed similar questions in their research, but they sought to find the answers by empirical methods. To Plato and Carlyle the leader was a superior character – a philosopher born with a sublime soul who underwent prolonged and profound training for their role (Plato), or a hero elevated above others in integrity, courage, originality and discernment (Carlyle). In psychological research (and generally in modern times) the leader is less romantic and much more one of the people. Not only do leaders emerge from all strata of society, they also vary in their education, knowledge, motivation and morality (we all know of highly charismatic leaders who were villains). Hence the psychology of leadership covers a broader range of possible leadership profiles and examines leadership far more empirically, using a wide variety of theoretical concepts and models. Furthermore, psychological research on leadership is not confined to political leaders or to those who have achieved fame in various spheres; it deals also with *leaders in everyday life* – in business, in the community, in the military, in fact in every social context.

The comprehensive survey of leadership studies compiled by the American leadership scholar Bernard Bass[6] reports on 10 000 studies conducted up to 2008. The survey mentions several developments. At first, following Terman, the researchers attempted to identify external features that characterized leaders. Then, with the growth of psychological knowledge they added more complex variables, such as intelligence, openness and several social skills. The research variables were often contradictory; traits that were identified in one study did not appear in others. It turned out that the *trait approach* (or the *Great Man Approach* as it was called in psychological journals) could not provide a reasonable explanation of the leadership phenomenon.

Their disappointment with the trait approach did not prevent scholars from continuing the attempt to understand leaders' influence. Adhering to the principle of pursuing a scientific approach, the psychologists continued investigating the leadership phenomenon, but this time they examined variables that were more given to observation and measurement, namely *behaviours*. They observed the behaviours of people who were clearly leaders in work settings, military structures and social networks, and attempted in this way to examine the behaviour patterns that characterized leaders. This approach, too, was criticized, on the grounds that in the name of scientific research they were taking a complex phenomenon, some said an emotional one, and dividing it into a set of behaviours. 'Is the statistical frequency of leaders' behaviours the story of leadership?' wondered some scholars.[7] In fact, this research approach soon lost its popularity, although it generated some concepts that were useful in later theoretical developments. One of these was the distinction between task-oriented behaviours and people-oriented behaviours. Task-oriented behaviours help the followers to make progress in task performance and are manifested in instruction, guidance and showing the right direction for successful performance. People-oriented behaviours are directed toward maintaining morale, pride and a sense of partnership.

This distinction was a practical contribution to research and it served as a basis for the development of instruments for measurement of leadership styles. At first, tools were developed for measuring the extent to which people in leadership roles (managers, army officers) were task oriented or people oriented. This had diagnostic significance because different tasks, as well as different followers, require different orientations. Two American scholars, Paul Hersey and Kenneth Blanchard,[8] found that the task-oriented style – direct, clear and instructive – achieves the best results with followers who have low motivation and scant knowledge for performing a task. On the other hand, when the followers have sufficient knowledge and skills for task performance but are in a state of motivational crisis (e.g., employees who have seen their workmates die in a fire) the people-oriented style is more effective.

The idea of leadership styles grew and expanded. New models of leadership styles were developed, with more detailed specification of situations, experiences and tasks. The typical research questions of these studies were: Which leadership style is more suitable in various situations? Which leadership style is more effective (i.e., produces better results) in comparative situations?[9]

The distinction that currently appears to predominate in the research on leadership styles was originally propounded by the political historian James MacGregor Burns,[10] who studied the leadership of several US presidents. Burns distinguished between two types of leaders, *transactional* and *transformational* leaders. Transactional leaders are those whose ability lies mainly in efficient management; that is to say they are very good at inducing people to perform specific tasks but they do not change the rules of the game, basic assumptions or aims. Leaders of this kind, as the name implies, know how to propose a 'motivational deal'. They know how to guide, explain and reward, how to motivate people to act on the basis of a give and take understanding in which endeavour leads to reward.

Leaders of the type that Burns called transformational leaders are those who generate change in the followers' ways of thinking, values, goals and standards. Such leaders, as some scholars have shown,[11] have transformed expectations (or at least they are credited with doing so). For instance, most historians agree that the thinking, the values and the social and ethical heritage of certain societies were all changed following the leadership of Abraham Lincoln, Franklin Roosevelt and Mahatma Gandhi – all leaders who, according to Burns, manifestly personify transformational leadership.

On the basis of Burns's distinction, the American psychologist Bernard Bass developed a model and a leadership measure, which has become the foremost measure of leadership styles and their effect on followers.[12] In order to characterize precisely the psychological meanings of the leadership styles that Burns proposed, Bass began his research with a simple and direct approach, using interviews to ask people how they perceived, remembered and described the influence of leaders. He also asked people from different spheres of life to choose individuals whom they perceived as leaders and describe why they perceived them as such. The respondents were asked to specify behaviours, words and actions of these leaders that influenced them. These reports were collected, analysed and classified into categories according to content. Bass did not stop at this; he wanted to turn this knowledge into a research tool. Using a statistical technique known as factor analysis he examined to what extent the different categories represented similarity of content. The analysis revealed three categories, one of which was non-leadership – statements and behaviours that do not motivate people, some even lowering the level of motivation. The other two categories identified were transactional leadership and transformational leadership. Transactional leadership is expressed in statements and behaviours that make people want to make an effort, to exert themselves to improve, motivated by the expectation of reward for their endeavours. Transformational leadership is manifested in behaviours and statements that influence people to endeavour beyond the conventional standards in their environment, sometimes even taking risks, acting without expectation of reward in the conventional sense.

The factors that were found to compose transformational leadership are values, credibility, personal example and the ability to be enthusiastic and to inspire enthusiasm. Some of these are 'parental' qualities related to developing and educating people, or the ability to create an atmosphere that encourages curiosity and enquiry. In other words, they succeed in creating the psychological conditions that foster originality and creativity. All of these factors have specific expressions that are represented in the research questionnaire developed by Bass.

The methods of analysing leadership as a psychological phenomenon have changed in recent years, and there is increasing criticism of the almost exclusive focus on the leader. The American scholar James Meindl[13] claimed that the leadership scholars had failed to shake off the practice of romanticizing the leader figure as described in glowing colours by Carlyle. According to Meindl, in order to understand the sources of leaders' influence we need to understand the psychology of the followers. After all, they are the ones who choose the political leaders, they are the ones who decide how far to comply with leaders, how hard to try to meet the expectations of leaders in organizations, whether to make efforts above and beyond expectations or to try just enough to avoid punishment. In fact, say Meindl and those of like mind, the followers not only determine the extent of the leader's influence, they also determine his or her image and his or her 'greatness'. A salient example of this is the case of Winston Churchill, who was seen as a dead horse in the 1930s, a political leader whose leadership days were over. In fact, he himself at the age of 66 assumed the lifestyle of a retiree, occupying himself with painting and writing.[14] And then, due to the exceptional international circumstances stirred up by Hitler, Churchill became prime minister. The man whom many considered a reckless and capricious militant led Britain and the free world to victory in World War II. The dead horse became a paragon of leadership – the most venerated leader of all times in Britain.[15] And then came another surprise. After the war and the military victory, Churchill, the model of leadership, lost the elections to Clement Attlee, a man who was seen as dull and devoid of charisma. Such a reversal arouses wonder about the elusive nature of leadership. It could not be explained by sudden dramatic changes in Churchill's character. The change was in the followers' perception of his leadership. His image as a leader for the post-war period did not match his image as a gifted and charismatic leader during wartime. This, like many other cases, shows that charisma is not a personality trait in the simplistic sense. As Max Weber remarked in a famous essay,[16] the followers endow the leader with charisma. And they are also the ones who divest them of it, as we see in Churchill's case. This argument is congruous with Meindl's basic assumption that in order to understand the leader's influence one needs to point the light of research at the followers. The main question that arises from this point of departure is: Why are people influenced by so-and-so whom they perceive as a leader instead of the question that has occupied most of the psychological research on leadership: What are the personality/behavioural traits of a leader?[17]

The inclusion of followers in the 'leadership formula' created options for new and more complex angles of vision than those that had prevailed during most of the years of psychological research on leadership. The cliché that a leader is one who captures people's hearts and minds became a research question from the opposite angle. What is it in the hearts and minds of people that is susceptible to the influence of leaders? What psychological components do leaders manage to touch, especially those leaders described as charismatic? This question has been examined in the research literature from diverse theoretical approaches.

THE UNCONSCIOUS ATTRACTION TO LEADERS

One of the scenes in a Japanese film, *Kagemusha* (1980), directed by Akira Kurosawa shows a troop of war-weary soldiers going towards the next battlefield. The camera lingers over the perspiring faces, tired eyes and dragging movements. They are totally exhausted. Suddenly, in the distance they notice their leader standing on a hilltop and waving his hand in greeting. The dramatic effect of the leader's presence is amazing. The soldiers' eyes sparkle, their backs straighten, the weariness disappears. With renewed energy they march into battle. Afterwards the camera turns away from the soldiers and slowly moves in to a close-up of the leader. When the camera hovers over the leader's face the viewer discovers that he is dead. Somebody is supporting him and waving his hand in the air.

I chose this powerful scene to illustrate one of the propositions in leadership literature, namely that the need for leaders is inherent in humans and they unconsciously create leaders for themselves. The most familiar approach that emphasizes totally unconscious processes is the psychoanalytic one, and in this conceptual framework it is possible to analyse the inherent need for leaders.

According to this approach leadership is related to processes of *projection* and *transference* (which is actually a form of projection). Projection in its general sense is a process whereby a certain person becomes a kind of clothes hanger on which others hang their wishes, fantasies and fears. This can be likened to the projection of a film on a screen. The film is the individual's private scenario – a web of wishes and experiences, mostly unconscious. The screen is the other (lover, leader...). Projection has many manifestations, some of them easily identified and explained and others anchored in the unconscious. For example, the common saying that people tend to see their own faults in others expresses the idea of projection. Children who are generous and gladly share their toys and games with others think that other children are also generous and act like them. At a more complex level, projections express hidden desires that are unknown even to the person who projects them. To illustrate this point, there is a well-known psychological test called TAT (Thematic Apperception Test) in which the people are shown pictures and asked to write what they see in them. One of the pictures shows a boy sitting alone in a room holding a violin and gazing at it. Everyone who takes the test sees the same picture but the stories they write are different. One writes about a lonely boy who is forced by his mother to learn to play the violin, and he is sitting in the room crying and feeling abandoned. Another, referring to the same picture, writes about a boy with outstanding musical talent sitting and stroking the violin lovingly, thinking of the brilliant future ahead of him. The stories reflect the writers' inner world – a projective expression of their hopes and fears.

Unconscious projection, according to Freud and his students,[18] is a psychological mechanism whereby people may, for example, fall in love with others who are the product of an unconscious inner scenario that responds to desires originating from their own history. In many cases the projection distorts reality, resulting in disillusionment that may be painful.[19] Freud's student (and later rival), the Swiss psychologist Carl Jung,[20] expanded the idea of projection and its expression at the individual level to the level of collective unconsciousness. Evidence of this can be found in the fact that different people have similar dreams, or in the mythology, legends, beliefs and literature of different peoples throughout generations. For example, the figure of the 'hero' or the 'sage' exists in many cultures. A mythical image (defined by Jung as archetypical) that is particularly relevant to the discussion on leadership is that of the 'saviour' who will deliver us from torment, protect us and guide us in the path of life. This archetype, according to Jung, exists in the unconscious mind and is projected onto authority figures such as priests, teachers, doctors and, of course, leaders.

Transference is a specific form of projection – an unconscious response to another person who in some way represents an authority figure (usually a parent) from early childhood.[21] The attempt by psychoanalytic scholars to explain the emergence and influence of leaders is totally sustained by the attempt to decipher the human enigma. According to psychoanalytic scholars, the (unconscious) internalization of the parents in their children's stream of consciousness is a process that is very powerful in forming the individual's 'internal emotional world'. Freud, in his book on Moses, a great Jewish leader, wrote:

> It is in the longing for the father which is common to all humans from their childhood days. Now it may become clear to us that the characteristics that we attribute to the great person are the characteristics of parents, and the essence of greatness of great people lies in this convention... Decisive thinking, willpower and energetic action are part of this image.[22]

Melvyn Hill,[23] in his descriptions of leaders, identified large numbers of 'parental' expressions. For example, the word father appears frequently in references to figures or representations of authority. Although there are specific titles for the clergy, many Catholic churchgoers call the priest father. When people ascribe great significance to a teacher, an educator or a religious leader, they often refer to them as 'my spiritual father'. Leaders who exist in the public awareness as founders of a given collective – a state, a community or an organization – are called the founding fathers, the city fathers and so forth. People praying to God often say 'Our father in heaven'. Nourishing, giving and supportive women are called motherly (nuns, Mother Teresa).

The association of a parental image (usually the father) with the leader occurs more intensively when the followers sense that a crisis is brewing. The prominent historical example of this is Hitler. In the hundreds of books and articles written in the attempt to solve the riddle of his leadership, the only explanation on which there is a consensus is the psychological effect of the severe crisis in Germany between the two World Wars. Despite the diverse explanations, one description is common to all – Hitler was carried on the waves of yearning for 'a strong man who will protect us'. Scholars of the Freudian and Jungian schools will offer similar explanations: that it is the longing for a primal father. They may support their argument with descriptions of the emotional reactions after the assassination of Abraham Lincoln, Mahatma Gandhi and Martin Luther King, or more recent descriptions of youngsters gathering in Tel Aviv's city square after the assassination of Prime Minster Yitzhak Rabin, weeping and murmuring 'they murdered our father'. In fact this argument is supported by research showing that some of the most charismatic leaders in history rose out of crisis situations.[24]

The point to be emphasized in all these examples is the primary importance of the need for security, one of the most fundamental and dominant needs in the entire range of human emotions.[25] This was recently exemplified by the American leadership scholar Jean Lipman-Blumen,[26] who cited statistical evidence from a national survey conducted by the *Los Angeles Times* in 2006. The results showed that when the need for strengthening security conflicts with the values of freedom and human rights, the need for security prevails. Only 40 per cent of the respondents thought that human rights should be protected in any circumstances. Regarding voting patterns, the data showed that although 62 per cent thought that the state should take other directions than those set by the ruling party, the majority of this group (46 per cent) declared that they would vote for the party they opposed because it gave them more physical security.

In the psychological literature the need for security is clearly connected with authority figures who can provide this security. According to some major psychological theories,[27] this is in many senses a construct inherent in humans, due to the fact that all human beings come into the world small and helpless, while large and powerful beings make their existence possible in the most basic senses – nourishment and physical security. This construct appears to be dormant in normal times, but in times of danger or crisis it awakens and becomes the psychological base for the yearning for a parent, a leader.[28] The mechanism is explained differently in various psychological theories. Some argue that it is an instinctive response originating from evolutionary and biological sources,[29] while those of the psychoanalytic trend argue that it is regression – a return to the unconscious emotional pattern of early childhood.

The idea of regression needs clarification because it expresses the essence of psychoanalytic thinking, which is hard to explain as it is not anchored in rational arguments. The psychoanalyst Vamik Volkan[30] shows the contrast between rational thinking and regressive emotions in the following example. A woman named Beth lived in his neighbourhood in Virginia. Her mother lived in New York, and after the terrorist attacks of 11 September 2001 Beth began to eat obsessively only macaroni and cheese. This was regressive behaviour, which had its source in her childhood. As a little girl, whenever she was overcome with fear her mother would give her macaroni and cheese to eat. Although Beth knew that her mother was still alive after the attack, she reverted to the early eating patterns that characterized her panic attacks in the past. It was only after she actually saw her mother that she was able to stop the obsessive eating. Needless to say, this story could be interpreted in different ways. Volkan's explanation was that this regressive pattern acted as a kind of internal mechanism to keep her mother alive.

Thus, according to the psychoanalytic approach crisis situations generate *collective regression*. The need for security (accompanied by the primary longing for someone who can provide it – the strong leader, the primal father) comes to the surface and erases the differences between people, differences in personality, education, income and social standing. Intellectuals, industrialists and manual labourers together crave for a leader who will respond to the primary needs of all living beings. 'It was quite frightening', thus Eleanor Roosevelt gave expression to this primary longing in describing the inauguration ceremony of her husband Franklin Delano Roosevelt (who was elected at the height of one of the most severe crises in the history of the United States). 'When Franklin said in his inauguration speech that he might have to assume presidential powers that are usually assumed by the president in wartime, just in that part of the speech he received the most thunderous applause'.[31]

There is abundant evidence to prove that regression to earlier emotions and behaviours at the collective level does not necessarily characterize only weak populations, as many tend to think. In the USA, for example, regressive behaviours related to feelings of insecurity have appeared in war situations. One hundred thousand Americans of Japanese origin were held in detention camps during World War II, although they had displayed no signs of disloyal behaviour.[32] And there is plentiful support for the argument that in severe crisis situations, primary, instinctive and perhaps unconscious feelings arise and may find a solution by projecting directly onto a 'leader and saviour' or by identifying with a group.[33] The French sociologist Emile Durkheim[34] claims that a group gives strength and security to the individuals and thus 'the personal identity becomes a collective identity'. It is common knowledge that team cohesion in combat units strengthens the individuals who are struggling with physical and mental difficulties in extreme stress situations.[35] A look at the emotion management processes carried out in combat units of the German army (which was considered an excellent army) during World War II can illustrate these emotional linkages. The officers were instructed to remember the soldiers' birthdays and their personal backgrounds, they were told to behave and express themselves like caring, loving and responsible fathers. This was the rhetoric they used. The soldiers were called children (*Kinder*), and the military unit was built as a family.[36] In a study conducted in the Israeli army, when outstanding battalion commanders (as evaluated by their senior officers and subordinates) were interviewed in order to examine their concept of command and their behaviour as outstanding leaders, it was found that the central concepts in their role description were based on their perception of the military unit as a family.[37] This kind of familial identification with a group based on emotional sources has served as the point of departure for several interpretations that link processes at the individual level, the centrality of the group and attachment to the leader.

The view of the leader as a source of identification processes was also presented by Charles Lindholm,[38] who compared leadership with romantic love. These two phenomena, according to Lindholm, are rooted in feelings of identity with others. The boundaries of the individual become blurred and the ego of one merges with the ego of the other. Charismatic leadership in this sense is above all relationship, and in its extreme form it is a relationship like falling in love, characterized by projection and blurring of the boundaries of the ego. This emotional process also takes place through identification with a group. The group becomes the object with which the individuals merge, and then it merges with the leader, and thus they all feel stronger. Using the concepts proposed by Mischel,[39] it became possible to generalize these individual and collective processes and formulate principles on the inherent attraction to leaders as 'providers of a sense of security'. Mischel distinguished between strong psychological situations – when people feel that there is security, order and high certainty – and weak psychological situations – when there is a large extent of insecurity and uncertainty. The most extreme of these situations is the state of war, described by Liddel-Hart as the realm of uncertainty.[40]

Therefore, in seeking to formulate more generalizable principles we may say that (unconscious) collective attachment to leaders tends to occur in weak psychological situations, when the reaction to the basic need for security is sharp and pervasive and reaches large groups. However, such extreme situations are infrequent; they simply stand out in the historical and psychological literature on leadership because people are drawn to drama, to exceptional situations. In any case, the psychoanalytical theories provide only one pair of spectacles for looking at leadership – spectacles that focus on the explanation of unconscious processes.

Psychology also offers other angles of vision that are not based on the assumption that attraction to leaders originates in unconscious feelings. One of these perspectives presents a basic assumption that is virtually the opposite of psychoanalytic thinking, namely the assumption that the human is a kind of 'naive scientist'[41] who gathers information, tests alternatives, formulates hypotheses and through these cognitive acts of information processing attempts to discover the causality at the basis of the various phenomena that he or she unveils. Hence we will examine how leadership is explained from this point of departure.

LEADERSHIP AS INFERENCE

Manfred Kets de Vries, an eminent leadership scholar,[42] used Jerzy Kosinski's book *Being There*[43] (which was later dramatized as a film starring Peter Sellers and Shirley MacLaine) to illustrate the process of creating a leader in the followers' eyes. The hero is Chauncey, a mentally retarded middle-aged man who has worked all his life as a gardener on the estate of an old man, dividing his time between tending the garden and watching inane TV programmes, trying to imitate the participants. After his benefactor's death, Chauncey has to go out into the world. Crossing a busy street for the first time in his life, he is overwhelmed by the distractions all around him and is hit by a limousine and slightly injured. The owner of the car, Mrs Rand, wife of the president of a giant corporation, takes him home with her to make sure that he is not seriously injured. In the conversation that ensues she is deeply impressed by Chauncey's intelligence and insight. Actually, in conversing with Mrs Rand the gardener does what he has learned from watching TV programmes; he simply repeats her words in a tone of empathy.

Mrs Rand is not the only one who is impressed. Her husband is wholly taken by Chauncey's wisdom. When Rand asks Chauncey about his business the following conversation takes place: 'It's not easy, sir. There are not many chances of getting a good garden where you can work undisturbed and cultivate it according to the changing seasons.' Mr Rand, assuming that Chauncey is referring metaphorically to the economic crisis in the US, responds enthusiastically: 'A gardener, uh? Well said! Isn't that a wonderfully apt description of a true businessman? A man who tills the soil with his sweat, waters the ground and harvests from it worthwhile products for his family, his community. Yes, Chauncey! What a wonderful metaphor! Indeed, a productive businessman is like a man of the soil, cultivating his vine.'

When the US president, who occasionally comes to visit and consult with the business magnate Rand, asks Chauncey about the slump in the American economy, Chauncey replies, 'There are always seasons in gardening. There is spring, there is summer, but there is also fall and winter, and then again spring and summer. So long as the roots are not seriously damaged everything is all right.' The president is profoundly impressed and adopts the feeble-minded gardener's seasons metaphor to use in his speeches. Chauncey's career advances quickly. He is invited to appear on an important TV show. Introducing the programme, the host remarks that the US president compares the American economy to a garden. When invited to talk, Chauncey speaks of the only thing he has ever known and done in his life. 'I know the garden well,' he says firmly, 'I have worked at this job all my life. The garden is good and healthy, the trees are healthy and so are the flowers and the other plants. And they will stay that way if they are watered and treated properly according to the seasons of the year. The garden needs proper care. I agree with the president. There is room for new trees and new flowers of different kinds.'

The audience responds enthusiastically to Chauncey's 'profound' statements. Asked by journalists which newspapers he prefers to read, Chauncey replies that he doesn't read any newspaper (in fact, he is illiterate). 'I watch TV programs all the time.' This reply is seen as one of the most honest statements ever made by a public figure. Chauncey becomes a celebrity, is chosen as best-dressed man of the year, and all the papers want to publish front-page stories about him. Kosinski's character Chauncey reflects the need of people to create authority figures for themselves even when the object of their admiration is an empty vessel. This story, although it is sarcastic and may be interpreted in different ways, can serve to demonstrate two approaches in explaining the creation of a leader. One, represented in the literature by Manfred Kets de Vries, is the psychoanalytic explanation discussed above. According to this approach, in situations of crisis, helpless and hopeless people are attracted to a character like Chauncey, an elderly, white-haired man who conveys the impression that he has experienced and seen everything, and therefore it is easy to project onto him the longing for security. Chauncey represents the response to the primary need for security. To those who project the longing for security, his fatherly figure gives the feeling that he will see to it that 'everything will be all right'.

The second approach (which leads to similar predictions) is the psycho-cognitive one, whereby leadership is simply a type of inference. In other words, the leader is not a solution to anxiety and unconscious feelings of stress, but an informative response to processes such as organization of information, causality and consistency – a process defined by the American scholar Karl Weick[44] as sense-making, an attempt to interpret events out of the glut of information that surrounds us. The law governing people's creation of interpretive models is a major subject of research in cognitive psychology.

From this theoretical point of departure the basic argument is that leadership is an accessible and convenient explanation category in interpreting reality, especially in the case of complex events. This is easy to see in election campaigns; although candidates in each party usually represent different ideologies, platforms and groups of people, in the end most of the people vote according to the characteristics that they attribute to the head of the party. A familiar instance of this is the phenomenon known as the 'Kennedy schema'.[45] To many Americans the ideal candidate is young, relatively moderate in his or her political views, intelligent, gifted with rhetorical ability and good-looking – all the characteristics that were attributed to John Kennedy. The fact that he was a war hero made him even more attractive to the followers. Kennedy's image was such a distinct prototype of leadership that candidates struggled to be nominated for election by endeavouring to imitate the 'Kennedy schema'. The prime example of this is Dan Quayle during his major television debate in the elections of 1998, when he claimed, in response to a remark concerning his lack of political experience, that he had as much political experience as John Kennedy had when he was a candidate. Quayle's adversary, Lloyd Bentsen, struck back with a retort that is considered one of the most insulting in the history of TV debates: 'Senator, I served together with Jack Kennedy. I knew Jack Kennedy, Jack Kennedy was my friend, Senator, you are not Jack Kennedy!'[46] During Bill Clinton's election campaign, a photograph was distributed of him as a boy in the Scout Movement in the early 1960s, shaking hands with John Kennedy. The picture was circulated throughout the United States on the assumption that it portrayed Clinton being 'anointed' by Kennedy. John Kerry, too, tried to emphasize his resemblance to Kennedy, although he looked nothing like him. The Republicans, on their side, endeavoured to eliminate the possibility that he might be regarded as similar to Kennedy. They did this in two ways: (1) by undermining his attempt to portray himself as a war hero (like Kennedy), and (2) by depicting him as having far more liberal positions than those of Kennedy. Thus, in the psychological sense, the (ascribed) image of the leader is a conspicuous, convenient and accessible informative category in the processing of information that has social psychological significance.[47] Studies on this issue have dwelt upon the phenomenon known as the *fundamental attribution error*, according to which people who find themselves in a situation when they need an explanation for what is happening attribute greater weight to people than to circumstances. An experiment conducted by the American psychologist Lee Ross and colleagues[48] demonstrates this error in information processing.

The experiment simulated a quiz in which the participants were divided randomly into questioners and respondents. The questioners were instructed to ask very difficult questions, and the rules of the game allowed them to ask questions about which none of the respondents possessed the relevant knowledge. Viewers who witnessed the experiment and the random allocation to questioners and respondents attributed more knowledge to the questioner than to the respondent, although they knew that the questioner's advantage was totally fortuitous. Similarly, two American scholars named Jones and Harris[49] conducted a study in which some of the participants were asked to read and deliver speeches supporting the Cuban leader Fidel Castro, while other participants were asked to learn and deliver speeches opposing Castro. The audience attributed to the speakers the attitudes presented in their speeches despite the fact that they were informed that the division of the participants was totally random. The participants simply acted the roles in their speeches.

Another fundamental argument that is common to psycho-cognitive theories is that the processing of information is based on clues which the individual receives, processes and interprets. These clues are filled out to form a picture of the leader based on leadership schemas that develop in the socialization process and help people to interpret reality.[50] For instance, the participants in a study who were shown a video of a leader tended to attribute to them behaviours that matched their leadership schema. Conger and Kanungo claimed that subjects attribute higher levels of leadership to characters according to leadership clues such as decisive speech or determined behaviour.[51]

Viewed from the psycho-cognitive perspective it is not hard to understand the construction of the ignorant gardener Chauncey as a leader also in terms of the fundamental attribution error and clues that represent leadership schemas. He is never agitated, he is too narrow and obtuse to be overcome by fear or anxiety, his calm demeanour is perceived as self-confidence. He never hesitates because he always repeats the same few sentences that he knows. Moreover, the public's attribution of leadership to Chauncey is reinforced by the information that he is a friend of the richest man in America, who is also a friend of the president. 'With friends like those', the follower could say to himself, 'he is certainly an important person.'

Political leadership, too, may be explained in terms of cognitive psychological biases. While the psychoanalytical school will argue, for example, that the American public's veneration for Franklyn Roosevelt (who was the US president for about 15 years) originated in projection and the longing for a father figure in a period of crisis, cognitive psychologists may claim that it is a question of attribution error and biased inference from clues. That is to say, the New Deal and its ideological or social implications (which were radical in that period) were too complicated for people to understand. The public paid attention mainly to the clues that, according to cognitive psychology models, would suffice to complete the picture of a leader: a confident speaker, radiating self-assurance and determination. In these Roosevelt was matchless. The reverence for Charles De Gaulle can be explained in the same way. The general's uniform and his unyielding resolve furnish the explanation as to why the public esteemed Charles de Gaulle as a great leader without needing to understand the complexity of the situation. Similarly, the upheaval that occurred in the Soviet Union in the 1980s and 1990s is attributed more to Mikhail Gorbachev's leadership than to the complex processes that had been occurring slowly and gradually over many years.[52] Furthermore, there is historical evidence showing that the decisions of political leaders are some-times influenced by the fundamental attribution error even if they reach these decisions after careful analysis and consultation with experts. The American historian Barbara Tuchman,[53] in her book *The March of Folly*, provides several examples of this. The 'folly' that she describes, the consistent human stupidity, may be explained as a common occurrence of processing or creating information that is simply the result of cognitive biases such as the funda-mental attribution error. An outstanding illustration of this, which involves more than one American president and several teams of advisors and experts, some of whom were brilliant people who had excelled in previous roles, is the USA's long-term dependence on Ngo Dinh Diem during the Vietnam War. The latter, an extreme nationalist from a Catholic Mandarin family, was a minister in the pro-French government who resigned because of his nationalist views and emigrated to Japan. The Americans saw him as the 'right leader' due to his resolute attitudes, especially the fact that he was anti-Communist. Diem moved to the United States, where he made contact with Cardinal Spellman from New York with the help of his brother, who was a Catholic bishop. The cardinal introduced him to influential circles, and thus he also met with Justice Douglas, who was deeply impressed by him and believed that he could replace the 'French puppet' (Prime Minister Bao Dai) and also Ho Chi Minh, the leader of the communists in Vietnam. Douglas reported his discovery to the CIA and presented his candidate to Senators Mansfield and John Kennedy, both Catholics. And thus, in Tuchman's words, the USA 'found a client' on whom American policy in Vietnam was largely based over a long period. In terms of cognitive psychology, we can see here the development of almost laboratory conditions for creating and deepening information based on the fundamental attribution error. The reality was extremely complex and unfam-iliar, the man made an impression on several important people who could be considered perceptive and objective thinkers (judges, bishops, senators). He was a Catholic and above all a staunch anti-communist; all of these psycho-logical conditions helped to create a fundamental attribution error, certainly among Americans in a period when communism was perceived as a danger-ous plague.

As mentioned earlier in this book, the proliferation of leaders' biographies may also be seen as another expression of the fundamental attribution error – the tendency of many historians to attribute more weight to the person and less to the circumstances.[54] The claim that these biographies are simply a popular genre, bestsellers rather than history books describing complex processes, simply reinforces the psycho-cognitive argument. People buy more books of this kind because they suit automatic biases in information processing, providing information that is easily available, simple and digestible. Leaders, as we have seen, can easily become such an informative category.

The discussion and research on psychological aspects of information processing, as well as helping to detect instances of informative inference regarding leaders, have also contributed to the understanding of how information processing is generated, how such information about leaders is built and processed. James Meindl[55] likened these processes to the spreading of a virus when people infect others with whom they are in contact. Meindl called this *social contagion*. It can be characterized as a certain kind of sense-making that originates mainly from the characteristics of the social network within which the leader functions.[56] In the absence of information about the leader, the information that is accessible within the social network provides the materials necessary for constructing the figure of the leader. This means that there are clues that match the leadership images existing in the social network (the images of leaders in paratrooper units, hi-tech, education or religious frameworks may all be different without regard to any specific leader).

The feature common to both the explanations presented hitherto (psychoanalytic and psycho-cognitive) is the focus on *processes*. The theories and models based on these approaches do not deal with the *contents* that occupy leaders and followers. Therefore we will now look at a type of psychological explanation that places contents first in the understanding of the relationship between followers and leaders.

LEADERSHIP AS A STORY

As I write these lines the 200th anniversary of Abraham Lincoln's birth is being celebrated. As well as demonstrating the American people's veneration of their leader, who was assassinated on 14 April 1865 only five days after the Civil War ended, the celebrations also reflect the ceremonial attitude towards the hallowed leader.

Barack Obama quoted Lincoln several times during his election campaign, declaring that Lincoln was his presidential model. After his election he began his inaugural tour in Springfield, Illinois, Lincoln's burial place. His keynote address was delivered on the steps of the monument erected in 1922 to commemorate Lincoln, the same place where Martin Luther King delivered his famous 'I have a dream' speech. Almost daily, TV channels broadcast programmes about Lincoln, including interviews with historians praising his greatness, wisdom and unparalleled leadership. Lincoln is the president most mentioned in the two leading US newspapers, *The New York Times* and *The Washington Post*, the president with the highest number of entries in the

Library of Congress and the president most mentioned in the important journals in academic libraries. Throughout the United States there are more towns, villages, streets and monuments bearing Lincoln's name than that of any other president.[57] Empirical evidence indicates that Lincoln is the most revered leader in American history, more than George Washington – which is somewhat surprising in view of the fact that the hallowed leaders in most countries are the founding fathers.

Lincoln's transformation over the years into a leadership icon, not only to the public but also to other leaders and to researchers and historians, is a fascinating and exceptional case. Clearly it is not a question of the man himself but of psychological processes related to the symbolization and construction of a national narrative of leadership. During his term in office Lincoln was one of the more controversial presidents and was barely re-elected for a second term. Moreover, President Lincoln, who was publicly identified with the abolition of slavery (and therefore was seen as a moral leader prepared to fight over moral issues) did not go to war to free the slaves. During his campaign for election to the Senate of Illinois in 1858 his greatest worry was that his personal opposition to slavery would be mistakenly perceived as a radical political stand of racial equality. He explained: 'I am not now, nor ever have been, in favour of bringing about in any way the social or political equality of the white and black races.' And he went on to say: 'There is a physical difference between the white and the black races which will forever forbid the two races living together in social or political equality.'[58]

In his inauguration address in 1861 Lincoln promised not to intervene in the issue of slavery in places where it existed, and he even adopted the suggestion that the Federal Government would never intervene in the question of slavery. Lincoln launched the Civil War for one reason alone (which he mentioned in his inauguration speech) – to preserve the unity of the Federation. When the southern states were threatening to secede, war was seen as a legitimate move to preserve the Union. The bloody war in which Americans fought Americans was not waged over values and ideologies but over control. Furthermore, this now highly revered president was almost forgotten for many years after his death. His construction as a venerated leader caught momentum in the twentieth century and reached its peak in World War I, when he became the ultimate symbol of moral leadership.[59] In other words, Lincoln after World War I was not the leader that he had been in his lifetime and during the nineteenth century. Others turned him into a symbol. His transformation into a symbolic narrative with which people could identify, and through which they could create solidarity and inculcate values calls for thorough examination and analysis because it exemplifies an important psychological question: Why do certain people become leadership narratives, and what are the rules that govern these processes?

The American scholar Barry Schwartz,[60] who has dealt with the symbolization of leaders, sees the psychological basis for the construction of a leadership narrative as the *need for meaning*, a need that many researchers regard as central in human nature.[61] There are some who argue that this need is as powerful as the human instincts. The American sociologist Charles Cooley argued that leadership is related to the inherent need for direction, and he formulated it thus: 'The function of the great, famous, man (the leader) is to be a symbol. The real question in mind is not so much "What are you?" as "What can I believe that you are?" "How far can I use you as a symbol?" '[62]

Jerome Bruner[63] of Harvard University gave concrete expression to some of these abstract ideas, expressions that have everyday reality as well as relevance to research. One of them concerns the centrality of the story in making meaning for people. Bruner claims that stories are an unparalleled means of making meaning. Evidence of this can be seen with children. Not only do stories fascinate children, they help them more than any other medium to construct the world and interpret it. In this basic sense, the desire for stories and the role of stories in interpreting and shaping reality do not end with childhood. The story is a major need that is expressed in many spheres throughout our lives.[64] In principle Bruner distinguishes between two types of reality. One concerns nature and is interpreted by logical and scientific thinking. The other concerns people and at its core is the story, the narrative. In this sense leaders can represent and be both stories and storytellers – a skill that is apparently vital in the choice of leaders. From this theoretical viewpoint Lincoln could not have been a revered leader in his lifetime because the appropriate circumstances for creating him as a story did not yet exist. It was only after the huge waves of immigration that started at the beginning of the twentieth century, when millions of immigrants came to build their lives in the New World, that Lincoln could become a narrative, a symbol. Lincoln, a small-town man from a farming family in the Midwest, who had worked hard from early childhood, acquired an education in law by his own efforts, and then became president, could serve as a perfect model of a self-made man, the American dream. His personal story included the elements of the collective story, of precious values that could be displayed simplistically. The personification of abstract values is an effective means of conveying messages that might otherwise be hard to explain.

History provides many examples of this psychological process. For instance, Yitzhak Rabin's story may be seen as an Israeli version of the development of Abraham Lincoln's leadership narrative. Like Lincoln, Rabin was elected to the premiership by a small majority. He too was assassinated for ideological reasons and he too during his lifetime was one of the more controversial leaders. He was harshly criticized as a pragmatist without a social and economic philosophy, a leader without vision. And like Lincoln, in the quality considered most important in a leader – the ability to make decisions – Rabin was perceived as hesitant and irresolute. Yet 15 years after his assassination Rabin was a paragon of leadership and, as with Lincoln, his reputation as a leader keeps growing. His name appears in memorial sites, streets, towns and villages, parks and in writing more than any other Israeli prime minister since the death of the founding father David Ben-Gurion. The mythology of Rabin's leadership (like that of Lincoln) was built (and could be built) *only after his death.* Only then did the circumstances and materials exist that could create a story with which people could identify.

The case of Nelson Mandela is an excellent illustration of the dynamics of the leader as narrative. This example is particularly clear because Mandela was in prison for 27 years and as soon as he was released he became the leader of the nation. The practical meaning of this fact is that very few people had actually met him (even distributing his photographs was forbidden). Furthermore, he barely appeared in public, so the people knew very little about him. In the absence of exposure to the public through election speeches, interviews with the media, meetings with voters and suchlike activities that are generally considered vital in election campaigns, one might think that it would be very difficult for the voters to make decisions concerning their choice of leader. In this case, a few parts of the general story were enough to generate mythologization through stories carried by word of mouth, conveying the image of a proud black man who did not bow to white people, who had spent many years in prison and, according to all the reports, not only did he not break but he even became stronger. This image was enough to construct him as a leadership narrative that the public wanted so much to believe in. They wanted to identify with this narrative and be strengthened by it. What is the mechanism driving such processes of constructing a leadership story? What is the connection between the processes of constructing a leadership story and reality? Why are certain leaders a better story than others? What can we learn from this about the leadership phenomenon? These questions will be addressed in the next chapter.

NOTES

1. Terman, L.M. ([1904] 1974), 'A preliminary study of the psychology of leadership', in R.M. Stogdill, *Handbook of Leadership Research: A Survey of Theory and Research*, Riverside, NJ: Free Press, pp. 58–95.
2. Ainsworth, M.D.S., M. Blehar, E. Waters and S. Wall (1978), *Patterns of Attachment: A Psychological Study of the Strange Situation*, Hillsdale, NJ: Erlbaum. The psychodynamic concepts developed by Freud and his followers dealt with the internal emotional world. Although they served in therapeutic practice, their validity was a source of contention with regard to research. Developments of the kind presented by Ainsworth and associates advanced the possibility of researching psychodynamic concepts by methods that were more conventional in empirical research trends.

3. Lewin, Kurt (1947), 'Frontiers in group dynamics: Concept, method, and reality in social science', *Human Relations*, **1** (4), 5–42.
4. Carlyle, Thomas ([1841] 1907), *On Heroes, Hero-Worship and the Heroic in History*, Boston: Houghton Mifflin.
5. Plato (1973), *The Collected Dialogues of Plato*, Princeton, NJ: Princeton University Press.
6. Bass, Bernard M. (2008), *The Bass Handbook of Leadership*, 4th edition, New York: Free Press.
7. Some scholars criticized the quantitative approach to leadership research, arguing that leadership is too complex a phenomenon for measurable research carried out by quantitative methods. They believed that leadership could and should be investigated by qualitative research methods. This view was expressed, among others, by Bryman, Alan, M. Stephens and C. Campo (1996), 'The importance of context: Qualitative research and the study of leadership', *Leadership Quarterly*, **7** (3), 353–71. And also Parry, Ken (1998), 'Grounded theory and social process: A new direction for leadership research', *Leadership Quarterly*, **9** (1), 85–105.
8. Hersey, Paul and Kenneth Blanchard (1969), 'Life cycle theory of leadership', *Training and Development Journal*, **23** (5), 26–34.
9. Bass (2008).
10. Burns, James MacGregor (1978), *Leadership*, New York: Harper & Row.
11. Popper, Micha (2005), *Leaders Who Transform Society: What Drives Them and Why We Are Attracted*, Westport, CT: Praeger.
12. Bass, Bernard M. (1985), *Leadership and Performance Beyond Expectations*, New York: Free Press.
13. Meindl, James R. (1995), 'The romance of leadership as follower-centric theory: A social constructionist approach', *Leadership Quarterly*, **6** (3), 329–41.
14. Best, Geoffrey (2001), *Churchill: A Study in Greatness*, London and New York: Hambledon & London.
15. Ramsden, John (2002), *Man of the Century: Winston Churchill and his Legend Since 1945*, London: HarperCollins.
16. Gerth, H. and C. Wright Mills (eds) (1946b), 'The sociology of charismatic authority', in *From Max Weber: Essays in Sociology*, New York: Oxford University Press.
17. Bass (2008). Most of the studies that appear in Bernard Bass's encyclopaedic survey deal with leaders. In many senses the empirical psychological research followed the tradition of studies conducted by social psychologists in the context of groups. The emphasis was on leaders' influence on task performance, work satisfaction and other variables that were later integrated in the general tendency of organizational psychology research to examine leaders' influence on variables related to concepts of effectiveness in organizations. Very few studies dealt with the psychology of the followers as a point of departure for their research.
18. Freud, Sigmund (1920), *A General Introduction to Psychoanalysis*, American edition, New York: Garden City Press, pp. 363–5.
19. Halpern, James and Ilsa Halpern (1983), *Projections: Our World of Imaginary Relationships*, New York: Putnam Publications. The psychological literature distinguishes between different types of projection, from those that are easily identified, such as the projection expressed in the saying 'the pot calling the kettle black' to complex and unconscious projections, some of which, according to psychoanalytic thinking, are generated by denial and are in fact defence mechanisms whose task is to defend the ego. Other projections are related to unconscious processes of identification (projective identification). I will not expand here on the various types of unconscious identification with leaders. Suffice it to say that it includes transference.
20. Jung, Carl Gustav (1986), *Analytical Psychology*, London: Routledge.
21. Rycroft, Charles (1995), *A Critical Dictionary of Psychoanalysis*, London: Penguin Books.
22. Freud, Sigmund (1939), *Moses and Monotheism*, London: Hogarth Press, standard edition of the *Complete Psychological Works of Sigmund Freud*, Vol. XVIII, pp. 109–10.
23. Hill, Melvyn A. (1984), 'The law of the father: Leadership and symbolic authority in psychoanalysis', in B. Kellerman (ed.), *Leadership: Multidisciplinary Perspectives*, Englewood Cliffs, NJ: Prentice-Hall.

24. Hertzler, J.O. (1940), 'Crises and dictatorships', *American Sociological Review*, **5** (2), 157–69.
25. Maslow, Abraham (1970), *Motivation and Personality*, New York: Harper & Row.
26. Lipman-Blumen, Jean (2007), 'Toxic leaders and the fundamental vulnerability of being alive', in Boas Shamir, R. Pillai, M.C. Bligh and M. Uhl-Bien (eds), *Follower-Centered Perspectives on Leadership*, Greenwich, CT: Information Age Publishing.
27. Freud (1920). See also Bowlby, John (1973), *Attachment and Loss, 2, Separation*, New York: Basic Books. Many psychological theories view the longing for security as the basis for emotional development or formation of mental constructs that are meaningful in various spheres. Freud and Bowlby are described as the formulators of influential theories that have led to the development of many models dealing with the claim that the longing for security explains many psychological processes. In some of the models the longing for a leader is related to these basic processes.
28. Davidovitz, Rivka, M. Mikulincer, P. Shaver, R. Iszak and M. Popper (2007), 'Leaders as attachment figures', *Journal of Personality and Social Psychology*, **93** (4), 632–50.
29. Lorenz, Konrad (1977), *Behind the Mirror: A Search for a Natural History of Human Knowledge* [trans. Ronald Taylor], London: Methuen. See also Bowlby (1973).
30. Volkan, a psychiatrist, has dealt in many of his works with the expansion of psychoanalytic concepts (which were originally formulated for the purpose of analysing processes that occur in the individual) to the level of collective discussion. He studied collective unconscious processes of broad populations and explained the development of famous political leaders (e.g., Ataturk and Richard Nixon) from a psychoanalytic perspective. His analyses are outstanding examples of psychoanalytic analysis of the relationship between leaders and followers. See for example, Volkan, Vamik D. (2004), *Blind Trust: Large Groups and Their Leaders in Times of Crisis and Terror*, Charlottesville, VA: Pitchstone Publishing.
31. Schlesinger, Arthur Meier, Jr. (1958), *The Coming of the New Deal*, Boston: Houghton Mifflin, pp. 1–2.
32. Volkan (2004).
33. Popper, Micha (2001), *Hypnotic Leadership: Leaders, Followers and the Loss of Self*, Westport, CT: Praeger.
34. Durkheim, Emile (1973), 'The dualism of human nature and its social conditions', in Robert N. Bellah (ed.), *Emile Durkheim on Morality and Society*, Chicago: University of Chicago Press.
35. Salo, M., M. Popper and A. Goldberg (2007), 'Pertinent research questions on group leadership', in A.J. Huhtinen and J. Rantapelkonen (eds), *Fundamental Questions of Military Studies*, Finland: Naval Academy.
36. Shils, Edward A. and Morris Janowitz (1948), 'Cohesion and disintegration in the Wehrmacht in World War II', *Public Opinion Quarterly*, **12** (2), 280–315.
37. Zakay, Eliav and Amir Scheinfeld (1993), *Mifakdei Gidudim Mitztayanim Bitzahal* [*Outstanding Battalion Commanders in the IDF*], research report, School of Leadership Development, Israel Defense Forces (IDF) [Hebrew].
38. Lindholm, Charles (1988), 'Lovers and leaders', *Social Science Information*, **16**, 227–46.
39. Mischel, Walter (1973), 'Toward a cognitive social learning reconceptualization of personality', *Psychological Review*, **80** (4), 252–83.
40. Liddel-Hart, Basil H. (1991), *Strategy*, 2nd edition, New York: Plume Books.
41. Heider, Fritz (1944), 'Social perception and phenomenal causality', *Psychological Review*, **51** (6), 358–74. Heider and his followers, who are classified under the general heading *cognitive psychologists*, believe that people formulate hypotheses regarding phenomena that they see in a manner similar to the thinking of scientists who formulate research hypotheses. These scholars attempt to describe and explain the law governing the formulation of these hypotheses. Assuming that thought is related to action, identifying patterns of thinking, or more precisely, pinpointing patterns of processing information, is beneficial to the understanding of adopting attitudes, taking decisions and so forth.
42. Kets de Vries, Manfred (1988), 'Prisoners of leadership', *Human Relations*, **41** (31), 261–80.
43. Kosinski, Jerzy (1972), *Being There*, New York: Bantam Books.
44. Weick, Karl. E. (1995), *Sensemaking in Organizations*, Thousand Oaks, CA: Sage Publications.

45. Popkin, Samuel (1993), 'Decision making in presidential primaries', in Shanto Iyengar and William McGuire (eds), *Explorations in Political Psychology*, Durham, NC: Duke University Press.
46. Houghton, David, P. (2009), *Political Psychology*, New York: Routledge, p. 163.
47. Lord, Robert G., R.J. Foti and C.L. Devader (1984), 'A test of leadership categorization theory: Internal structure, information processing, and leadership perception', *Organizational Behavior and Human Performance*, **34** (3), 343–78.
48. Ross, Lee D., Teresa M. Amabile and J.L. Steinmetz (1977), 'Social roles, social control, and biases in social perception', *Journal of Personality and Social Psychology*, **35** (7), 485–94.
49. Jones, Edward E. and Victor A. Harris (1967), 'The attribution of attitudes', *Journal of Experimental Social Psychology*, **3** (1), 1–24.
50. Lord et al. (1984). Schema, mental model, scenario and cognitive map are major concepts in cognitive psychology, which describes patterns of organizing information that serve preference, decision and action. The prevailing concept is schema, and the argument is that schemas are constructed and created in the socialization process and serve as the basis for action. A common example in the literature is the 'restaurant schema'. A person learns the order of actions performed in a restaurant and thus has a ready-made schema for such situations.
51. Conger, Jay A. and R.N. Kanungo (1987), 'Toward a behavioral theory of charismatic leadership in organizational settings', *Academy of Management Review*, **12** (4), 637–47.
52. Mazlish, Bruce (1984), 'History, psychology, and leadership', in Barbara Kellerman (ed.), *Leadership: Multidisciplinary Perspectives*, Englewood Cliffs, NJ: Prentice-Hall. See also: Westlake, Martin (ed.) (2000), *Leaders of Transition*, London: Macmillan Press.
53. Tuchman, Barbara (1984), *The March of Folly: From Troy to Vietnam*, New York: Knopf.
54. Mazlish (1984).
55. Meindl (1995).
56. Pastor, Juan-Carlos, James R. Meindl and M.C. Mayo (2002), 'A network effects model of charisma attributions', *Academy of Management Journal*, **45** (2), 410–20.
57. Schwartz, Barry (2000), *Abraham Lincoln and the Forge of National Memory*, Chicago: University of Chicago Press.
58. Basler, Ray (ed.) (1953–55), *The Collected Works of Abraham Lincoln*, 9 vols, New Brunswick: Rutgers University Press, vol. 3, pp. 145–6.
59. Schwartz (2000, p. 125).
60. Schwartz, Barry (1987), *George Washington: The Making of an American Symbol*, New York and London: Free Press/Collier Macmillan; Schwartz (2000).
61. Mead, George H. (1934), *Mind, Self and Society*, Chicago: University of Chicago Press; Frankl, Viktor (1959), *Man's Search for Meaning*, Boston: Beacon Press; Maslow (1970); Durkheim (1973).
62. Cooley, Charles H. (1964), *Human Nature and the Social Order*, New York: Schocken, p. 341.
63. Bruner, Jerome (1986), *Actual Minds, Possible Worlds*, Cambridge, MA: Harvard University Press.
64. A salient expression of the centrality of the story is the place that it occupies today in therapeutic practice. In this context, the argument in essence is that human life is a story that one tells oneself and by which one lives. This frame of reference naturally has therapeutic implications, as described in a book by Omer and Allon (see below). Nevertheless the very mention of this possibility presents the story as a powerful means of making meaning in its deeper senses, including aspects that tend to be classified as psychopathological. See Omer, Haim and Nechi Allon (1997), *Ma'aseh Hasipur Hatipuli [The Therapeutic Story]*, Tel Aviv: Modan [Hebrew].

3. Fictionalization of leadership

> Our senses don't deceive us: our judgment does.
> (Goethe)

ONCE A LEADER, ALWAYS A LEADER?

It is surprising to what extent people in the Western world who are diverse in age, education, gender and socioeconomic status cite the same names when they are asked to give examples of leadership. Winston Churchill, Franklin Delano Roosevelt, George Washington, Charles de Gaulle, Mahatma Gandhi, Martin Luther King, Nelson Mandela, Mustafa Ataturk, David Ben-Gurion, Thomas Jefferson, Pierre Elliott Trudeau and John Kennedy are always mentioned. Many people think that great leaders belong only to the past; they long for them and refer to them as a standard by which to compare the leaders of today and explain why they are not real leaders like those who existed in the past.

This list of names[1] arouses some questions to which I alluded in relation to the psychological explanations presented in the previous chapter. Was Churchill a projection screen – a source of unwitting attraction of the followers to the leader – whose psychological validity was relevant only during wartime? Why were leaders like Thomas Jefferson and George Washington, who kept slaves, considered symbols of leaders with high moral principles? Were they carved out of the 'right' narrative materials that made it possible to ignore these facts? In general why do some people and not others constitute the materials for the 'right story', which becomes a narrative of leadership that lives beyond their time? And what are these narrative materials? How is it that a certain person (e.g., Lincoln) becomes a revered leader many years after his death, while leaders who are incomparably charismatic during their lifetime (such as Vladimir Ilyich Lenin, Andrew Jackson) are gradually forgotten over the years? How do some people who are admired as leaders in social, military or business spheres become dull and grey when they accede to political leadership? In order to explain the psychological law that governs these processes, I will attempt, through analysis of their stories, to formulate more accurate models of acceptance, response and even reverence of leaders.

To begin this analysis, let us take an example that was discussed in the previous chapter – the story of Abraham Lincoln. Using Lincoln's story I will demonstrate the contents that can turn a leader into a myth, as well as the social contagion processes whereby the mythologization of the leader figure occurs.[2]

ABRAHAM LINCOLN – THE EVOLUTION OF A LEADERSHIP MYTHOLOGY; AN ILLUSTRATIVE EXAMPLE

From the beginning of the twentieth century Lincoln was an increasing subject of discussion, first in the media and later in growing social and political circles. Analyses of the contents of these discussions have identified three major themes: *simplicity, accessibility, and compassion.*[3] The following documented examples illustrate how these themes found expression in descriptions relating to Lincoln.

Simplicity: The *Chicago Daily Tribune* of 12 February 1908 published a report (p. 7) by sculptor Leonard Volk of his visit to Springfield, the hometown of President-elect Lincoln. Volk, who had come to Lincoln's home immediately after his election in order to take measurements for a sculpture of the new president, was overwhelmed by Lincoln's direct approach. He reported that when the time came for a cast to be made of the forearm, he asked Lincoln to choose and grasp some object. The president-elect went out to the yard, sawed off an old broom handle, and returned with it. 'Would it not have been more fitting for a servant to do that kind of work?' the sculptor asked. Lincoln could only laugh and say, 'We are not much used to servants about this place; besides, you know, I have always been my own wood sawyer.'

Anecdotes related by Lincoln's friends also emphasized his simplicity. For example, the *Chicago Tribune* of 1 February 1909 featured a story reported by Billy Brown, a friend of Lincoln from Springfield, on a visit he had made to the White House. When he arrived at the president's residence he was prepared to wait, assuming that the president would be busy. He gave his name to the doorman and within a minute Lincoln appeared and embraced him warmly, urging him to stay for dinner. After dinner the guest prepared to leave for his hotel in the city centre, but the president invited him to stay the night. When Billy insisted on returning to the hotel, explaining that he had to get up early in the morning in order to travel back to Springfield, the president shook his hand warmly and with tears welling in his eyes, said, 'You don't know how happy you have made me, Billy. You have no idea how much I miss home.'[4]

Stories of this kind appeared in the press more and more frequently. At one point they were not only introduced as 'anecdotes worth reading' but presented almost as an educational imperative. For example, in a manner typical of that period, the above anecdote on Billy Brown was preceded in the *Chicago Tribune* by a statement that could be seen as editorial opinion: 'Everyone, whether man, woman, or child, will be a better person after reading this story.'

This tendency grew noticeably in the second decade of the twentieth century. The rhetoric in the press soon merged into the official political discourse and thus, for instance, Woodrow Wilson (who besides being president of the United States was also a professor of political science at Princeton University) used the theme of Lincoln's simplicity as a desirable political image: 'The great voice of America does not come from the seats of learning, it comes from the hills, the forests, the farms, the factories, the mines, in a desire that is snowballing and gathering momentum. It comes from the homes of simple people.'[5]

Accessibility: Among the hundreds of anecdotes about Lincoln that circulated during the first two decades of the twentieth century, the following appeared in the *Chicago Daily Tribune* of 7 February 1909:

> Many persons noticed three little girls, poorly dressed, the children of some mechanic or laboring man, who had followed the visitors into the White House to gratify their curiosity. They passed around from room to room and were hastening through the reception room with some trepidation when the president called to them, 'Little girls, are you going to pass me without shaking hands?' Then he bent his tall, awkward form down and shook each little girl warmly by the hand. Everybody in the apartment was spellbound by the incident, so simple in itself.[6]

Numerous stories described how Lincoln greeted widows and orphans, showing warmth and empathy. Especially numerous were the accounts of his visits and talks with wounded soldiers in hospitals. Such gestures by leaders are not uncommon today and are almost an unavoidable ritual, but that was not the case in those days. There is sparse evidence of such behaviours on the part of past leaders (including the most revered). George Washington, who headed the army for eight years in the struggle for independence, is never described as paying attention to the wounded, certainly not visiting them in the hospital and having long conversations with them.

Compassion: From the beginning of the twentieth century innumerable anecdotes began to spread referring to Lincoln's kindness, forgiving nature and empathy. Even romantic episodes in his life were described in a manner that accentuated his humanity. One story goes that when he was living in a rented apartment in New Salem, Illinois at the age of 26, he fell in love with his landlady's daughter, Ann. She was already engaged to a man called John McNamara who had come from the East Coast to start a new life in Illinois.

McNamara went to visit his family in the East and was supposed to return in time for the wedding. After some months had passed and nothing was heard of him, Lincoln declared his love to Ann. Although she returned his love she was torn between her commitment to her absent fiancé and her love for Lincoln. According to the story, this dilemma affected Ann's health and her mental state deteriorated. She became seriously ill and finally died of complications in the brain. Her death was a severe blow to Lincoln, and there are some who believe that he suffered all his life from guilt feelings. Others say that he never loved another woman (although he married later), and there is a version that his health was ruined by this event. Whatever the case may be, the grief and sorrow motif is dominant in his most famous pictures and statues, and in published descriptions of him Lincoln is portrayed as a grieving mourner.[7]

One of the many stories illustrating Lincoln's compassion is that of the 'sleeping sentinel', which was actually dramatized as a movie. The story tells of a young soldier called William Scott who came from a family of farmers in Vermont. Caught sleeping on guard duty while substituting for a sick friend after an exhausting day of military exercises, William was court-martialled and sentenced to death. Lincoln heard about the case from William's friend and hurried to see the soldier in his prison cell. After questioning William at length about his family, his friends and neighbours, and the management of the farm in Vermont, Lincoln reached the conclusion that this was a worthy young man and ordered his release, urging him to be a pride to his mother. Later, William died in battle. All the versions of this story praise the warm and caring relationship that Lincoln maintained with the family of the dead soldier who had really become a source of pride to them, especially to his mother.[8]

From the point of view of psychological analysis of the leader's image construction, the emphasis on compassion in Lincoln's image raises an interesting and important question when we compare Lincoln's leadership with that of President Andrew Jackson, who was more open to the masses and whose biography, deeds and decisions show him to be a man of the people more than Lincoln. Jackson, the son of Irish immigrants, grew up in North Carolina in a poor family. He lost his entire family (parents and two brothers) before he was 14. He worked hard (in a store), acquired an education in law and became an attorney, and later a delegate to the Tennessee Constitutional Convention. When Tennessee achieved statehood, Jackson was elected its US representative. In 1797 he was elected to the US senate and resigned within a year. In 1798, he was appointed judge of the Tennessee Supreme Court, serving until 1804. In 1829 he was elected as the seventh president of the US and was the first president to invite the public to attend the White House ball honouring his inauguration. His contribution to the democratization of America is highly praised by historians, some of whom see him as a president who was ahead of his time in his democratic outlook. Among other things, he was responsible for strengthening the power of party conventions and for the direct election of presidential candidates. He initiated regulations such as rotation of roles in the administration.[9] In addition to his legal and political career, Jackson prospered as a slave owner, planter and merchant (during his lifetime he owned as many as 300 slaves). At the same time, Jackson was appointed commander of the Tennessee militia in 1801 (he was a Major General) and won two victories – in 1812 against the Indians, and in 1815 in New Orleans against the British. He was known as a brave, tough commander who had direct and close contacts with the common soldiers; they admired him and called him 'tough as old hickory'.[10] Although Jackson was more open to the masses than Lincoln and his attitude to the wealthy and privileged classes was less tolerant, and although he contributed much more to the democratization of society than Lincoln and was very much admired in his term whereas Lincoln was the subject of controversy, today Lincoln is the most revered president in American history and Jackson, in comparison, is quite marginal and forgotten. This retrospective comparison of two leaders from peripheral states with similar family backgrounds, who showed genuine interest in the common people illustrates the process of construction of a leadership narrative and also contributes to our understanding of the changing nature of the contents and processes that create leadership myths. The case of Lincoln, which is so distinct and prominent, can serve as a suitable 'laboratory study' for analysis of the psychosocial processes that facilitated the construction of his image as a revered leader.

A good starting point, then, is examination of the processes that occurred in the first two decades of the twentieth century, the period when the veneration of Lincoln grew rapidly.

First let us look at the facts and then examine their sociological and psychological significance in the context discussed. Between 1861 (the beginning of Lincoln's presidency) and 1910, the population of the United States more than tripled, from 30 million to 92 million, and the urban population rose from 20 per cent to 46 per cent of the population as a whole. This means that by 1910 approximately half of the population was urbanized (a trend that was to grow in the following years). In other words, the American society of Lincoln's lifetime, which was largely rural and agrarian, had become much more urbanized and industrialized. New York City, for example, grew sixfold in less than 25 years, from half a million citizens in 1867 to 3 million in 1900. The population of Chicago grew from 30 000 in 1861 to more than 2 million in 1910.[11] Furthermore, the urban population growth was not only numerical; it also reflected the development of large urban centres – a fact that had significant sociological effects, mainly in terms of social stratification but also in the sphere of culture. For example, hereditary status symbols that were dominant in the agrarian society of the nineteenth century lost their exalted meaning.

Money became the most important thing, even as a status symbol. Money was also a universal and more accessible resource to the millions of new immigrants. The lifestyle and the cultural symbols were different in the urban centres. With the expansion of economic and social mobility, the familiar features of an urban society began to appear – growing gaps between rich and poor, slums versus luxury neighbourhoods, rich financial corporations and the emergence of a new class – managers versus unions of workers without rights. The changes that occurred in the 50 years after Lincoln's assassination may be summarized using the terminology of the American sociologist Edward Shils, '*center and periphery*', center being the sociological term for the elite – people, organizations and entities that symbolize the major values to which people aspire in a given period.[12] All these had changed significantly. The symbols of the centre in Lincoln's period resembled those of the Old World, meaning Europe, and particularly Britain. The symbolic centre of the urban industrialized American society that began to take shape in the early decades of the twentieth century was very different. It emphasized values such as universality, equal rights, individualism, populism and laissez-faire – values that were totally opposed to the ascribed values of the Old World. In the light of these concepts it is easier to see the sources of the leader's charisma. Charismatic leaders who arouse feelings of identification are in fact concrete manifestations of abstract values and concepts such as symbolic centre. Thus, just as George Washington was perceived as a leader because he was the personification of the symbolic centre in his period (a ranch owner and army officer, born and married into the 'right families'), Lincoln personified the values of the New World. This perspective clarifies how the characteristics attributed to Lincoln that made him so controversial in his lifetime facilitated his transformation into a revered leader 50 years later. First of all he had a life story that matched the changes that had occurred in American society. He did not come from a noble family, nor had he studied in prestigious schools. He came from a small town in the Midwest, from a family of farmers, and together with his family had worked hard to earn a living while studying to acquire an education in law by his own efforts. His biography could well serve as a symbol of the American ideal of the self-made man, but so was Andrew Jackson's story. However, unlike Jackson, the anecdotes about his humane and compassionate approach were the right materials for a society that had rapidly become urbanized and industrialized, with the concomitant alienation, loneliness and poverty alongside the struggle for opportunities and mobility in an immigrant society. Against the background of this nascent society, the people and movements that led social struggles found in Lincoln the most persuasive images for advancing their agenda.

Yet despite the fact that the leader's image is in accord with the period, the people's deep yearning in a certain period is necessary but not sufficient. The development of a person's image as that of a charismatic and revered leader requires informal assimilation processes, which are widely described in research on phenomena such as gossip, rumour diffusion and reputation building. These processes are part of what is described as *social contagion*.[13] Let us look at some typical examples of how they occur.

First, leading figures in the political system used Lincoln as a personification of their ideas and initiatives. An example of this is the rhetoric of Theodore Roosevelt, an extremely activist president in the early twentieth century, who strove to promote a more progressive agenda than any previous president. He acted to achieve regulation of the price system, protective taxes, regulation of private corporations, income tax, preservation of natural resources, laws granting compensation for employees, legislation concerning the work of women and children, and more. Roosevelt used Lincoln as a model for the purpose of promoting and 'marketing' his progressive doctrine, mentioning Lincoln's name in almost every programmatic statement. He stated repeatedly that he was merely Lincoln's follower and executor of his progressive platform: 'The Progressive platform of today', he argued in one of his addresses, 'is but an amplification of Lincoln's. Lincoln and Lincoln's supporters were emphatically the Progressives of their day.'[14] Roosevelt's many followers knew that he was a great admirer of Lincoln. His admiration for Lincoln was typically portrayed in a caricature that appeared in the *New York Mail* of 3 August 1904 with the caption 'Led by Lincoln's principles', showing Theodore Roosevelt holding Lincoln's hand while the latter leads him with arm outstretched as if guiding a blind man. Reminiscent of the old cliché that a picture is worth a thousand words, the caricature shows clearly that Lincoln is the one who sets the direction. The fact that a revered president venerates another leader undoubtedly arouses great esteem for the latter.

Second, regarding the psychological image described, Lincoln was eminently suitable for symbolic use by social movements, which were increasingly prevalent in the demographic and social reality of the early twentieth century. The most salient example of this is the struggle for women's rights. Lincoln, apparently after the manner of agrarian societies, had not dealt with women's rights, nor had he spoken or written very much about this issue. Nevertheless, the movements that were struggling for women's suffrage sought to prove the justice of their claims by likening their struggle to the Civil War (which was seen as a battle for values and justice initiated by Lincoln). The women envisaged themselves as 'Lincoln's soldiers' fighting for a new, modern version of liberation from slavery. At numerous rallies, demonstration marches and in the press, they called for the 'fulfilment of Lincoln's legacy'. His 'maternal' qualities of compassion, simplicity and accessibility, which depicted him as a controversial leader in the tough, masculine stereotype-ridden society of nineteenth-century America, were embraced by the social activists as positive expressions of concern and sympathy, justice and social responsibility. Indeed, when women achieved the franchise in 1920, they saw this as a manifestation of the fulfilment of Lincoln's wishes.[15] Similarly, other social movements fighting for their rights or opposing the privileges or excessive power of government or financial bodies (e.g., the anti-corporate movements) used Lincoln's image from the Civil War and his humane expressions as weapons in their struggle. The social contagion processes were intensified by those powerfully resonant channels – the media, particularly the printed press, which was then the main medium of mass communication. Lincoln's image was enhanced by numerous newspaper items that extolled him as an agent of the progressive agenda that was supported by the important newspaper editors. According to the *Reader's Guide to Periodical Literature*, during that period 575 articles about Lincoln appeared in 58 different publications. Half of the articles appeared in eight publications, which openly declared their commitment to the progressive agenda.[16]

Thus, the massive population growth and the dramatic transition in socio-demographic characteristics, together with changing values and social unrest marked by a search for relevant symbols and a suitable agenda effectively pursued by its proponents, gave rise to processes and contents of social contagion that turned Lincoln into a leader with a message, a story that contained all the elements necessary for transforming him into a *narrative of collective identity*. This man, who was criticized harshly during his lifetime, who won the presidency with a majority of only 4 per cent of the vote, whose term in office was probably the most difficult period in the history of the USA, when Americans were killed by Americans on American soil, this leader who did not go to war to free the slaves, who was profoundly hated by many and eventually assassinated, this man 50 years later became the most charismatic, moral and highly esteemed leader in the history of the United States. It is rare to find such a clear example of the twists and reversals that play a part in the construction of a leader figure, but analysis of the psychological processes occurring among the followers can certainly show that it is not a question of fortuitous and meaningless changes but of processes governed by psychological laws. Let us look, then, at these psychological laws.

THE PLACE OF NEED AND MEMORY IN A LEADER'S IMAGE CONSTRUCTION

Two theoretical points of departure will serve for examination of the laws governing the construction (or disappearance from memory) of charismatic leaders. One is based on the concept of need and the other on memory.

In discussing the concept of need we can refer to Abraham Maslow's famous theory,[17] which is clear and compact, and above all poses a central idea that serves as a conceptual scaffolding – *hierarchy of needs*. This means, for example, that the motivation and behaviours of someone who is busy looking for a solution to the basic needs of his or her physical existence differ in their expression and intensity from those of someone living in a Fifth Avenue apartment in New York. Maslow's theory served the famous leadership scholar James MacGregor Burns in developing his major ideas on leadership. Since Burns's book *Leadership*[18] has had considerable influence on leadership research in the past 30 years, the use of Maslow's theory as a conceptual starting point can provide a relevant basis for comparative analysis. At the bottom of Maslow's hierarchy of needs are the basic needs – physical survival and safety – that motivate every living creature. In humans they reach full expression in infancy. Babies can be observed responding mainly to hunger, heat, cold, dangers and physical contact. Thinkers such as Sigmund Freud or John Bowlby,[19] whose theories had a powerful impact on psychological research, saw the manner in which these needs were fulfilled (usually by the parents) as the basis for understanding the emotional development of humans in the course of their lives. They conceptualized and investigated the existence of a psychological substructure that causes the basic instincts from early childhood to return to the fore, especially when doubts and fear arise. Then the primary yearning for the big, strong, omnipotent figures that we knew in our early lives is aroused. From this point of view, the more threatening and distressing the situation, the stronger the attraction, the wish and the readiness to follow a leader who is perceived as able to supply these basic needs.

Apparently it was not in vain that Hillary Clinton's advisors sprang into action during her electoral battle with Barack Obama over the Democratic Party leadership, in order to create the clip in which the president's hotline rings at 3 a.m. and the voiceover asks the voters who they would rely on at that moment. It appears that the fear and drama involved in such situations reduce the entire leadership phenomenon to this specific criterion – the ability to provide security. This principle bridges inter-situational and inter-organizational differences. The soldier in the battlefield will stick to a leader who makes them feel that they can extricate them from the inferno. And the citizen who is unemployed (or afraid of losing their job) will tend to support a leader they see as capable of providing an answer to their fears. This basic level in the hierarchy of needs encompasses behaviours that may be described as instinctive behaviours.

However, a hierarchy by definition consists of different levels, and many people have either passed the stage of basic needs or are more concerned with other needs at a higher level in the hierarchy. Some of the higher-level needs are associated with abstract and symbolic manifestations that distinguish humans from other creatures. Some of this can be seen in the expression of *the need for belonging*, namely wanting to be part of a group, community or other framework that grants identity.

In this sense leaders are figures who help people and groups in consolidating the psychological processes of forming a sense of identity. The example cited in the previous chapter – Nelson Mandela's transformation into a national leader – illustrates symbolization processes unconnected with intimate knowledge of the man himself. Mandela was incarcerated as a young man and released at the age of 71. An analysis of the process in terms of the need for belonging and identity[20] indicates that Mandela's story contains all the materials of a leadership symbol. He was the symbolic embodiment of the blacks in South Africa – unyielding in the face of oppression. His isolation and inaccessibility only helped to magnify his image as a leader and his construction as a narrative, a tangible symbol of a social identity. In point of fact the agitation, the pressure to release the blacks from the oppressive rule of the white government, all happened while Mandela was in prison. He himself was not present at the actual events for almost 30 years, but the story, the myth, was present, and with a force that could not be stopped.

A comparison of the personalities or visions of leaders like George Washington, Nelson Mandela, Mahatma Gandhi, David Ben-Gurion or Mustafa Ataturk – all 'fathers of nations' – reveals differences that are enormous in some cases. The personality of George Washington, the landowner and 'majestic officer', was very different from that of Nelson Mandela, a man of the people who had grown up in a remote village in South Africa. Furthermore, an analysis of the vision of these leaders reveals differences that are not conducive to the formulation of a comprehensive theory of similarity between leaders. Gandhi saw *truth* (*Satyagraha*) as a source and a means of struggle against the British. Not only was his approach non-militant, his apparel and his ascetic way of life, as well as his words, were oriented towards spirituality (*Brahmacharya*) as a personal and national source of power.[21] In contrast, Ataturk, a dandy who liked women and alcohol, regarded military strength, Western progress and separation of state and religion as the sources of power of modern Turkey. Yet despite these differences in the contents and style of their leadership, analysis from the followers' point of view reveals the similarity of the psychological substructure. The crumbling of the Ottoman Empire created a vacuum and yearning for national identity. Ataturk, a military man who had led the battle of Gallipoli and was seen as a hero by the Turks, began to be constructed as a legend that grew and became more powerful as the empire and sultanate weakened. Apparently a military legend was what suited the national yearnings that surged in Turkey during that period.[22] David Ben-Gurion's activist approach aroused dissension during the early years of his leadership, but he became a legendary leader due to the need and the desperate longing to build a national home for the Jews after the Holocaust in Europe.[23] These leaders' messages differed and the symbols, too, acquired diverse expressions, but the essence was the same – each of them (in the specific contexts, which will be analysed) represented the powerful need for a distinctive collective identity. From this point of view it may be argued with some degree of speculation that, like Abraham Lincoln, who only started to become a revered symbol of leadership at a certain time, some of these founding fathers matured into their symbolic status in circumstances connected with the palpable dominance of the issue of collective identity during their period.

Why, then, is the need for identity manifested in such different modes of leadership? Why does one society choose and follow a leader who represents spiritual values (Gandhi) while another chooses a leader who represents more militant ideas (Ataturk)? And more, why do leadership prototypes change over time (as in the case of Lincoln)? It is important to address these questions in order to formulate psychological principles that can help to provide a more precise and detailed answer to the question: what are the materials from which the leadership narrative is constructed?

A useful integrative concept for discussion of this subject is *community of memory*,[24] according to which, just as memories of experiences, people, stories and facts affect the interpretation of reality at the personal level, so do such memories influence interpretations of reality at the collective level. Since different collectives have different experiences, histories and memories, these naturally have different meanings, which also concern leadership. This argument is congruent with analyses conducted by scholars, revealing the existence of processes of interpreting reality based on meanings derived from collective memory.[25] Furthermore, observation and analysis of memory functions lead to a further distinction concerning the permanent and temporary elements that influence the choice and acceptance of a leader – namely short-term memory and long-term memory. The difference is clear: short-term memory relates to items and events close to the present time, while long-term memory relates to past events that occurred in the collective and are burnt into the collective consciousness, and have different implications regarding the strength of the attraction to different leadership images.

Perhaps it will be easier to understand the leader's location in the collective memory if we return to the metaphor of the leader as a story. In these terms the question is: why is a certain book a bestseller in one period and then forgotten in the long term? And on the other hand, why do certain books become immortal, some of them crossing national boundaries and living on as universal treasures? Analogically, why is a leader venerated in a certain period (Andrew Jackson) and almost forgotten in the course of time, while others become legendary leaders for generations? What is the psychological law that explains the location of a leader in the short-term collective memory, and the processes of forgetting or locating leaders in the long-term collective memory?

The sociologist Karl Mannheim,[26] in a well-known article on *generational units* provides a conceptual frame suitable for the discussion on collective memory, at least short-term memory. According to him, a generational unit is characterized by the fact that its members are exposed to the same historical experience and therefore tend to display similar manners of thinking, emotional reactions and behaviour patterns. The attitudes and ideas that are really formative in the life of a collective in a certain generation are not consciously transmitted but permeate people's minds without their knowledge and become the natural world view of the adult. This is reflected in the feelings described by representatives of different generations. For example, many people in Israel from the generation of 1948 (people who lived during Israel's War of Independence) report that their way of thinking was profoundly affected by their daily experiences such as blacking out the rooms, obsessively following the news on the radio, discussions in the school and youth movement, the songs and books, and accounts of personal experiences from the army.[27]

Mannheim's explanation appears to cast light on the formation of myths, values, preferences and also of leadership concepts in periods that may be delineated as generational units. In addition, this angle of vision shows more clearly the power of the social contagion processes mentioned earlier.[28] For one thing, as described by researchers on collective memory, we can see that the primary condition for the formation of a collective memory is the transformation of the personal memory to a narrative that is related in social and public contexts.[29] An unusually clear example of this is the incorporation of the Jewish Holocaust in World War II into the Israeli collective memory. Although hundreds of thousands of Holocaust survivors reached Israel after World War II, during the first 15 years of Israel's existence as a state this accumulation of painful private memories was not reflected in the public discourse. Perhaps the memories were suppressed because the subject was too painful to bear. Perhaps the mythologized image of the Jewish warrior was preferred to the image of the Jew dragged to the slaughter, and in this public atmosphere the survivors of the ghettoes and death camps were ashamed and preferred to keep silent. Whatever the reason, the undisputed fact is that the Holocaust was not a part of the collective memory of the new nation, whereas today it is a significant component, perhaps the major component, in the Israeli collective memory.[30] How did this come about? How did suppressed private memories become a component that has such a powerful socializing effect in the shaping of the collective identity?

Although there are different opinions regarding the process, the consensus is that the turning point was the trial of Adolf Eichmann, whom Hitler had entrusted with the implementation of the Final Solution (the annihilation of the Jewish people). Eichmann was found in Argentina by Israeli espionage agents and brought to trial in Israel in the early 1960s. Only then did the deeply suppressed stories come into the public domain. The evidence of Holocaust survivors was broadcast daily on the radio, journalists reported extensively on the trial proceedings and published the accounts of victims who laid bare their hearts following the trial. Students in schools listened to the broadcasts of the trial together with their teachers and discussed it with them. Encouraged by their teachers, children began to ask their parents about the Holocaust. Survivors' personal memories became the topics of the day. People who had hidden or suppressed the memories of their Holocaust experiences began to talk of them openly on various platforms. Survivors addressed audiences of soldiers or members of youth movements, or spoke with young people who wanted to hear first-hand accounts of what had happened. During the year of the trial, the entire Israeli population seemed, directly or indirectly, to be sharing the experience of the Holocaust, which had clearly become part of the collective memory.

The view of leaders as a narrative taking place within a generational unit may, for the sake of illustration, cast light on the enigma of two Israeli leaders who were highly charismatic in their time and almost completely forgotten later: Yigal Allon and Moshe Dayan. These two may be seen as the ultimate embodiment of the aspirations of their generation, the personification of a generation that longed to erase the image of the 'old Jew', the ghetto Jew, the merchants living in fear of their surroundings. They symbolized the new Jew, a symbol that their generation was so eager to adopt – strong people of the soil and brave fighters, a new breed.[31] However, the arrival of millions of immigrants from many different countries within a short period of time changed Israeli society completely as it underwent a process similar to the transformation of American society from an agrarian to an urban industrialized society, bringing in its wake changes in values, myths and also leadership images. From a small homogeneous society seeking to live as pioneers and fighters, it became a heterogeneous émigré society. This perspective may explain why Menachem Begin, whom many saw as the 'eternal opposition', a pre-eminent representative of European Diaspora Jewry, a man who mentioned the Holocaust on every public platform, suddenly became the leader of the nation, the prime minister. Begin, Allon and Dayan, like Lincoln, did not undergo dramatic upheavals in their personality. The upheavals took place in the society of which they were leaders.

These examples may help us to understand the principles underlying the growth of generational leadership stories, but the question remains as to the psychological law relevant to long-term, *intergenerational* memory. This question is the hub of discussion among researchers of collective or social memory,[32] an elusive area whose meaning is derived from the cultural consensus.[33] It has no precise definition but most historians are agreed that collective memory, its formation, its ongoing existence, as well as the research on it, differ from formal history as studied in academic institutions. As implied in the examples presented earlier, biographers, poets, playwrights, journalists, authors, scriptwriters, film directors, art curators, curriculum writers, tour guides, and, of course, electronic communications media – all contribute to the diffusion of stories, some of which become components in the collective memory.[34]

Which components are retained in the intergenerational memory, and why those in particular? And how does it happen? These are cardinal questions that occupy scholars from various disciplines, who largely agree with Durkheim's statement that components of the collective memory become social fact that affects the consciousness like a geographical and physical experience, and that the components of the collective memory become part of the identity of the collective.[35]

A familiar example of the existence of long-term collective memory and the manner of its formation and preservation is the development of the concept of military heritage in combat units. In these units' messages are transmitted from one generation to another through a variety of channels, the purpose being to shape the character, values, motivation and ways of thinking of the soldier, particularly of the commander – the leader who is in essence an intergenerational figure. Thus, soldiers completing their basic training might be sworn in at the site of heroic battles fought by their units, visit battle sites from earlier generations, participate in arduous marches 'in the footsteps of warriors', visit heritage centres in their units, meet with former fighters to hear their stories and read about past heroes of the unit. All of this helps to promote esprit-de-corps in the unit, feelings of pride and mutual loyalty expressed in their emotions, ways of thinking and characteristic behaviours.[36]

This example of the history, symbolization and identity formation of a military unit as a community of memory highlights the centrality of the story in general, and the leader's story in particular, in creating the intergenerational collective memory, and shows how this is analogous to the entrance of literary works into the canon. The story, as we can see from the example of memory building and identity building processes in military units, is a major means of transmitting messages. In fact, the study of stories is a valuable source for examining the creation and preservation of organizational cultures,[37] which may be seen as the civilian equivalents of military heritage in military units. Take, for example, this military heritage-like story that circulated in IBM.[38] An engineer approached the CEO with an idea for developing a new product. 'Go for it!' said the CEO, and sure enough, backed by appropriate funding, the engineer worked devotedly and enthusiastically on developing the idea. After considerable endeavours, he arrived at the conclusion that his idea was not feasible. With a letter of resignation in his pocket he went back to the CEO to offer his resignation due to his failure. The CEO refused to accept the resignation, claiming angrily that the man had no right to leave the company after gaining so much knowledge at the company's expense.

The important thing in analysing the circulation and resonance of this story is the messages it conveys: in our company we encourage risk-taking; failure is something to learn from; nothing ventured, nothing gained – messages indicating the behaviours that are desirable 'in our company'. Stories like this, generally referring to leaders, become, so to speak, coordinates on a road map showing the best route to take, based on knowledge from the past, from the collective memory.

Edgar Schein, a researcher of organizational cultures,[39] argues that the components of long-term memory are retained and become part of the culture because they have functional value in the sense of existential survival. The essence of his claim is that the roots of a culture are grounded in the formative influence of the generation of the founders. The latter laid the foundations of the culture and identity, including the guiding values, etiquette, ceremonies, symbols and other things that create the forms of thinking and the behaviours characteristic of a given organization. These components are preserved and passed on from one generation to another so long as they constitute an internal language and an effective tool enabling the organization to contend successfully with its environment and major challenges. As a matter of fact, this thinking was the point of departure for the study of successful organizations.[40] For example, the American scholars Collins and Porras investigated commercial companies, which they called champions, that were indisputably and by measurable criteria the most successful in their fields over decades. These scholars found that the key to success was the values passed down from the founding generation to their successors, values that they likened to a clock or a compass guiding them.[41]

On the other hand, when organizations are not successful the first thing to be done, according to the man who replaced the founder of Digital (a company that prospered for many years and then began to decline in the 1990s), 'You have to show the old values the door.' The clearest practical link between values and leadership is the sequel to this statement: 'You have to send the leaders home.'[42]

Another explanation, which in many senses represents a different side of the collective experience that is retained in the intergenerational collective memory, is that of the *collective trauma*. The effects of this have been extensively discussed by the Turkish-American psychoanalyst Vamik Volkan.[43] Volkan first explains the idea of intergenerational transmission at the intrapersonal level, and then goes on to discuss the manifestations of this phenomenon at the collective level.

Based on his therapeutic work with refugees of the war between Abkhazia and South Ostia, Volkan wrote about an Abkhazian refugee named Marli who had escaped from her home and lived with her three children in poor conditions in a hotel that had been converted into a temporary shelter for war refugees. Within a short time the eldest daughter, Downa, age 16, grew inordinately fat. In the psychological diagnostic process, Volkan discovered that Downa understood very well her mother's daily struggle to find food for her children. Becoming fat, according to Volkan's psychodynamic interpretation, was simply an unconscious physical reaction to the mother's worries, a message to the mother saying, 'You don't need to worry about finding food for me. There is enough food; in fact I'm getting fat.' Volkan assumed that if the mother was open and shared her anxiety with her daughter, this would put an end to the unconscious process of intergenerational transmission, which indeed happened, as he reported. According to the theory, intergenerational transmission may become collective, particularly after severe traumas. Volkan distinguishes between disasters that have no element of malicious intent (e.g., acts of God) and deliberately instigated disasters such as genocide. Disasters of this kind become collective traumas, accompanied by ceremonies, stories, films, public discussions and rituals, all fixing the event in the collective memory, which shapes the identity of that community of memory, as demonstrated in the case of the Holocaust in Europe.

The descriptions and explanations presented thus far highlight the importance of a psychological component defined by the Canadian psychologist David Aberbach[44] as *homogamy* – psychological resemblance within a collective in terms of needs, aspirations and perceptions. Such resemblance is more evident at the level of small communities of memory – military units, clans, tribes or organizations. Clearly, the more psychologically, socially and culturally homogeneous the collective, the more intensive the processes of social contagion. As mentioned, social contagion processes have been likened to the spread of a virus; this analogy makes it easier to understand the expansion of leadership concepts in a given social network. As an illustration of this, let us take the followers of the Lubavitcher rabbi, a highly dedicated group that operates as a social network in all corners of the world. Their astonishing ability to act together and achieve results stems largely from their unquestioning obedience to the leader and his or her messages. 'The rabbi said' is not just an undisputed imperative that guides them in their daily activities. The rabbi's leadership has been described in hundreds of stories and anecdotes praising his leadership skills and his wisdom. From a psychological perspective, the point that demonstrates (with great clarity in this case) that the key to understanding the leadership is the social network itself and not the leader's personality; it is the fact that the leader – the Lubavitcher rabbi – died many years ago.

Thus, small communities of memory possess many characteristics of social networks; stories and anecdotes circulate and create an atmosphere and images that influence the network, sometimes directly.[45] In a military unit, a clan or a religious congregation, this also happens at the intergenerational level. Officers know their troops, authority figures like rabbis, priests, khadis and mukhtars (heads of villages) pass on stories that are not only documented in writing but also transmitted directly by word of mouth.

Homogamy processes also exist in commercial organizations. The American organizational psychologist Benjamin Schneider[46] argues that a consensual organizational culture is eventually formed, among other things because the fact of people staying together in an organization generates a kind of natural selection based on compatibility and adjustment. If a certain organization exists in a highly competitive environment, the people in the organization are expected to be suitably competitive and aggressive; otherwise the organization will not survive. People who are not sufficiently competitive and aggressive will either not be drawn to organizations of this kind or will leave them quickly. In the end, says Schneider, the people who remain in the organization are those with similar psychological characteristics. This explanation complements the social psychological explanations discussed above. The leaders in these communities are not just the prototypical expression of the group; they are also the ones who choose people similar to themselves.

Culture scholars have offered explanations with similar logic at broader levels, namely societies or nations. These collectives are shaped to a large extent by their struggle with challenges that call for internal mobilization (expressed in language, culture, identity) in order to enable the collective to strive for its existence and uniqueness. The discussion of questions as to which challenges are the most formative in developing the national character and how it all happens is largely speculative and involves the examination of many possible causes. Some argue that climate has considerable impact on the development of cultures, myths and naturally of leadership prototypes. For example, it was found that populations in cold countries such as those in Scandinavia, where the main threat to survival was from nature and where humans developed the faculties necessary for finding alternatives to agriculture, were characterized by more egalitarian views concerning authority than those in hot countries like Malaysia.[47] These differences are manifested in the everyday practices that shape people's conceptions regarding authority and leadership. In countries that are more egalitarian, for example, the attitudes, typical behaviours and messages transmitted by parents, teachers and principals differ from those in less egalitarian countries. In the latter, children are brought up to obey their parents unconditionally. The teacher is seen as a kind of guru whom the child has to respect, listen to and learn from unquestioningly. Unequal relations between people are the required and accepted pattern (for instance, an employee obeys his or her manager without question). In egalitarian countries on the other hand, children, students and workers are all encouraged to criticize and question. In their eyes those in authority are not necessarily always right.[48] Clearly, differences in socialization influence their leadership concepts, patterns of choosing leaders and the extent of their obedience to the leaders. In a study comparing Druze teachers (whose culture stresses respect for authority in the family and the community, a value imprinted in socialization processes from childhood) with Jewish teachers, it was found that the Druze teachers' attitude towards the principals was more respectful and obedient than the Jewish teachers' attitude to principals, even when they fulfilled the same role functions.[49]

Needless to say, the climatic explanation is only one among many. Most of the explanations concern the influence of certain groups over others that they dominated. Research has found that nations ruled by the Roman Empire adopted different values than nations that were under the rule of other conquerors. It seems, therefore, that the answer lies in different combinations of factors – climatic, historical and geopolitical. And even if it is difficult to pinpoint one explanation or evaluate the relative weight of the different explanations, intercultural comparative research shows clearly that different societies have different cultures, which have been referred to as the *software of the mind* that provides the basis for routine applications.[50] One of the more dominant software programs in terms of influence on ways of thinking, symbols and those who represent them, is religion. Max Weber, in his early writing, remarked that Protestant values encourage diligence and achievement, and therefore Protestant societies succeed more than others.[51]

Religion is a conspicuous illustration of primary philosophical conceptions summarized in a book or related through legends passed down by word of mouth until they eventually become sanctified and guiding. At the beginning of Greek culture we find two sacred books – the *Iliad* and the *Odyssey*. The *Book of Changes* (*I Ching*) became the foundation of the Chinese culture. The Jewish culture is based on the *Torah* (Old Testament), and the New Testament is the foundation of Christianity. Many of the ideas embodied in these books became constitutive stories, and some of them were dramatized in order to convey their messages more powerfully.

The *Iliad* and *Odyssey* contain stories of the Olympic gods who, like humans, are controlled by fate. Fate is the fundamental idea in the classical Greek culture. In cultures where authority is the representative of the gods or of fate, the followers cannot conceive that it is possible for them to cross the boundaries of determinism.

A closer and more dramatic example of the reality represented by a story in the interpretation of a culture and of the collective attitude to leadership is the Faust story of Mephistopheles, a German folk tale originating in religion.

The folk tale of Faust who sold his soul to the devil was dramatized by Goethe. In the prologue we already see a concept of deity different from that described in books. God is portrayed as bored with the society of his good angels, who keep singing his praises. God sends Mephistopheles to spur idle humanity to activity. Unlike the stories that appear in other religious myths, here there is no message of redemption or of improving the world, of hope, mercy or love, only a message of *action*. God only wants his beloved son Mephistopheles to descend into the world and spur on the humans who are idling in their work. The protagonist in the play, Faust, the man who made a pact with the devil, was an alchemist who lived during the time of the Reformation. In life he was a marginal person who was tired of dialectics and the study of philosophy and theology, which did not solve his problems. He did not want to remain bound by ethical discussions that demanded restraint; he longed to begin life anew. He wanted action! Faust made a pact with the devil in order to gain all the pleasures of life and receive supernatural powers. A decision like that could not derive from most of the familiar religious stories because, although there are differences, the religious archetype matches the way in which the human consciousness functions, and it is clear to the human mind that there is a price to be paid for everything. There are indeed differences between religions and cultures as to the manner of payment. Some choose penance; others offer sacrifices to placate the gods. There are some who associate sacrifice with the idea of redemption. In Goethe's drama, Faust signs an agreement with the devil but also avoids payment.

It would be possible to relate to this story as just another tale that may perhaps interest folklore scholars but has no substantive meaning. But some observant scholars and writers, such as the German author Thomas Mann, pointed to the thread linking Martin Luther, the story of Faust and the pragmatism referred to by many as a central attribute in German culture.[52] The fact that the myth of Faust occupied writers and artists in Germany to an inordinate extent (at least 20 adaptations of the Faust legend appeared in Germany, including musical adaptations) along with the fact that this very play that was highly acclaimed in Germany met with a cool reception at best in other places, does not seem accidental to some scholars. It reflects cultural differences that affect, among other aspects, different approaches to authority.[53] In this respect God and his representatives are just a metaphor illustrating the relation to authority in a particular collective.

Societies that share collective memories rooted in continuous life in the same territory, similar theological roots, collective traumas, a common language and a common history of struggles for survival tend to be homogeneous, whereas societies in which there is considerable divergence in all or some of these areas (e.g., different languages, different theologies) tend to be more heterogeneous, as can be seen in countries of large-scale immigration, and there will not always be complete congruence between concepts such as social identity and national identity. In psychological terms we may say, somewhat simplistically, that the more homogeneous the society in the aspects mentioned above, the more similar it is to small communities of memory with regard to the psychological processes of collective memory and social contagion. This understanding may help to clarify the transition from a local leadership story (generational and intergenerational) to a more universal transgenerational leadership narrative. The psychological processes that explain why the Faust story was well received in Germany but not in England recall the question as to why a certain leader is the story of a local hero while another leader becomes a universal narrative.

A clue to the understanding of this is provided by no other than Leo Tolstoy, an author whose work is part of the canon of world literature. Tolstoy, a tempestuous anti-establishment character, was known for his uncompromising views on leadership and leaders. He was in the habit of declaring repeatedly that 'to see leaders as heroes is an invention, it's a lie! There are people, just people, and nothing else.' Yet he of all people argued in an interview that took place in 1909 that 'Lincoln was bigger than his country. His example is *universal*' [my emphasis]. In this sense, 'as long as the world exists, Lincoln's greatness as a humanist and a prophet of freedom will live and not just in the American memory.'[54]

Looking at Lincoln's story or, more precisely, at Lincoln as a story, in terms of collective memory, we see that he is remembered mainly for his image as the emancipator of slaves (although, that was not the purpose for which he embarked on the Civil War). In other words, Lincoln is identified with the struggle against exploitation and inequity and the gross violation of natural justice, a theme that crosses boundaries. A more contemporary example that may help to explain the psychological processes involved here is the sacred status ascribed worldwide to Nelson Mandela. The psychological mechanisms that were constructed under his influence, such as the Truth and Reconciliation Commission (a judicial body before which people accused of cruel acts appeared to plead publicly for forgiveness, and received forgiveness), emphasized the theme of forgiveness in the basic sense of absolution, or equality between people (like the image attributed to Lincoln). The emphasis on metaphors such as rainbow, meaning equality between people of different colours, transformed his image from that of a local leader into a more universal symbol of leadership in a manner similar to stories that crossed the boundaries of the local culture in which they were written. Hans Christian Andersen became a famous author outside Denmark because the 'Emperor's New Clothes' does not deal with a local incident but with a common psychological trait – hypocrisy. *Uncle Tom's Cabin* is not simply a story that characterizes the southern states of the USA in a certain period, but a story of struggle against injustice. Dostoevsky's *Crime and Punishment* is not a Russian story but rather deals with more universal issues of right and wrong. These are all themes that transcend nations and cultures. Similarly, certain leaders, whether they were universal and timeless leaders in reality, or were constructed as such through a narrative that was built around their image, became, according to Tolstoy, precious assets to civilization as a whole.

The argument that some ostensibly local cultural manifestations in fact contain messages with universal drawing power is not new.[55] It was articulated by the Swiss psychologist Carl Gustav Jung, who studied dreams, ceremonies and folk rituals in various cultures and found that similar motifs exist at hidden levels of diverse cultures.[56] Moreover, from the perspective of cognitive psychology, a theoretical perspective opposite to that of Jung, scholars reached conclusions of universal significance regarding certain values. For example, Lawrence Kohlberg, an American psychologist who studied cognitive aspects of moral development, found that at the higher developmental levels moral thinking splits away from local inference (e.g., 'What will those around me think of my actions?') to inferences based on universal values.[57] Andrei Sakharov, the renowned physicist who was imprisoned by the USSR government, was not just a local hero, he became a symbol of the battle for freedom of the human spirit, transcending national borders. As social psychologists have pointed out, people are not motivated only by pragmatic considerations but also by expressive needs, such as the wish to 'be worthy'. According to various studies, the components of self-worth are rooted in the human motivation to retain self-consistency, meaning a sense of consistency based on continuity between the past, the present and the projected future, and on the correspondence between their behaviour and self-concept and a need to locate the self in socially recognizable categories (such as nations, organizations, occupations) in order to derive meaning from being linked to social collectives.[58] Hence, leaders' articulations of visions, their presentation of the right life stories and their execution of symbolic acts serve as a *schema of interpretation* linking the individual self-concept with broader entities.

These effects on the self-concept represent three common processes of possible attachment to the leader: personal identification, that is, identification with a specific person (e.g., a son with his father), social identification, meaning identification with a social group (e.g., with Ataturk as national symbol) and value internalization – the incorporation of values within the self as guiding principles beyond a specific group. In social identification, leaders constitute narratives embedded in a well-defined community of memories. In value internalization they serve as narratives representing more general values (e.g., Lincoln as representing ideas of freedom and equality).

Identification with a leader who is a worthy story is related to the formation of the self-concept, and specifically to the dynamics of self-enhancement. This area has been studied extensively in social psychology, and the findings mostly show that humans have a universal tendency to enhance the positive components and diminish the negative components in their self-concept.[59] Identification with a leader who is a worthy story makes the follower more worthy in his or her own eyes.

The view of the leader as narrative thus illustrates the fact that the leader may be a small local story engraved in the memory of a given collective, or a story with which people identify due to processes related to the construction of their own self-concept. In this respect, to return to the analogy of literary canonization, the psychological basis of the attraction to leaders (as stories) lies in the extent to which they represent themes and values that can potentially enhance the followers' self-concept.

POLITICAL LEADERSHIP AND LEADERSHIP IN EVERYDAY LIFE: ON THE EVOLUTION OF LEADERSHIP CONCEPTS AND IMAGES

A look at the popular literature on leadership and at manuals on leadership development shows that leadership is described in similar ways. The message that emerges is that 'leadership is leadership is leadership'. In the business and financial press, leaders of start-up companies receive lavish praise of their vision, their special ability to predict major changes in the world that are hidden from the eyes of ordinary mortals. Steve Jobs, the founder and leader of Apple, appeared on the cover photo of the *The Economist* wrapped in a cloak like a religious prophet (5 February 2010) and was described in terms amazingly similar to those that were used to describe Winston Churchill, who foresaw the dangers from Germany long before most leaders had seen them.[60] Leaders in sports are described in the press and in popular literature in terms similar to those used in descriptions of army officers who commanded thousands of soldiers and changed the course of history. The manuals in some junior and senior military academies describe the leadership that is required of company or regimental commanders similarly to the recommendations of Von Clausewitz, who attempted to unravel the secret of the successful military strategy.[61] Hundreds of books written about leaders (usually successful ones, and not by chance, a fact whose psychological significance will be discussed later) describe leaders who are so similar that the reader may wonder whether a basketball coach, a military commander, a human resources manager, a company president, a chief of general staff and a prime minister must all be (albeit to different extents) visionaries or strategists who are irresistible, charismatic or possess similar attributes that fill the leadership literature from cover to cover.

A perusal of the psychological research literature on leadership reveals some apparent attempts to shatter the monolithic view of the leader and examine it in

more specific contexts. As mentioned earlier, in a review of leadership literature (Chapter 2), the distinction between people orientation and task orientation was adopted by scholars in the 1950s and 1960s and served as the basis
for dozens of models and studies on leadership. According to these models
leaders were measured by their ability to adapt to changing circumstances,[62]
and the criterion for successful adaptation was *effectiveness*, the keyword for
some kind of accepted evaluation of successful performance. Models were
developed mapping the conditions for success. For example, in situations such
as military operations an authoritarian leadership style was found more effective than others. For performance of a task requiring innovation (e.g., R&D
projects), a democratic, people-oriented style with a high level of participation
was considered more effective.[63]

As mentioned in Chapter 2, the idea of leadership styles branched in several
directions. The most prevalent model in the research literature on effectiveness
of leadership styles is the one that distinguishes between transactional leadership and transformational leadership. This model was developed and perfected
in the late 1980s and the 1990s by Bernard Bass and colleagues from
Binghamton University, New York.[64] A scrutiny of the process of conceptualization and development of this important model can show how biases about
leadership may occur even in research literature.

The terms transactional leadership and transformational leadership were
coined by James MacGregor Burns in his book *Leadership*, published in
1978.[65] Burns, a political historian who studied the leadership of some US
presidents (he was awarded the Pulitzer Prize for his book on Franklin Delano
Roosevelt),[66] demonstrated his proposed distinction between transactional and
transformational using political leaders as examples. The reader of his analyses and illustrations cannot avoid the impression that the really meaningful
leadership is transformational leadership, since it genuinely leads to change in
the status quo. Through the examples of leaders like Roosevelt (in fact, both
Roosevelts, Theodore and Franklin Delano), Burns shows how transformational leaders differ from transactional leaders who, in fact, are the majority.
The latter can perhaps be seen as generating success in the areas of economy
and industry, but that is not enough to express the transformative element that
Burns sees as possessing normative value.

Transformational leaders, then, are leaders who cause their followers to
think and act in the light of principles that are mostly more social and ethical.
Jefferson, Lincoln and both the Roosevelts exemplify transformational leaders
because new, more moral and more social norms emerged in the wake of their
leadership. The conceptualization of transactional leadership in many senses
serves only to emphasize the unique contribution of *real* leadership – transformational leadership, which transforms people and elevates them. As I
mentioned briefly earlier, Bernard Bass, the encyclopaedist of leadership stud-

ies, reported in the introduction to his 1985 book that in a chance meeting his attention was drawn to a new book by Burns (published in 1978). Bass was profoundly impressed by the book and a few years later, in 1985, he published his book, *Leadership and Performance Beyond Expectations*, which was not only dedicated to Burns but in fact translated his ideas and conceptualizations into research tools that have since been used in thousands of studies on leadership in everyday life, particularly in organizations. There is barely a doctoral dissertation, MA thesis, or a paper in a psychology journal from the 1990s that is not based on the tools developed by Bass to diagnose and distinguish between non-leadership, transactional leadership and transformational leadership. However, a careful scrutiny of the items composing the questionnaires that were so painstakingly developed by Bass, and validated statistically and elaborated by research teams led by his outstanding students[67] indicates that the core of Burns's argument, namely the normative moral influence of transformational leaders, has largely disappeared. In the development of these concepts into instruments for evaluation and measurement of leadership in organizations, the major criterion for evaluation of leadership became success *in performance*. Transformational leaders, as shown in hundreds of studies based on statistical correlations, are those who bring better results. Furthermore, all of this leadership and its influences are reduced to measurable dimensions of very specific behaviours. Transformational leadership has become a behavioural profile by which to evaluate leaders of all kinds in any organizational context and at every level. A foreman in a car factory, a head nurse in a hospital, a company commander in an infantry corps, the commander of an air force squadron, the mayor of a city, a plant manager, government minister and head of government – all can be measured by the same scale. Moreover, as leadership is measured by a behavioural scale it is also possible to train leaders and improve their leadership style to make it 'more transforming', an academic term for more successful. Given that most of the research on transformational leadership is done in business organizations, it is largely a question of financial success. This kind of success has thus become an overshadowing criterion of the concept of transformational leadership in general.

Exploration of the deeper meaning of the process of developing leadership concepts into models and tools thus indicates that the centrality of the concept or perception of success may be an expression of the cultural bias of writers and researchers. It is not just a question of automatic linkage of leadership with success but the characterization of success in specific ways. Is success expressed only in behaviour? In performance? In business? Do leaders always generate success? Jim Jones bewitched his believers and persuaded them to commit suicide. Two hundred children were poisoned by their parents at the request of the adored leader in the largest mass suicide in modern history. In the 1960s a group of young people in California brutally murdered innocent people just because of the hypnotic influence of their charismatic leader, Charles Manson.[68] Can this, too, be called success? History is full of examples of leaders who were incomparably charismatic and all they brought with them was destruction. Charisma, then, may lead people in different directions and sometimes may lead to results that are disastrous.

Burns's concepts were mostly the fruit of observation and analysis of political leaders, and their development into a widely used model for research and application regarding leaders in an organization was a puzzling conceptual leap. This is clearly demonstrated in a study conducted by Boas Shamir, a leadership scholar from the Hebrew University of Jerusalem. Shamir's study comparing people's perceptions regarding political leaders and leaders in everyday life may clarify the arguments presented here and help in the formulation of theories relating to the types of psychological bias that were discussed in Chapter 2.[69]

The 320 students who participated in Shamir's study were asked in an interview to describe a charismatic leader with whom they had no direct contact, a *distant leader* (81 per cent of the distant leaders chosen were political leaders) and also to describe a charismatic leader with whom they were acquainted and had direct contact, a *close leader* (28 per cent chose teachers and leaders in educational frameworks, 26 per cent chose officers whom they had known personally in the army and 24 per cent chose friends). A comparison of the perceptions and concepts relating to various characteristics attributed to the distant and close leaders revealed that the participants attributed a larger number of characteristics to the close leaders and that these characteristics were more specific and more behavioural than the ones they attributed to the distant leaders, whom they described as larger than life figures. The salient characteristics attributed to distant leaders were rhetorical skills, ideological orientation and sense of mission, determination and consistency in pursuing their mission, courage and equanimity in the face of social criticism. The close leaders were described more in terms of concern for people, social skills, expertise in their field and similar aspects that may be linked directly to performance of tasks for the improvement of group cohesion or individual attention.

The differences between the followers' perceptions of distant and close leaders, added to the fact that most of the distant leaders chosen were political leaders, have important psychological implications, the most basic of which is the possibility that close leadership and distant leadership call for different psychological explanations. The fact that the distant leaders were described mentioning fewer characteristics, and that these characteristics were more general and prototypical than those mentioned in the more behavioural and detailed description of the close leaders indicates that distant leaders are constructed from inferences derived from information that is less comprehensive and is not the result of direct observation. Anecdotes spread through suitable channels, a confident appearance in the mass media, resolute statements (some of which could be written by speech writers) and similar effects can infiltrate the public awareness (by chance or manipulation) and act as clues creating the informative stimuli for the completion of a leadership figure – completion that is achieved by the followers themselves without a firm basis of fact, as evidenced by cognitive psychological theories. In contrast, in close leadership, as in the case of direct command of a military operation, the officer and those in their charge know and understand the mission and the circumstances of its performance, and can discern clearly who and what caused the success or failure of the operation. In other words, the closer the leader the less room there is for attribution processes based on partial or biased information.

Also from the psychodynamic (especially psychoanalytic) point of view, according to which the leader's main function is primarily emotional – to provide a sense of security – distance from the leader has various psychological implications. The sight of George Washington radiating authority was enough for him to be viewed as a charismatic leader even though he was in fact a failure as a military leader until his appointment as commander in chief of the continental forces.[70] In the perspective of psychological distance, the principle is that the more distant the leader, the better he or she can serve as a projection screen. Therefore it is easier to dress distant leaders in images that make them larger than life. Close leaders with human weaknesses are not easy material for exciting stories. This may also explain why it is easier to revere dead leaders, especially those who were assassinated because of their ideological stand (see, for example, Martin Luther King, Mahatma Gandhi, Abraham Lincoln, Yitzhak Rabin).

Thus, a closer scrutiny of just one aspect – distance from the leader – is enough to show that there are diverse psychological phenomena related to leadership, all of which require discussion using different concepts and models of analysis. The closer the leaders, according to implicit leadership theories, the more behavioural the followers' criteria for judgement and evaluation of them (personal example, manner of treating people, steadiness in stress situations). The psychological meaning of this argument in the terms presented in Chapter 2 is that in the space of close leadership there are fewer projections, fewer attribution errors than in relations with distant leaders. Therefore, outstanding leaders at lower levels will not necessarily be outstanding at higher levels as distant leaders. An excellent company commander who is a model of close leadership will not necessarily be perceived in the future as an excellent political leader, and vice versa, outstanding political leaders would not necessarily have passed the test of behavioural leadership of a company commander or leader of a small group.

The importance and the psychological implications of real proximity between followers and their leader are illustrated in the analogy between good

parents and transformational leaders. Characteristics that were found important in studies on good parenting were also prominent in studies on transformational leaders.[71] Parenting in fact is not just the clearest and most everyday
expression of transformational leadership[72] but also the ongoing practice of its
development. A study comparing young army officers who were parents with
officers of about the same age who served in similar roles but were not parents
showed that the officers who were parents were more transformational as leaders in their military role. The extent of their transformational leadership in
their military role grew as they accumulated experience of parenting.[73]

It appears that the analogy between transformational leadership and good
parenting illustrates clearly the everyday manifestation of transformational
leadership and also reveals the differences between distant and close transformational leadership in the expression of its symbolic aspect. For instance, due
to the powerful effects of projection, attribution and giving meaning in the
space of distant leadership, the ability to formulate visions and create images,
as well as the rhetorical skills, are more dominant. See, for example, the
hugely influential speeches of Winston Churchill, Martin Luther King,
Thomas Jefferson and George Washington. In contrast, the symbolic influence
of the close transformational leader is expressed in daily interactions and
behaviours,[74] such as the personal example of the direct commander or the
parent.

Can just anybody in a position of authority and responsibility be a transformational leader? This appears to be one of those biases that are most
ignored in research literature and at the same time most disputed in popular
literature. On the one hand there is a kind of leadership development industry;
various institutes, from summer camps, through residential schools, to prestigious universities, pride themselves in 'training the leaders of the future'. On
the other hand, as Burns found, in the end very few pass his proposed test of
transformational leadership. But there again, good parenting is described as
transformational leadership, so how can we bridge these conceptual gaps?
What are the boundaries of this metaphor?

The distinction between motivation and commitment can provide a conceptual criterion for this discussion. The question as to what motivates people has
been the subject of countless discussions. Some scholars have dealt with motivation in relation to needs,[75] while others have referred to cognitive processes
that motivate people.[76] In the context of transformational leadership, the most
economical and efficient distinction is between motivation based on instru-
mental considerations (i.e., pragmatic), which consciously benefits the individual in the broad sense (supplying his or her existential needs, providing
wealth, status symbols and power) and motivation based on commitment,
which is not pragmatic in essence. People who are motivated by commitment
may pay the price of conventional benefits. The soldier who volunteers for a

dangerous mission risks the thing that is worth most – their life. The activist fighting for civil rights who goes out in torrential rain to demonstrate in the city square sacrifices his or her comfort. The anonymous volunteer working day and night for the election of a leader will not necessarily see a personal reward for his or her endeavours. These are people who are usually committed to an idea, a social principle. This kind of motivation, as various psychological theories have attempted to explain, stems from different sources, originating from self-concept and self-esteem, and leading to altruism.[77] Whatever the case, this is commitment to something that is more ideological and abstract than simple profit based on cost–benefit considerations. In this space, as articulated by Burns (and later confused by others who followed him), transformational leadership has clear psychological boundaries – it always involves commitment. The basic question of people who are characterized by a high level of commitment is not 'What's in it for me?' but 'What is a worthy thing for a person like me to do?' (sometimes expressed in practical terms using the mirror image: 'What do I say to myself in the mirror?'). Transformational leaders do not impact on the cost–benefit formula of the follower, but they impact on the level of his or her commitment to a cause, the ability to move from commitment to values of freedom and justice, through a social or national ideology, to collective, community or organizational values. One way or another, the point is that this commitment goes beyond considerations of immediate practical benefit.

Expansion of the discussion on the distinction between 'ordinary' motivation and commitment raises the idea of mapping the various possibilities of charismatic leadership in everyday life. Using terms formulated by the sociologist Amitai Etzioni,[78] we can distinguish between three types of compliance that are relevant to follower–leader relationships:

1. *Compliance based on fear of punishment.* This is the kind that typically exists in prisons and certain hospitalization institutions, where the existence of formal authority is enough to ensure compliance.
2. *Utilitarian compliance based on cost–benefit considerations.* This type characterizes most business organizations. Transactional leaders, who know how to diagnose followers' expectations and set clear game rules of reward for effort (usually in terms of material or psychological benefits), can obtain maximal compliance from employees in these organizations.
3. *Commitment – compliance based on identification and internalization of ideological values that form the conceptual basis for the centrality of symbols.* Needless to say, there are areas and organizations in which the probability of this kind of compliance is higher, such as organizations dealing with education, social issues, the environment, quality of life, certain military units, intelligence services, R&D organizations and so

forth. These organizations have the psychological 'raw material' to emphasize commitment to 'a story bigger than yourself'. By way of illustration, a study on patterns of motivation of workers in metal industries compared workers in a plant that manufactured commercial products (water taps, irrigation equipment, etc.) with workers in a plant producing equipment vital for the security of their country. Even though the type of work, wages, work hours and working conditions were identical, the employees in the latter plant showed much greater commitment to the organization than those in the former. In interviews, the workers in the security plant emphasized that they were doing 'important work for the country'. They were doing something that they considered vital and more important than just 'profit for the boss'. This feeling was a significant component in their perception of their work and their self-concept, and it was evidently a major factor in their commitment to the organization, expressed in such things as willingness to make greater efforts, less absences from work for health reasons or others, more punctuality and less turnover of workers.[79]

All this does not mean that leadership in business organizations will inevitably be transactional. A look at the patterns of motivation that organizations attempt to develop indicates that business organizations do not generally just settle for the give and take dynamic of transactional leadership but attempt to create commitment, which entails more loyalty, effort and productivity. And in fact both the extensive research literature on commitment to organizations and the rhetoric of business leaders reflect this endeavour. It is clear to see how business leaders attempt, through the use of rhetoric and symbols, to link the work of the organization with aims that may be perceived as a broader and more moral contribution in the sense of giving meaning. For example, pharmaceutical companies stress their contribution to humanity, and telephone companies adopt slogans that emphasize motifs such as connecting people, creating a small, cosy and conversational world. Even finance companies that have difficulty showing a concrete product adopt such aims as 'giving to the community', emphasizing the expressive need to be a good person as a central component in human motivation.[80]

The above analysis and the comparisons cited show that human motivation has diverse sources, some of which are symbolic. At different psychological distances between the leader and the followers the distinction between these sources is evident. Examples such as those of Lincoln, Mandela and Gandhi demonstrate that from a large psychological distance the leader's daily behaviours do not carry great weight, as do those of close leaders. The attribution, the metaphor and the symbols that represent a collective narrative anchored in aspects of the memory such as tradition, history or transcendent principles communicated mainly through rhetoric – these are what touch the followers' emotions and mobilize them. On the other hand, at a close psychological distance (as we saw in the case of parents), the leader's behaviours, especially those that constitute a frame of reference for role modelling, are the major messages that he or she communicates.

Another point whose psychological significance is most relevant to political leaders concerns the distinction between *leadership emergence*, which is mainly the leader's ability to charm his or her public, to touch their feelings (an ability that is cardinal in election campaigns) and *leadership effectiveness*, namely the leader's ability to govern and especially the ability to change goals, values and norms. The absence of thorough discussion of this point is one of the major sources of biases about leadership. The eminent journalist Walter Lippmann argued that political leadership (in the USA) is mainly manifested in the effort to be elected in election campaigns rather than in the ability to govern after being elected.[81] A leader, and especially a distant leader, may be charismatic, venerated and irresistible not only irrespective of any real achievements but even when he or she causes failures and destruction. Thus, the connection between leadership and success is a bias that merits deeper analysis.

ARE LEADERS BORN OR MADE?

The question as to whether leadership is a gift or a skill that can be learnt is almost as old as the larger question that has occupied scientists for many years: heredity versus environment, or in colloquial terms, nature or nurture. This question has been discussed endlessly in many domains; nevertheless I have chosen to raise it again with regard to leadership because it seems to me that in this domain there are also many biases and myths. Using some of the concepts relating to intercultural differences discussed throughout the book can help to shed more light on the issue.[82]

A conceptual frame that allows for more precise distinctions regarding the development of leaders has been proposed by several scholars.[83] The argument in principle is that outstanding human performance in any sphere, be it art, science or sport, requires three constituents: *potential, motivation and development*. Thus, for instance, an individual who lacks the suitable potential will not reach excellent scientific achievements, but the potential for success in a given sphere is not in itself a precursor of success because motivation is a vital component. There is considerable evidence of people with exceptional talent in sport, science or the arts who were not sufficiently interested or motivated to continue their training and disappeared into the recesses of memory although great things had been predicted for them in their childhood.[84]

Development in a particular sphere requires a necessary degree of potential and motivation. Furthermore, an individual who has outstanding talent in a certain area as well as great interest and motivation, if trained by the best teachers will develop more successfully than someone else with similar skills and motivation who studies with inferior teachers. The former has better prospects of being exposed to excellent role models and quality experiences that are more conducive to his or her development.

This basic distinction can further our understanding concerning the growth and development of leaders. It may also increase our understanding of the development of different types of leaders. The distinction between leadership ability and motivation to lead simply means that there are people who can lead but do not want to. In fact, questions such as why people want to be leaders (sometimes obsessively so), how the motivation to lead is formed and where it originates are of profound psychological significance. No less significant is the question as to the implications of motivation to lead in the context of the leader's aims, vision and style of influencing people. Evidence of this may be found in the life stories of some famous leaders, but it needs to be discussed beyond the anecdotal level that appears in biographies.

I will begin with a subject on which there has been scant psychological research: the distinction between negative leaders, known in the literature as personalized charismatic leaders (Hitler is the icon of this category), and positive leaders, known as socialized charismatic leaders and represented by such sanctified figures as Nelson Mandela and Mahatma Gandhi.[85] All of these were charismatic leaders with great influence who were formally elected to power, but the differences between them were vast. Examination of the sources of these leaders' motivation may help to broaden the understanding of the differences.

If Hitler's classmates had tried to predict which of them would reach a position of leadership one day, Hitler would most likely not have been among the candidates. Like many leaders who turned out to be destructive, Hitler was a lonely child with a deep inner feeling of marginality.[86] Not only did he not reveal seeds of leadership, there is no evidence of such aspirations.[87] Until his military service in World War I he did not think of himself as someone capable of being a leader. Furthermore, unlike Winston Churchill, Nelson Mandela and Franklin Roosevelt, to name a few examples, his family history did not include any direct or indirect encouragement to choose a path of leadership. His ambition and his intention were to be an artist – an occupation that does not involve social interaction or the wish to have direct influence on people. What became known in time as Hitler's charisma was revealed to him during his military service as a corporal in World War I. There he discovered that people were gripped by his words, especially when he spoke with great fervour (which he did mainly when speaking about Germany's enemies).

Hitler himself was first surprised by his rhetorical skill,[88] which he discovered by chance, and which later became overpowering in his speeches in the city squares, but once discovered, it became an addiction. A similar dynamic of chance discovery of rhetorical skill and persuasive ability has appeared among other negative charismatic leaders, such as Jim Jones.[89]

The term addiction is apt because it characterizes this uncontrollable desire to be a leader, which is similar to the addiction of drug addicts or alcoholics, who see shaking off their habit as a kind of death. This was aptly described by Charles Manson, the charismatic leader of a gang that committed a cruel murder in California in the 1960s, in recalling his attitude towards his people, who utterly adored him. 'I often had the urge to get my things together and head for unknown places, but I was so caught up with those kids and the role I played in their lives, to leave them would have been like ripping my heart out.'[90] The key to this addiction was provided by Manson himself in an interview reported in the press: 'I began to enjoy the sense of power that I received from those around me, but it was not power as an aim in itself. Do you understand, I enjoyed that I was needed and never felt better.'[91]

A psychological source underlying the passionate desire to be a leader is ascribed by many scholars to *narcissistic deprivation*, meaning the wish to compensate for an internal experience that originates in most cases from a feeling of marginality, lack of adoration from the mother, deprivation of love and attention or relations with a narcissistic mother, lacking warmth and intimacy.[92] People characterized by narcissistic deprivation are motivated by compensatory character formation, as defined in the psychological literature.[93] Certain occupations can compensate more than others for the feeling of inner emptiness. Actors, for example, have the opportunity to appear on the stage and capture the attention of an applauding audience. Leadership too provides opportunities to receive adoration and applause. A study comparing actors and leaders with research workers functioning in relative anonymity showed a significantly higher level of narcissism in the first two groups.[94]

Does this mean that leadership is simply a response to narcissistic needs? Does being a leader necessarily mean being a narcissist? It appears, as with most psychological phenomena, that this is not a question of dichotomous categories but of a continuum whose extreme end is pathological. Manfred Kets de Vries, who examined psychodynamic aspects in the development of leaders, argues that some measure of self-aggrandizement is necessary not only in order to want to be at centre stage but also in order to create, change things and lead. Thus, a certain degree of narcissism is vital to the expression of initiative, and leadership is one of its possible expressions.[95]

Leaders such as Adolf Hitler, Charles Manson and Jim Jones (the cult leader who persuaded hundreds of his believers to commit the largest mass suicide in history) are examples of the extreme end of the pathology that characterizes solely negative leaders.[96] Their behaviour matches the symptoms described in the *Diagnostic and Statistical Manual of Mental Disorders* (DSM) as symptoms of narcissistic disturbance, including lack of empathy, illusions of grandeur and excessive self-importance, and the demand for constant admiration.[97]

This perception, which has yet to be thoroughly discussed in the psychological literature,[98] means that, contrary to the common myths, leaders need followers no less than the followers need a leader. The connection between the leader and the followers resembles that between an actor and his or her audience. Surprising as it may seem, in terms of development many leaders need followers in order to build and strengthen their self-concept. In pathological cases drug addiction is perhaps the appropriate metaphor, with the followers serving as the leader's drug. They give meaning to his or her life, meaning that is sometimes essential to keep him or her alive.

This perception is also relevant to the development of the self-concept as leader. Ian Kershaw's biography of Hitler[99] reveals the surprising fact that Hitler in his early days did not think of himself as a great leader. In the 1930s he saw himself in the role of a drummer (*Trommler und Sammler*) summoning the troops to prepare for the arrival of the victorious leader. At this stage he regarded himself as an intermediary between the masses and the great leader who would lead them to victory. Just a few years later he found himself in the role of that leader. According to Boas Shamir's analysis, the followers' admiration and expectations, in fact their psychological demand to see him as a great leader became a self-fulfilling prophecy. Hitler began to believe in what the public wanted to see in him – an unparalleled leader gifted with exceptional qualities.[100] And indeed, the grandiosity component, which is a known characteristic in the narcissistic profile, became increasingly evident in the growth of Hitler's personality cult. The other, less familiar, side of the narcissistic leader is the gnawing fear of losing the adoring masses who, in Hitler's case, were the basic confirmation of his worth. He demanded loyalty, admiration and submission from those around him and, like other leaders characterized by pathological narcissism, he was capable of behaving cruelly when his leadership was challenged (e.g., his treatment of Von Stauffenberg and the group of officers who plotted to kill him on 22 July 1944).[101]

On the other hand, the narcissistic psychological constructs that exist in leaders who embody a positive mythology are more refined and complex. In analysing the leadership of Ataturk, Vamik Volkan uses the term *reparative narcissism*. According to Volkan's analysis, Ataturk's narcissistic needs were not fed by the adoration of the masses but mainly by the admiration of esteemed others – an elite whose admiration he needed for the maintenance and development of his self-concept as a leader.[102]

The extreme cases of motivation to lead arising from narcissistic deprivation, even if they achieve great resonance, do not in statistical terms represent
the leadership phenomenon, and most leaders do not belong to the pathological categories of narcissistic deprivation. Yet the extreme cases demonstrate
very clearly the impact of the followers and their influence on the development of leaders' self-concept. In the extreme cases, as we have seen, the
followers' influence may be significant to the extent of rendering the leader
dependent on them. Hence it is possible to formulate a psychological principle stating that the more the leader is characterized by narcissistic deprivation,
the more dependent he or she is on the followers. Somewhat paradoxically,
this insight is important for deepening our understanding of the dynamic of
positive leadership, particularly transformational leadership.

A transformational leader, by definition, is less dependent on the followers.
The political leaders who are often cited in the literature as examples of transformational leaders, for instance Franklin Roosevelt, Mahatma Gandhi and
Nelson Mandela, represent developmental processes that are psychologically
different from those experienced by destructive leaders like Hitler. Their motivation to influence people, to be in leadership positions, does not stem from
narcissistic deprivation, from the reparative principle, or from chance discovery of the power to influence, which becomes an addiction. Their development
as leaders can be described as an ongoing evolutionary process marked by
multidimensional developmental variables. As regards parental care and
warmth, although they grew up in very different environments these three
leaders received mother love in abundance. All three had fathers who were
highly esteemed and who served as role models in their development as leaders. In more generalized terms we can say that these leaders demonstrate the
existence of the emotional infrastructure that is essential for the growth of a
transformational leader (emphatically, transformational, not just charismatic).
This secure emotional base leads to the formation of a positive self-concept,
curiosity and learning ability, which are characteristic of secure people. Unlike
the narcissistically deprived, secure people are less concerned with their
reflection in the eyes of others; they have better prospects of emotional independence and are more open to exploration and learning. In fact, studies
conducted in recent years based on attachment theory, which is one of the
major theories on psychological development, clearly support these arguments.[103, 104, 105]

In view of the existence of a broad range of research based on attachment
theory, it is worth expanding somewhat on the psychological rationale behind
this research. The underlying assumptions of attachment theories are based on
biological, evolutionary and psychological processes related to survival.
Whereas most animals are able to fly, run, crawl or emit poison, the human
baby is totally helpless for a long period. His or her entire ability to survive

depends on help from outside. To be fed, to be clean and not to catch infectious diseases, to feel the world around them, the baby needs the help of adults. Usually it is the mother; when the baby is hungry or thirsty, feels cold or hot, is afraid or alarmed, the mother responds to all these primary feelings. Hence, this proximity to the mother is existential in the most basic senses.

The central claim of this theory is that these primary instinctive relations that are created during the critical period of dependence have psychological meanings for the whole of our lives, especially in the sphere of emotional relationships with people, including romantic relations,[106] friendship[107] and also leader–follower relations, as shown by research conducted over the past decade.[108] The basic argument is that the dynamic of the baby's dependence and the mother's appropriate and warm response to his or her needs creates *internal working models*, which affect humans' attitude to themselves and to other people throughout their lives. When the mother is attentive to the baby and quick to notice signs of distress (mostly expressed by crying, whimpering or wriggling) and readily and gently satisfies all his or her needs, then the baby at the level of primary sensations can feel that he or she has a secure base. Babies who have a sense of security reveal a greater extent of exploratory behaviour. They venture more to move away from the mother, try to examine things and touch them – all behaviours expressing attempts at discovery.

Different patterns of response are found when the mother (or the caregiver) is inattentive, insensitive, inconsistent or simply ignores the baby's distress signals. These situations lead to insecure patterns of attachment in the infant. Differences in the psychological foundations of emotional security have developmental significance in many areas, but predominantly in the area of emotional relations.

Given that leadership is in fact social influence, its conceptualization as relationship is useful and also accentuates the relevance of attachment theory to the understanding of leaders' functioning and development, particularly in the case of close leaders – leaders in everyday life.[109] To illustrate this point, a comparison of research studies conducted on good parenting and on transformational leaders revealed that the qualities that characterize good parents are identical to those that characterize transformational leaders in organizations.[110] This similarity has many practical and conceptual implications. The meticulous documentation in the research on good parenting not only enlightens us regarding the typical behaviours of transformational leaders but also makes it possible to examine more thoroughly the psychological profile of these leaders. Like good parents, transformational leaders were found to have a secure attachment style and their level of narcissism was found to be lower than that of people with insecure attachment styles.[111]

Besides personality traits and typical behaviours, the analogy between good parents and transformational leaders also casts light on motivational characteristics. Both groups generally want to make their mark. For example, in a study conducted among battalion commanders who were found to be outstanding transformational leaders, one of the commanders quoted some typical sayings, such as 'I'm like the chief of the tribe, I have older children (deputy commanders) and young children, and I have to take care of them and make sure that the older ones take care of the young ones.' Or 'Before everything else, technical or operational, I am above all an educator. My major task is to make the people believe in the aims and importance of what they are doing.'[112]

The secure attachment style is not only an emotional psychological substructure that enables the individual to be more open to others and hence better able to maintain relationships of a higher quality. It also has implications for learning and development processes, especially for two types of learning that have been found central in the development of leaders: experiential learning and vicarious learning.[113]

In research conducted among managers of organizations in order to discover their perception of the sources and processes that were important for their development as leaders, the participants reported that early experiences, such as being captain of the school basketball team or head of the student council, youth movement leaders or summer camp counsellors, carried great weight in their self-discovery as leaders. In a study comparing leaders with non-leaders, one of the leaders typically described the basis of his development as a leader as follows: 'My parents have a guest house and even when I was very young, whenever they went away to the big city for a few days they always left me in charge. I was responsible for my small brothers, for the household, and for making sure that everything was in order. They gave me the feeling that I was a responsible adult who was capable of taking care of everything. Also, I didn't want to disappoint them and the fact that I always managed gave me great confidence.'[114] Although the word leadership was not mentioned even once in this interview (the participants did not know that the research was investigating leadership; as far as they knew, it dealt with other matters), when the interviews were analysed it was clearly evident that their preparation for leadership began early in childhood experiences such as these, which afforded them the opportunity to take responsibility and make decisions. But above all, these experiences generated a developmental component of the utmost importance – *experiences of success*. Many studies have shown that experiences of success have powerful influence on the individual's motivation and self-concept in the relevant spheres[115] and contribute to the building of self-efficacy (belief in one's own ability). A person who experiences success, whether in sport, mathematics or leadership, will have considerable belief in his or her ability to succeed.[116] On the other hand, in many cases students who failed in mathematics at an early age (sometimes due to an impatient teacher) are afraid all their lives to engage in occupations that involve mathematical calculations.[117]

It is clear to see how the cycles of security building in infancy, processes of learning and building self-efficacy, and influence on followers are interrelated. The secure pattern that is formed in infancy is expressed, among other things, by the level of curiosity and the urge for discovery.[118] In other words, children with a secure attachment style are more ready to face new experiences, that is to say, experiential learning. From the start they will tend more than others to be in a site where they are likely to undergo experiences in general and experiences of success in particular. Successful experiences of leadership strengthen the self-efficacy in this sphere.[119] This kind of self-confidence is transmitted to the followers more than any other psychological characteristic. Indeed, the security transmitted by the leader enhances the leader's image in his or her people's eyes. When followers were asked to grade the characteristics that made them 'ready to follow the leader', the most important category was 'they give me a sense of security'.[120] People who lack security or belief in their ability to lead cannot transmit this sense consistently over a long period and in changing circumstances. This is a test that singles out leaders in everyday life (unlike distant leaders, who can choose when and where to appear in public). Thus, we see that, contrary to many perceptions of leadership that ascribe great importance to academic training programmes (especially in prestigious universities), the basic foundations of leaders' development are usually laid earlier, in daily life, especially in the family, in groups of friends, in the neighbourhood and often by figures who do not necessarily match the stereotypical definition of leaders. The experiences and the learning that are more important in the acquisition of leadership are not defined as such. Most of the influences on leaders' development are identified in retrospect; in many cases it is only discovered in hindsight that everyday people and events played a decisive part in their shaping as leaders.[121] Recalling Monsieur Jordain's surprised remark in Molière's play *The Bourgeois Gentilhomme*: 'Good heavens. For more than forty years I have been speaking prose without knowing it,' leadership develops in various ways through diverse experiences and forms of learning. Like Molière's character, while it is happening those who experience it do not know that they are 'speaking prose', that is, developing their leadership.

Another bias that exists in the psychological literature on leadership is the emphasis placed on process aspects. In fact this bias is characteristic of psychology in general and is particularly salient in social psychology, which abounds in research dealing with aspects such as first impression, attractiveness, primary effect and group processes, with minimal reference to content.[122] The psychological research on leadership has also focused on process variables such as impression management, the salience of the leader's behaviours or the leader's ability to appear attractive on a podium or in the media.[123] The concern with charisma in the original literal sense of magic, grace or gift of God strengthens the feeling (as described incisively in the case of the Kennedy schema; see Chapter 2) that the leader's good looks and charm in a TV talk show are the standards for evaluating his or her leadership. This bias, if stretched to the extreme, means that there is no essential difference between charismatic leaders (e.g., between Mandela and Hitler). Charisma in this sense is sufficient for the candidate to be elected in the case of political leaders, and enough to motivate people in general, and that's all there is to it! This bias in fact leads only to the idea of recruiting or inspiring the followers by the leader's charming personality. But what about the content of his or her messages? Have they no importance?

In his autobiography, Gandhi gives a fascinating account of his development as a leader and describes how his world view was formed. One of the descriptions in his reminiscences is that of himself on a train journey reading John Ruskin's book *Unto This Last* (1860). 'The book changed my life,' he wrote in his autobiography.[124] The central argument in Ruskin's book is that the true basis of society is not wealth, as the classical economists then thought, but companionship. These messages became part of Gandhi's vision, in fact part of his influence as a leader. When this episode is presented, most of the listeners (or the readers of his autobiography) take it at face value. A person who happens to be a renowned leader read a book that influenced his world view and his messages as a leader. What is special about that? But examination of the deeper and more hidden meanings raises the question: why did this specific book have so much impact? Why does the content of one book and not another have such a strong effect? Obviously people (including Gandhi of course) read many books, most of which are probably forgotten leaving no mark, and certainly do not become the reader's world view or an obsession, as Gandhi said of himself. He himself provides the answer based on insights that became clear in retrospect only when he was an adult. John Ruskin's messages were simply the embodiment of Gandhi's internalized image of his mother. According to his autobiographical account, his mother was an 'angel', an ascetic for whom giving was the essence and purpose of life. Hence Gandhi was, so to speak, fertile soil ready to receive a certain kind of plant. This emotional substructure, with its links to world views, contents and messages of leaders, tends to be neglected by psychological research and left outside the discussion on leadership development.

From the followers' point of view, in this frame of content the leader's influence becomes more clearly defined. Without this perspective it may be inferred (as happens in the psychology literature) that the sole purpose of leadership is to activate people. However, activation without direction means that, to quote Lewis Carroll, if you do not know where you are going, any road will get you there. The direction indicated by this message inconsequentially makes a charismatic person a leader. Contents expressing certain moral values turn a charismatic leader into a transformational leader. Distinctions of this kind are not usually discussed in an integrated manner. Historians study contents without sufficiently analysing psychological processes, while psychologists focus on processes and pay little attention to contents.

Furthermore even if we assume that the adult Gandhi simply chose to offer a developmental explanation as an afterthought so that his leadership would appear coherent to the followers, his words still convey an important theoretical statement concerning the significance of leadership contents and messages. This means that highly influential transformational leaders (of whom Gandhi was one) understand that in order to influence people it is necessary to construct a suitable message. One of the ways of doing this is through a suitable personal story.[125]

It appears then that different perceptions of leadership also arise due to the disciplinary structure, and therefore there is a constant need to examine other relevant variables beyond those automatically studied by scholars in the existing structure. This limitation is particularly prominent in the case of leadership because it is one of the more complex phenomena, which cannot be addressed by one discipline alone. It is enough to look at leaders, to listen to the followers or to the leaders themselves in order to identify the biases and the diminution of the leadership discourse. The following example can illustrate this. Winston Churchill, who retired to his family estate from a position of leadership (First Lord of the Admiralty), described his feelings in his customary graphic style: 'the change from the intense executive activities of each day's work at the Admiralty to the narrowly-measured duties of a counsellor left me gasping. Like a sea-beast fished up from the depths, or a diver too suddenly hoisted, my veins threatened to burst from the fall in pressure.'[126] In other words, contrary to the conventional thinking, although leaders work harder than most people and are presumed to be exhausted by constant stress situations, what exhausts them in fact is inactivity and absence of pressure, whereas the leadership position 'creates energies'.

Churchill's description of his feelings is not unique; it appears in other biographies, and many leaders when asked about it identify with these feelings.[127] Nevertheless there is a dearth of research investigating in depth this kind of psychophysiological energy,[128] perhaps because psychology lacks the concepts and tools to discuss and explore variables whose meaning is psychological although their foundations are inherent or biological. This area, which has been studied to some extent in certain fields of developmental psychology (such as attachment theory), is still in its infancy in leadership research. It appears, therefore, that some of the perceptions of leadership simply stem from the boundaries imposed by the structure of disciplines that leads to certain forms of thinking. In an attempt to see what exists and what does not in this discussion, which is meant to be more multi-disciplinary, we can now turn to look at the big picture and attempt to map the theoretical thinking underlying the concrete manifestations of leadership hitherto discussed.

NOTES

1. Popper, Micha (2005), *Leaders Who Transform Society: What Drives Them and Why We Are Attracted*, Westport, CT: Praeger.
2. James Meindl's groundbreaking contribution to the study of the psychological processes that occur in the followers is well-known. His works advanced forms of thinking and methods such as examining how business leaders' images are shaped in the press. His thought and his research created a big step forward in the study of the psychology of followers. See, for example: Meindl, James R. (1990), 'On leadership: An alternative to conventional wisdom', *Research in Organizational Behavior*, **12**, 159–203; Meindl, James R. (1995), 'The romance of leadership as follower-centric theory: A social constructionist approach', *Leadership Quarterly*, **6** (3), 329–41.
3. Zerubavel, Yael (1995), *Recovered Roots*, Chicago: University of Chicago Press.
4. Schwartz, Barry (2000), *Abraham Lincoln and the Forge of National Memory*, Chicago: The University of Chicago Press, p. 164.
5. Wilson, Woodrow (1917), *Compilation of the Messages and Papers of Presidents*, 20 vols, prepared under the direction of the Joint Committee of Printing of the House and Senate, New York: Bureau of National Literature, vol. 17, pp. 7868–70.
6. Schwartz (2000, p. 172).
7. Schwartz (2000, p. 181).
8. Chittenden, Lucius Eugene (1909), *Lincoln and the Sleeping Sentinel: The True Story*, New York: Harper and Brothers.
9. Gullan, Harold I. (2004), *First Fathers: The Men Who Inspired Our Presidents*, Hoboken, NJ: John Wiley & Sons.
10. Remini, Robert V. (1999), *The Battle of New Orleans*, New York: Penguin, p. 28.
11. Schwartz (2000, p. 123).
12. Shils, Edward (1975), 'Ritual and crisis', in *Center and Periphery: Essays in Macrosociology*, Chicago: University of Chicago Press, pp. 153–63.
13. Meindl (1995). Diffusion processes are widely described in studies dealing with the spread of rumours (Rosnow and Fine) and reputation building (Fine). Such psychological mechanisms are incorporated in Meindl's integrative notion of 'social contagion'. See: Rosnow, Ralph L. and Gary A. Fine (1976), *Rumor and Gossip: The Social Psychology of Hearsay*, New York, Elsevier; Fine, Gary A. (2001), *Difficult Reputations: Collective Memories of the Evil, Inept and Controversial*, Chicago: University of Chicago Press; see also Meindl (1990).
14. Roosevelt, Theodore (1913), *Lincoln Day Speech*, Progressive Service Documents, New York: Progressive National Committee.
15. Sklar, Kathryn K. (1988), 'Organized womanhood: Archival sources on women and progressive reform', *Journal of American History*, **75** (1), 176–83.
16. Schwartz (2000, p. 135).
17. Maslow, Abraham (1970), *Motivation and Personality*, New York: Harper & Row.
18. James MacGregor Burns's book of 1978 is considered a turning point in the study of psychological aspects of leadership. Although Burns, a political historian, dealt mainly with the study of some of the US presidents, the concepts that he introduced regarding leadership, particularly the distinction between transactional leadership and transformational leadership, changed the paradigm of psychological research on leadership. The

main paradigmatic change originated in the pinpointing of the leader's position as a transformer of expectations. See Burns, James MacGregor (1978), *Leadership*, New York: Harper & Row.

19. Bowlby, John (1969), *Attachment and Loss: 1, Attachment*, New York: Basic Books; Freud, Sigmund (1920), *A General Introduction to Psychoanalysis*, American edition, New York: Garden City Press.

20. Hogg, Michael (2001), 'A social identity theory of leadership', *Personality and Social Psychology Review*, **5** (3), 184–200.

21. Chadha, Yogesh (1997), *Gandhi: A Life*, New York: John Wiley & Sons.

22. Volkan, Vamik and Norman Itzkowitz (1984), *The Immortal Ataturk – A Psychobiography*, Chicago: University of Chicago Press.

23. Shapira, Anita (1997a), *Yehudim Hadashim, Yehudim Yeshanim* [*New Jews, Old Jews*], Tel Aviv: Sifriat Ofakim and Am Oved Publications [Hebrew].

24. Schwartz, Barry (1986), *The Battle for Human Nature. Science, Morality and Modern Life*, New York: Norton.

25. The coining of the term collective memory and the first systematic discussion of its nature and sources are attributed to the French philosopher Maurice Halbwachs. Sociologists have dealt extensively with collective memory because on the one hand it is important for understanding the symbolism of the collective and on the other hand it is not a classical historical subject in the methodological sense. Beyond the different approaches, it is argued that the study of collective memory is relevant to the understanding of elements of identity and ways of interpreting attitudes towards issues of identity within a given collective. This thinking is consistent with the conceptual developments suggested by Max Weber regarding the centrality of understanding the subjective view in the interpretation of reality – an opinion that is shared today by most of the writers in the social sciences. See Halbwachs, Maurice ([1926] 1950), *The Collective Memory* [trans. F.J. and V.Y. Ditter], London: Harper Colophon Books.

26. Mannheim, Karl (1952), 'The problem of generations', in *Essays on the Sociology of Knowledge*, New York: Routledge and Kegan Paul, pp. 276–322. See also: Weber, Max (1946), *From Max Weber: Essays in Sociology*, in H. Gerth and C. Wright Mills (eds), New York: Oxford University Press; Stryker, Sheldon (1980), *Symbolic Interactionism: A Social Structural Version*, Menlo Park, CA: Benjamin Cummings.

27. Some examples illustrating the influence of the 'spirit of the generation' on the way of thinking are presented in Avirama Golan's book, in which women of different generations speak of the socializing effects emanating from the period. In this sense the interviews with these women demonstrate at the personal and everyday level Mannheim's arguments on the generational unit that is shaped by the spirit of the period. See Golan, Avirama (1988), *Al Da'at Atzman* [*Of Their Own Accord*], Tel Aviv: Am Oved (Ofakim) [Hebrew].

28. Meindl (1995).

29. Misztal, Barbara A. (2003), *Theories of Social Remembering*, Philadelphia: Open University Press.

30. Shapira (1997a).

31. Shapira, Anita (1997d), 'Hamitus shel hayehudi hehadash' ('The myth of the new Jew'), in *Yehudim Hadashim, Yehudim Yeshanim* (*New Jews, Old Jews*), pp. 155–74.

32. Halbwachs ([1926] 1950). See also Misztal (2003).

33. Shapira (1997b p. 8).

34. Gelber, Yoav (2008), *Historia, Zikaron Ve ta'amula* [*History, Memory and Propaganda*], Tel Aviv: Am Oved (Ofakim) [Hebrew].

35. Misztal (2003).

36. Micha Popper demonstrates how symbols such as military heritage are used for the purpose of inculcating certain concepts and values in the Israel Defense Forces (IDF). Beyond the military units themselves, mnemonic processes are initiated through bodies that are set up especially for this purpose. See: Popper, Micha (1998), 'The Israeli Defense Forces as socializing agent', in Daniel Bar-Tal, D. Jacobson and A. Kleiman (eds), *Concerned with Security: Learning from the Experience of Israeli Society*, Stamford, CT: JAI Press, pp. 167–80.

37. Martin, Joanne, M.S. Feldman, M.J. Hatch and S.B. Sitkin (1983), 'The uniqueness paradox in organizational stories', *Administrative Science Quarterly*, **28** (3), 438–53.

38. Lipshitz, Raanan, Victor Friedman and Micha Popper (2007), *Demystifying Organizational Learning*, Thousand Oaks, CA: Sage Publications, p. 187.

39. Schein, Edgar (1985), *Organizational Culture and Leadership*, San Francisco: Jossey-Bass.

40. Peters, Tom and Robert Waterman (1982), *In Search of Excellence: Lessons from America's Best-Run Companies*, New York: Harper Business.

41. Collins, James C. and Jerry I. Porras (1997), *Built To Last*, New York: Harper Collins.

42. Popper, Micha (1994), *Al Menahalim Kemanhigim* [*On Managers as Leaders*], Tel Aviv: Ramot Publishing House, Tel Aviv University, p. 87 [Hebrew].

43. Volkan, Vamik, Gabriele Ast and William Greer (2002), *The Third Reich in the Unconscious: Transgenerational Transmission and its Consequences*, New York: Brunner-Routledge.

44. Aberbach, David (1995), 'Charisma and attachment theory: A crossdisciplinary interpretation', *International Journal of Psychoanalysis*, **76** (4), 845–55.

45. Mayo, Margarita and Juan-Carlos Pastor (2007), 'Leadership embedded in social networks: Looking at inter-follower processes', in B. Shamir, R. Pillai, M.C. Bligh and M. Uhl-Bien (eds), *Follower-Centered Perspectives on Leadership*, Greenwich, CT: Information Publishing, pp. 93–114.

46. Schneider, Benjamin (1987), 'The people make the place', *Personnel Psychology*, **40** (3), 437–53.

47. Hofstede, Geert and Jan Hofstede (2005), *Cultures and Organizations: Software of the Mind*, New York: McGraw-Hill, p. 43.

48. (Ibid., p. 57).

49. Popper, Micha and Salman Khatib (2001), 'Intercultural differences and leadership styles of Druze and Jewish school principals', *Journal of Educational Administration*, **39** (3), 221–32.

50. Hofstede and Hofstede (2005).

51. Max Weber's work on the influence of values (the Protestant Ethic) is regarded as ground-breaking in its attempt to identify a link between manners of thinking and acting. Weber claimed that the values of Protestant societies are more conducive to economic success than those of other societies. In fact the analyses that are so common today (especially in the American literature) on the link between culture and economic or managerial success are simply more specific expressions of the manner of thinking presented by Max Weber. See Weber (1946).

52. Schechter, Rivka (1990), *Hashorashim Hateologiim shel Hareich Hashlishi* (*The Theological Roots of the Third Reich*), Tel Aviv: Ministry of Defense Publishing House [Hebrew].

53. Ibid.

54. Stalker, S. (7 February 1909), 'Tolstoy holds Lincoln world's greatest hero', New York: *The World*. Story based on interview with Tolstoy about Lincoln.

55. Martin et al. (1983).

56. Jung, Carl Gustav (1986), *Analytical Psychology*, London: Routledge.

57. Kohlberg, Lawrence (1971), *From Is to Ought: How to Commit the Naturalistic Fallacy and Get Away with it in the Study of Moral Development*, New York: Academic Press.

58. Models and studies dealing with the association between individual identity and collective entities are discussed in: Shamir, Boas, Robert J. House and Michael B. Arthur (1993), 'The motivational effects of charismatic leadership: A self-concept-based theory', *Organizational Science*, **4** (4), 577–93.

59. Beauregard, Keith and David Dunning (1998), 'Turning up the contrast: Self-enhancement motives prompt egocentric contrast effects in social judgments', *Journal of Personality and Social Psychology*, **74** (3), 606–21.

60. Kershaw, Ian (2008), *Fateful Choices: Ten Decisions That Changed the World*, New York: Penguin Books.

61. Keegan, John (1987), *The Mask of Command*, New York: Jonathan Cape Ltd.

62. Fiedler is considered the father of the approach known as the *contingency model*, according to which the effective leader is one who has style flexibility, meaning that he or she knows how to adapt to changing situations. In the 1960s the paradigm associated with Fiedler was dominant in the psychological research on leadership. See: Fiedler, Fred E. (1964), 'A contingency model of leadership effectiveness', in L. Berkowitz (ed.), *Advances in Experimental Social Psychology*, New York: Academic Press; Fiedler, Fred (1967), *A Theory of Leadership Effectiveness*, New York: McGraw-Hill.

63. Lewin, Kurt, Ron Lippitt and Robert White (1938), 'An experimental approach to the study of autocracy and democracy', *Sociometry*, **1**, 292–300.

64. The full-range model of leadership was first introduced in Bernard Bass's book. The research method, the items and the many examples presented in the book point to the lack of discrimination in using a questionnaire when leaders who are at different degrees of distance or proximity to the followers are measured by the same instrument. References to the research instrument that was constructed on the basis of the full-range model appear in the following: Bass, Bernard M. (1985), *Leadership and Performance Beyond Expectations*, New York: Free Press; Bass, Bernard M. and Bruce J. Avolio (1990), 'The implications of transactional and transformational leadership for individual, team, and organizational development', in R.W. Woodman and W.A. Passmore (eds), *Research in Organizational Change and Development*, Greenwich, CT: JAI Press.

65. Burns (1978).

66. Burns, James M. ([1956] 2002), *Roosevelt: The Lion and the Fox*, New York: Mariner.

67. Avolio, Bruce J., Bernard M. Bass and Dong I. Jung (1996), *Construct Validation of the Multifactor Leadership Questionnaire MLQ-Form 5X. CLS Report 96–1*, Center for Leadership Studies, Binghamton University, State University of New York.

68. Popper, Micha (2001), *Hypnotic Leadership: Leaders, Followers, and the Loss of Self*, Westport, CT: Praeger.

69. Shamir, Boas (1995), 'Social distance and charisma. Theoretical notes and explanatory study', *Leadership Quarterly*, **6** (1), 19–48.

70. Ellis, Joseph J. (2004), *His Excellency George Washington*, New York: Random House.

71. Popper, Micha and Ofra Mayseless (2003), 'Back to basics: Applying a parenting perspective to transformational leadership', *Leadership Quarterly*, **14** (1), 41–65.

72. Popper (2005).

73. In a comparative study conducted by DellaPergola the participants were paired in such a way that the subjects (the officers) in the comparison group were of the same age, command experience and similar professional background. This was done in order to ensure as far as possible that the only differences measured between the groups would be in parenting experience. See: DellaPergola, Shulamit (2002), 'Leadership and fatherhood', MA thesis submitted to University of Haifa, Department of Psychology [Hebrew].

74. Shamir et al. (1993).

75. Maslow's theory is apparently the predominant theory representing a trend of thought and research that places the concept of need at the centre of the explanation. All of these theories posit gratification of need as the motivating force. The differences between theories in this trend are in the classification of needs or the extent of importance attributed to the various needs. See: Maslow (1970).

76. As opposed to the motivation theories that focus on content, on need, such as Maslow's, some other motivation theories deal only with the process of motivation formation, irrespective of the contents of the motivation. A representative example of this is Adams's equity theory, according to which the level of motivation is determined by some formula weighted by the individual, who calculates the rewards he or she receives in exchange for the contributions he or she makes. However, the calculation is done in comparison with relevant ascription groups (for example, labourers do not compare themselves with physicians). See: Adams, John Stacey (1965), 'Inequity in social exchange', in L. Berkowitz (ed.), *Advances in Experimental Social Psychology*, vol. 2, pp. 267–99.

77. A major discussion is currently taking place in various disciplines, from biology to psychology and sociology, regarding the causes that make people behave seemingly against

their own interests. Social psychologists have also examined this issue in research on altruism. Many of the explanations for such 'irrational' behaviours derive from the concept of the self, which has social and expressive dimensions in addition to the individual's cost–benefit considerations. See for example: Markus, Hazel and Elissa Wurf (1987), 'The dynamic self-concept: A social-psychological perspective', *Annual Review of Psychology*, **38**, 299–337. Also: Shamir et al. (1993).

78. Etzioni, Amitai (1975), *A Comparative Analysis of Complex Organizations*, New York: Free Press.
79. Vardi, Yoav, Y. Wiener and M. Popper (1989), 'The value content of organizational mission as a factor of the commitment of members', *Psychological Reports*, **65** (1), 27–38.
80. Popper (1994).
81. Lippmann, Walter (1913), *A Preface to Politics*, New York: Mitchell Kennerly.
82. Dorfman, Peter W. (1996), 'International and cross-cultural leadership', in Betty J. Punnett and O. Shenkar (eds), *Handbook for International Management Research*, Oxford: Blackwell, pp. 267–349. See also: Den Hartog, D.N., P.J. House, D.J. Hanges, S.A. Ruiz-Quintanilla and P.W. Dorfman (1999), 'Culture specific and cross-culturally generalizable implicit leadership theories: Are alternatives of charismatic/transformational leadership universally endorsed?', *Leadership Quarterly*, **10** (2), 219–57.
83. Popper, Micha, Karin Amit, Reuven Gal, Moran Sinai and Alon Lisak (2004), 'The capacity to lead: Major psychological differences between "leaders" and "non-leaders"', *Military Psychology*, **16** (4), 245–63. See also: Amit, Karin, A. Lisak, M. Popper and R. Gal (2007), 'Motivation to lead – research on the motives for undertaking leadership roles', *Military Psychology*, **19** (3), 137–60; Amit, Karin, M. Popper, R. Gal, T. Mamane-Levy and A. Lisak (2009b), 'Leaders and non-leaders: A comparative study of some major developmental aspects', *Journal of the North American Management Society*, **4** (2), 2–19.
84. Storr, Anthony (1972), *The Dynamics of Creation*, London: Secker and Warburg.
85. House, Robert J. and Jane M. Howell (1992), 'Personality and charismatic leadership', *Leadership Quarterly*, **3** (2), 81–108.
86. Popper (2001).
87. Kershaw, Ian (1998), *Hitler: 1889–1936 Hubris*, New York: W.W. Norton.
88. Fest, Joachim (1974), *Hitler*, New York: Harcourt Brace.
89. Popper (2001).
90. Emmons, Nuel (1988), *Manson in His Own Words*, New York; Grove Press.
91. *Maariv*, 14 March (1997), 'I am Charles Manson', interview with Manson, weekend supplement [Hebrew].
92. The psychology literature contains extensive discussion on narcissistic deprivation and its sources. Its linkage with motivation to lead was emphasized by Manfred Kets de Vries. A point worth mentioning is that ostensible proximity between the narcissistic leader and his or her mother is not an expression of love in the sense described as healthy parenting, but of the mother's adoration that has no intimate elements of giving. In these cases it is usually the narcissism of a mother who sees her child as an extension of herself. See: Kets de Vries, Manfred (1995), *Life and Death in the Executive Fast Lane*, San Francisco: Jossey-Bass; Kets de Vries, Manfred and Elisabet Engellau (2004), *Are Leaders Born or Are They Made? The Case of Alexander the Great*, London: Karnac. See also: Popper, Micha (1999), 'The sources of motivation of personalized and socialized charismatic leaders', *Psychoanalysis and Contemporary Thought*, **22** (2), 231–46; Popper (2001).
93. The idea of compensatory character formation with regard to leadership was first used by Alexander in analysing Woodrow Wilson's motivation to lead. See: George, Alexander L. and Juliette L. George (1956), *Woodrow Wilson and Colonel House: A Personality Study*, New York: Macmillan.
94. Sher, Moran (2008), 'Keshe'orot habama nidlakim (When the stage lights go on): On leadership and acting', MA thesis submitted to University of Haifa, Department of Psychology [Hebrew].
95. Kets de Vries (1995).
96. Popper (2001).
97. The DSM (1984 4th edition (*Diagnostic and Statistical Manual of Mental Disorders*) is a

guide used by psychiatrists and psychologists for clinical diagnosis. The symptoms of pathological narcissistic deprivation appear in the manual. See DSM, 1984, p. 661.

98. Popper (2001).
99. Kershaw, Ian (2001), *Hitler 1936–1945 Nemesis*, New York: Norton.
100. Shamir, Boas (2007), 'From passive recipients to active co-producers: Followers' role in the leadership process', in B. Shamir, R. Pillai, M.C. Bligh and M. Uhl-Bien (eds), *Follower-Centered Perspectives on Leadership*, Greenwich, CT: Information Publishing, pp. ix–xxxix.
101. Popper (2001).
102. Volkan, Vamik (1980), 'Narcissistic personality organization and "reparative" leadership', *International Journal of Group Psychotherapy*, **30** (2), 131–52.
103. Rholes, Steven W. and Jeffrey A. Simpson (eds) (2004), *Adult Attachment: Theory, Research, and Clinical Implications*, New York: Guilford Press, pp. 159–95.
104. Davidovitz, Rivka, M. Mikulincer, P. Shaver, R. Iszak and M. Popper (2007), 'Leaders as attachment figures', *Journal of Personality and Social Psychology*, **93** (4), 632–50.
105. Bowlby, John (1988), *A Secure Base: Clinical Applications of Attachment Theory*, London: Routledge.
106. Hazan, Cindy and Philip Shaver (1987), 'Romantic love conceptualized as an attachment process', *Journal of Personality and Social Psychology*, **52** (3), 511–24.
107. Mayseless, Ofra, R. Sharabany and A. Sagi (1997), 'Attachment concerns of others as manifested in parental, spousal and friendship relationships', *Personal Relationships*, **4**, 255–69.
108. Davidovitz et al. (2007).
109. Popper, Micha (2004), 'Leadership as relationship', *Journal for the Theory of Social Behaviour*, **34** (2), 107–25.
110. Popper and Mayseless (2003).
111. Popper, Micha (2002), 'Narcissism and attachment patterns of personalized and socialized charismatic leaders', *Journal of Social and Personal Relations*, **19** (6), 796–808.
112. Zakay, Eliav and Amir Scheinfeld (1993), *Mifakdei Gidudim Mitztayanim Bitzahal* [*Outstanding Battalion Commanders in the IDF*], Research Report, School of Leadership Development, Israel Defense Forces (IDF) [Hebrew], p. 12.
113. McCall, Morgan W. Jr., Michael M. Lombardo and Ann Morrison (1988), *The Lessons of Experience*, Lexington, MA: Lexington Books.
114. Amit, Karin, M. Popper, R. Gal, T. Mamane-Levy and A. Lisak (2009a), 'Leadership shaping experiences: A comparative study of leaders and non-leaders', *Leadership and Organizational Development Journal*, **30** (4), 312.
115. Bandura, Albert (1977), 'Self-efficacy: Toward a unifying theory of behavioral change', *Psychological Review*, **84** (2), 191–215; Bandura, Albert (1982), 'Human agency in social cognitive theory', *American Psychologist*, **44** (9), 1175–184.
116. Popper (1994).
117. Bandura, Albert (ed.) (1995), *Self-efficacy in Changing Societies*, New York: Cambridge University Press.
118. Rholes and Simpson (2004).
119. Day, David V. (2000), 'Leadership development: A review in context', *Leadership Quarterly*, **11** (4), 581–613; Day, David V., Stephen J. Zaccaro and Stanley M. Halpin (eds) (2004), *Leader Development for Transforming Organizations: Growing Leaders for Tomorrow*, Mahwah, NJ: Erlbaum.
120. Smith, Jeffrey A. and Roseanne J. Foti (1998), 'A pattern approach to the study of leader emergence', *Leadership Quarterly*, **9** (2), 147–60.
121. Popper et al. (2004); Amit et al. (2009a).
122. Collier, Gary, Henry L. Minton and Graham Reynolds (1991), *Currents of Thought in American Social Psychology*, New York: Oxford University Press.
123. Gardner, William and Bruce Avolio (1998), 'The charismatic relationship: A dramaturgical perspective', *Academy of Management Review*, **23** (1), 32–58.
124. Gandhi, Mahatma (1957), *An Autobiography: The Story of my Experiments with Truth* [trans. Mahadev H. Desai], Boston, MA: Beacon Press.

125. Some recent works have presented the construction process of leaders' biographies as part of the actual experience of influence, claiming that leaders construct their stories in a way that does not necessarily represent the actual biographical story but rather creates messages that the leader wishes to convey through his or her story. See, for example: Shamir, Boas, Hava Dayan-Horesh and Dalia Adler (2005), 'Leading by biography: Towards a life-story approach to the study of leadership', *Leadership*, **1** (1), 13–29; Shamir, Boas and Galit Eilam (2005), 'What's your story?' A life-stories approach to authentic leadership development', *The Leadership Quarterly*, **16** (3), 395–417.
126. 'Painting as past time', initially in the *Strand Magazine* (Dec. 1921, Jan. 1922), next published in *Thoughts and Adventures* (1932).
127. Popper (1994).
128. Bass, Bernard M. (2008), *The Bass Handbook of Leadership*, 4th edition, New York: Free Press.

4. The big picture

A rock pile ceases to be a rock pile the moment a single man contemplates it,
bearing within him the image of a cathedral.
(Antoine de St. Exupery)

LEADERSHIP – BETWEEN THE LOCAL AND THE UNIVERSAL

Two children who felt ill were taken to hospital. After they were examined the father of one of the children was told that his son had been diagnosed with a severe disease that might prove fatal. The only thing that could save his life was orange peel. The father of the other child was also told that his son had a severe disease (a different one) and the only thing that could save him was the flesh of an orange. This was the background story given to two participants who were about to engage in a role-playing exercise that is often used in workshops on interpersonal communications. The story was told to each participant separately without their knowing of each other. During the role-playing the two participants 'find' an orange at the same moment (handed to them by the facilitator) and from then on, through their interactions, they are expected to decide what to do. The situation is characterized by the fact that the orange has crucial meaning for both sides. Each one feels that their child's life depends on the orange, and each feels that the orange is theirs. In most cases the participants regard this exercise as a kind of Judgment of Solomon story, a zero-sum game. The people observing the role-playing are expected to observe the patterns of communication between the actors. In the briefing they receive before the workshop session (without the presence of the actors) they are told categorically that the problem is resolvable. Effective communication between the actors can lead them to understand that one of them needs the orange peel while the other one needs the flesh, so they can peel the orange and each one can save their child. Effective communication is also tested by the time it takes to reach the conclusion that there is no real problem here, but in many cases they do not reach this insight quickly.

This little story (to which I will return later) demonstrates at the most simple level (1) the complexity of social communication, and (2) the importance of the emotional baggage that each participant brings to a game. It determines the meaning ascribed to the subject of discussion and thus affects the interaction between the actors. These basic 'diagnoses' are at the core of broad cogitation in the history of ideas concerning man, his nature, his development and his aspirations. Now, having focused on the trees – in looking at leadership mainly from the point of view of social psychology – I will attempt to expand the view of leadership from the perspective of the entire forest. This more panoramic view may broaden our understanding of the deeper theoretical foundations of the discussion on leadership.

In a book composed of interviews with eminent scholars and researchers in social psychology,[1] the more veteran psychologists (whose works were published in the first half of the twentieth century) described Freud's influence as more dominant than that of all the other thinkers. On the other hand, the psychologists who were born after 1914 (most of whose works were published in the second half of the twentieth century) ranked Freud's writing in twentieth place. A survey conducted in the mid-1980s contains no mention of Freud among the ten most studied and influential works in psychology and sociology in a sample of universities in the USA.[2]

These facts reflect extreme fluctuations in the manner of thinking within the ongoing theoretical and empirical attempt to unravel the human enigma (especially the social human) with all its stratifications. The earlier expressions of this thinking were based on a biological conceptual foundation. Darwin's theory served researchers to explain not only the survival of individuals and societies (see the literature on social Darwinism),[3] but also complex psychological phenomena such as love and altruism. It was argued, for example, that romantic love, which is an inexhaustible source of poems and songs, movies and books, is no more than a sophisticated social expression of the evolutionary urge to spread one's genes through procreation.[4] The American psychologist David Buss,[5] who examined the patterns of preference in choosing a life partner, found that people from different cultures generally gave similar replies and showed specific preferences for mating with similar people. The men generally preferred beautiful young women to women who were older and wealthier, while the women preferred older and wealthier men to young and poor ones. The explanation is that these matings were selected in the evolutionary past, which determined that people chose partners with the attributes that would enable them to bear children and raise them. Men prefer a woman who is healthy and fertile, characteristics reflected in their youth and beauty, while women want a man with resources (money and power, which are generally accumulated over time), who can provide for them and their children.

Even actions that appear to be purely social and altruistic, when helping others may involve risking one's life, such as saving a drowning person; even these actions are explained as having a biological source. For example, the

Harvard ethologist Edward Wilson argued that the willingness of individuals to come to the rescue of people drowning in a river increases proportionally to their blood relations with those whom they are about to save. A person will risk their life, often without hesitating, when their children are drowning. They will be ready to take risks in order to save their cousins, although they will be slower than in the case of their own children, and increasingly slower to risk their life for others proportionally to the decreasing closeness of their blood relations with them. According to Wilson there is a kind of inherent formula that calculates the reaction time based on proximity of relations. The calculation is not done mathematically, but people behave as if such an inborn formula really existed.[6] In evolutional terms the need to help others is simply a 'selfish gene' designed to preserve one's kin. In other words this expands survival concepts to broader circles of families and groups that are interrelated.

Later developments in psychology that were also grounded in biology, such as behaviourism,[7] dealt with predicted behaviours of humans generated on the basis of reinforcement of behavioural responses. According to the logic of this approach, there is basically no difference between a dog or a dolphin jumping through a hoop and being rewarded by the food given to them by the trainer, and the employee who receives a cash bonus for 'behaving well' in the workplace. The only difference is in the degree of sophistication and abstraction of the reinforcement. While the animal needs tangible positive reinforcements, particularly food, for the human being a pat on the shoulder, a letter of appreciation and especially promotion in status and prestige are the positive reinforcements that encourage and instil desirable behaviours.

Some more complex psychological theories concerning man's inner world, such as those of Sigmund Freud and John Bowlby, also claim that complicated psychological developments in the course of life are based on instincts of biological origin. The parents' responses to the child's instincts, particularly during infancy (a period when the human most resembles other animals and is focused on the palpable sensations of hunger, pain, fear, pleasure and physical comfort) will affect his or her future life, especially in emotional and social contexts such as couple relationships, friendship, parenthood and also leadership.

The fluctuation in theoretical thinking on humans, which is central to our discussion on leadership, can be described somewhat simplistically on the axis of distance from the biological sources. For example, Ruth Benedict and Margaret Mead, who represent new disciplines such as cultural anthropology, clearly depart from the biological source, arguing on the basis of their comparative research projects that the personality of a human being in every aspect (including the attitude towards sex) is definitely shaped by his or her environment. Benedict demonstrated three totally different personality types: (1) Apollonian, exemplified by her observations of American Indians from New

Mexico; (2) Pueblo Indians, a completely opposite type, which she called paranoid, presented in her reports on the Dodu tribe that lived in North Guinea; (3) Dionysian, a type demonstrated by Kwakiutl Indians living in the northwest of the Pacific Ocean.

The first model (Apollonian) describes an environment in which the women are the property owners and breadwinners. Divorce is achieved simply by the woman putting the man's few possessions outside the door. In this environment people avoid competition and relationships are characterized by the absence of conflict and aggression. The men are 'delicate' and they are occupied with spirituality and religion.

In the second model (paranoid) the winner by the Dodu tribal standards is the manipulator who manages to accumulate more property than others. This society is largely characterized by suspicion and violence, and a woman will not go into the forest alone for fear of being raped.

The Dionysian model places considerable emphasis on competition and status struggles. Benedict shows how every culture creates different personality types. It is evident from her writing how an individual who grew up in a certain culture would find it difficult to adjust and function in a different culture.[8]

Margaret Mead's work presents a similar research direction. Her celebrated research on Samoa[9] emphasizes the *negative instance* methodology, which demonstrates more clearly the influence of the environment on personality development. For example, she compares the Arapesh, whose life pattern is characterized by cooperation between men and women and absence of aggression, with the Tchambuli tribe in which, contrary to the Western world, the women are dominant and provide for the family, while the men have no real responsibility and are emotionally dependent. Mead's conclusions are similar to those of Benedict – the ways of thinking, the emotions and the behaviours of people reflect the cultural differences between them.

I have expanded somewhat on these examples in order to show that (1) these theoretical poles, aggression, sex, family, parenthood – classical subjects that derive from biological origins according to instinct-based thinking – are presented here as distinctive and formed in a way that is patently different in different cultural environments, and (2) the formulation of leadership models is just one instance of more comprehensive theoretical propositions concerning human nature in a broader sense.

In more biologically biased thinking, such as that of Darwin or Freud, leadership models tend to be universal. In fact some leadership scholars have attempted to prove that the leader's role is to support survival and adjustment processes.[10] On the other hand, the more distant they are from the biologically based concept, the more the leadership models are culture-bound. Clearly, the probability of a man (certainly an aggressive and cunning one) becoming a leader in the Pueblo tribe in New Mexico is minimal. However, if he succeeded such a man would fully meet the expectations of a leader in the Dodu tribe. This dilemma between the universal and the circumstantial-cultural characterizes the social sciences in general and is particularly evident in psychological research on leadership.

How can these differences be resolved? I argue that when considering leadership theories the notion of *hierarchy* provides a bridge that permits the formulation of models that are more universal in certain circumstances, as well as models that are more bound to the context and culture relevant to different circumstances.

Instinct-bound thinking provides a major contribution to the understanding of leadership emergence in times of danger. Let us take the example of Moshe Dayan, who was forced by public pressure in Israel to become defence minister prior to the Six Day War. The public saw him as the right leader during a period of great existential fear and uncertainty preceding the war. This illustrates how the need for security calls to those leaders who are perceived as a suitable response to existential anxiety. Dayan's example clarifies two points: (1) it shows who has a better chance of being perceived and chosen as a leader in a time of existential insecurity; (2) existential anxiety is not a static condition and is not unique to weak societies. In certain circumstances developed societies may also regress to this kind of collective consciousness.

On the other hand, when collectives are in other situations or stages, far away from the instinctive stage, different aspects that are clearly unique to humans come to the fore. This is manifested at the level of the human group; here the theoretical leap between analysis at the individual level and at the group level is clearer in the sense that scholars, especially social psychologists, have successfully demonstrated how a group constitutes a source of reference for authority and leadership.

SYMBOLS, LEADERSHIP AND DIFFERENT CIRCLES OF INFLUENCE

The social psychologist Solomon Asch[11] was one of the first scholars to demonstrate the psychological status of the group as an analysis unit that not only influences the individual's identity in many cases but is also the component that determines his or her identity. Asch showed the subjects in an experiment three lines of different lengths. As expected, when each subject separately was asked the length of the lines their assessment was precise. Each of them ranked the lines according to their real length. This was the pre-experimental stage. Then the researcher brought in, unbeknown to the subject participating in the experiment, six more 'participants' who were in fact actors on his behalf. After every few rounds of estimating the length of lines shown to the genuine subject, the actors (secretly instructed by the researcher) claimed that the lines were of equal length, although this was patently incorrect. The results of the research showed that 75 per cent of the participants in a series of experiments of this kind changed their assessments after hearing the answers of the group. This research, which showed unequivocally the power of group conformity, led to many other studies examining the power and influence of the group. One of the well-known studies, which is also relevant to leadership, is Stanley Milgram's experiment dealing with the group dynamics of obedience to authority.[12]

Milgram's experiment purportedly concerned punishment by teachers. The participant who was asked to assume the role of teacher was permitted to administer an electric shock to the 'learner' who was sitting behind a thick wall. Every time the learner was given an electric shock he started shouting and crying as if in great pain. In fact, the learner did not receive any electric shocks and was playing the part as instructed by Milgram. To ensure a 'clean' experiment examining only the effect of the situation, Milgram held interviews and conducted personality tests prior to the experiments in order to filter out people who were liable to have unstable or sadistic personalities. The assumption was that the subjects in the experiments were normative people and therefore the results could be attributed to the situation and not to pre-existing personality differences.

In addition, before commencing the experiment Milgram conducted an opinion poll among psychiatrists and psychologists. They predicted that only 1 per cent of the participants in the experiment would give the learners electric shocks at the highest voltage indicated on the instrument under the word 'danger'. In fact, 65 per cent of the subjects reached this stage and did not stop even when the learner screamed and cried that he or she wanted to stop and leave the experiment (incidentally, this percentage was the same in the case of men and women). Milgram followed the responses of the 'shockers' (the subjects) and reported that they found different ways to avoid feeling responsible. Although some of them felt uncomfortable and showed clear signs of confusion and nervousness, the majority simply said that they had obeyed instructions.

The power of social conformity and its effect on obedience are clearly demonstrated in these experiments, and the inferences that serve to explain the subjects' behaviour in experiments such as those of Asch and Milgram are manifested in real life. Hannah Arendt, a prominent journalist and author, who observed and recorded the Eichmann trial, gave Milgram's psychological inferences a name that became common parlance – 'the banality of evil'. According to Arendt, what leads to evil is the social effect of conformity on obedience, rather than satanic urges or inherent personal wickedness. Evil, she claimed, is part of a chain in which the individual has no real sense of responsibility for the results. In such circumstances obedience is in a certain sense 'what everyone does' without thinking too much.[13] This was most aptly described by the historian Christopher Browning in a book in which he describes a regular military unit reaching horrifying levels of cruelty simply through processes of group conformity – being swallowed up in the group identity and totally casting off any feeling of personal responsibility for the results.[14]

These processes can be explained not only in terms of social psychology but also in sociological terms of role behaviour.[15] The argument basically is that people behave according to the role costumes that they wear, and these costumes are tailored according to social expectations. A salient example of this is the behaviour of a 20-year-old who becomes a platoon commander in the army. At home he may be the pampered son of a doting mother, a young man who enjoys going to a pub with his friends, bashfully attempting to chat up a girl. But when he puts on his uniform and appears before his new recruits he behaves in the manner that he understands is expected of him and as he has internalized from observing role models – his commanders. In donning the uniform (actually and metaphorically), he adopts the behaviour patterns of company commanders, which are manifested in many ways, including posture, manners, modes of speech and even slang. This example helps to explain behaviours that were revealed in another noted experiment, conducted by Philip Zimbardo at Stanford University.[16] Zimbardo created a simulation of a prison in which the participants (students) were allocated the roles of jailers and prisoners. A short time after the beginning of the experiment the jailers began to behave so punitively that it was necessary to stop the experiment after six days although it was planned to continue for two weeks. This experiment aroused a great deal of controversy, particularly around the question of natural cruelty and whether it was inherent in humans. Like Milgram, Zimbardo had screened the participants in order to rule out mentally disturbed individuals. His major argument was that the situation (or the role in a sociological view) is the key to the understanding of behaviour. Indeed, one of the major disputes in the social sciences concerns the weight of personality tendencies compared with the effect of the situation, and this dispute reverberates in the discussion on leadership.

According to the environmental/social role perception, people fill their role according to the expectations of a group, and the leader is merely an actor with a role to perform on the social stage. This view is common to many leadership theories, especially in sociopsychological and sociological trends.[17]

There are abundant explanations, experiments and field studies at the level of the group, the community or the social network, all of which can provide theoretical answers to the question of followers' attraction to the leader. And despite the differences between the theoretical explanations, the central place ascribed to norms, conformity, social self-concept, formative expectations and similar variables indicates the power of a social setting that is not too large (a group or an organization) in shaping the psychology of the followers. This also helps in understanding the influence of leaders in such settings.

The more complicated and less comprehensible issue is the attraction to leaders in the case of populations larger than groups, organizations or small communities. In the psychological literature on leadership this issue is discussed mainly at the level of instincts, as expressed in mass psychology. In the nature of things, psychoanalytic thinking, which places instinctive aspects at the centre, has devoted more attention to this question. From this angle of vision the mass is seen as an entity in itself. It is neither a 'moral domain' nor a structure of norms and social order. It is the form that precedes all social order and thought, a form full of desires, without any defined goal and totally lacking in meaning. That is to say the mass is not simply a collection of individuals; it has a psychology of its own and a dynamic of its own. Furthermore one of the conditions for an emotional outburst inspired by a leader is the *anonymity* provided by the mass. Thus, mass psychology allows space for man's aggressive and violent emotions to erupt. Such anonymity does not exist in small groups.[18] Freud, whose main concern was the inner world of the individual, was not optimistic about man's 'true nature' and saw culture primarily as an expression of the collective superego – a restrictive frame that directs the acceptable behaviours in a given society. When the superego breaks down, as in conditions of stress and anonymity, the aggressive impulses come to the forefront and in these circumstances the leader may be a powerful catalyst.[19]

Another psychodynamic explanation for the yearning of broad collectives for leaders was offered by the psychoanalyst David Aberbach.[20] His explanation is less universal and relates to the psychology of *trauma*, arguing that in crisis situations there may be congruity between the feelings and traumas of the charismatic leader and those of the collective. In this situation the leader becomes a kind of refuge.

The basic proposition is that collective trauma engenders a natural psychological potential for attachment to a leader who has undergone a similar trauma in his or her private life. Unlike most people, they have already experienced a similar trauma and learned to cope with it. Thus, at this rare meeting point they know how to display effective struggle with the crisis and, what is no less important from the followers' point of view, they understand from personal experience the psychological nuances of the situation. One of the explanations offered for the German people's attraction to Hitler was the following psychodynamic interpretation. First, life in Germany between the two World Wars was marked by existential uncertainty, severe unemployment and galloping inflation. Furthermore, the legend of the stab-in-the-back that purportedly caused the defeat in World War I was deeply humiliating. Many Germans believed that the defeat was not inevitable and that Germany had surrendered without putting up a real fight. In this atmosphere millions of German children grew up feeling afraid and disappointed with a father who could not provide for them, who perhaps was a soldier who had not fought properly and was not strong enough. In these emotional circumstances of a collective traumatic experience with a disappointing father, Hitler could emerge as a leader. A disappointing father was a familiar experience to him. He had the most obsessive and strongest urge to compensate for this personal trauma. He knew how to play on all these themes, on the pain and disappointment, on the sense of pride and security, and at the most fateful and tragic time in the history of the period this had powerful resonance.[21]

This brings us back to the discussion on needs and Abraham Maslow's definition of primary and higher-order needs. Considerable theoretical attention has been paid to the question of yearning for leaders, resulting in two types of theories: (1) theories that are instinct oriented, relating to primary needs or regressive processes, and (2) theories that relate to broader ranges of influence based on higher needs that can be manifested only in social and organizational contexts.

The concept *symbol* appears to be relevant to this discussion above the instinctive primary phase because it has the potential for analysis of leadership both in its political manifestations and as expressed in daily social life. It may also be relevant to comparative intercultural analyses. One of the fundamental distinctions between humans and other animals is the ability to use symbols. This is most clearly expressed in language, through which humans can create meaning.[22] But it is not only language that has symbolic power; so do physical objects and behaviours; and unlike other animals, who basically respond simply to stimuli, humans respond to the meanings attributed to various stimuli. Generally an orange is just a type of fruit, but in the story that opened this chapter it acquired a different meaning when it was perceived as a life-saving remedy. This meaning could be attributed to the orange by virtue of the human ability to understand representations of complex and abstract phenomena, an ability that can turn certain objects into social objects.[23] For example, a huge sheet of cloth painted with red and white stripes and stars on a blue background hanging in the middle of a remote path deep in a jungle in Africa constitutes an object that obstructs the field of vision of a leopard who is lying in wait for the prey that is expected to appear on the path. The same sheet of cloth can bring tears to the eyes of an American zoologist who finds himself in this area in the course of his research. To him, this cloth is a flag, an object with symbolic meaning that can arouse deep emotions. The same sheet of painted cloth is a source of patriotism and pride for soldiers on parade and a source of anger and hatred for another population that sees it as a symbol of oppression. Theoreticians who study symbolization processes claim that when objects are used for communication between people they serve as symbols. But as stated, not only objects serve as symbols; certain behaviours and actions also have symbolic meaning. In this sense, beyond living in a physical reality we also live in a reality that is full of symbols. In fact, the question as to how symbols are created has occupied many thinkers.

The historical and philosophical foundations of this enquiry have appeared in the works of many scholars.[24] A relevant contribution to the study of leadership was made by Blumer and some of his followers,[25] who dealt with symbolization processes. The orange described above would not have become meaningful if the actors had not come into the game with past baggage that gave the orange its unique meaning at that point in time. Such baggage is created in communication processes with significant others, with reference groups and social worlds that surround us and influence our self-concept. According to the scholars, the self-concept is shaped mainly in social contexts wherein processes such as vicarious learning,[26] social comparison[27] and performance of social roles occur, and through these processes, norms and the social self-concept are internalized.[28]

The prevalent opinion among the scholars is that the formation of the social self begins at an early age. Two social psychologists, one American (Hazel Markus) and one Japanese (Shinobu Kitayama), demonstrate how different foundations of the social self are created.[29] They present an everyday event in which a mother attempts to feed her small child who refuses to eat. The American mother tries to persuade her son to eat with arguments such as 'If you don't eat you won't be strong enough to be good at sports'. The Japanese mother describes to her little boy the sources of the food she wants him to eat. She tells him about the people who milked the animals, the people who made the cheese from the milk, the farmers who grew the wheat that was used to make dough, and those who baked the dough to make the bread. After enumerating all the people who worked to prepare the portion of food placed in front of the child, she asks: 'Won't you respect all those people and their work?' Thus, we see how social values begin to be formed from such early interactions. In the American society the values of individualism and achievement are fostered, while collective values are nurtured more in Japanese society.[30] There is indeed considerable research evidence showing the effect of familial and social interactions on the formation of the self-concept and on the understanding and interpretation of processes and symbols.[31]

Leadership, especially political leadership, can be a kind of social symbol. The leaders' rhetoric, the figures of speech and images they use, their biographies (at least those that are made known to the public) and their lifestyle all create what I have referred to as a 'story'. The extent of symbolism of the story derives from the expectations and the socialization that characterize the various *communities of memory*. Hence, looking at leaders as social objects, as symbols, can help to clarify differences in followers' attitudes towards the leaders.

It appears that some well-known political leaders intuitively discern the psychological mechanism underlying the creation of persuasive symbols. When asked to explain the secret of his leadership, Churchill used to say that all his strength was in his pen and his tongue. Clearly his persuasive skills stemmed partly from his deep understanding of the power of symbolism in recruiting people. This was mainly expressed in his excellent use of words. His meticulously prepared speeches established him in the public awareness as a symbol of leadership. A notable example is the famous speech that he delivered to the nation immediately after forming the government, promising only blood, toil, tears and sweat.[32]

Symbolic effects were the sources of empowerment of some of the most outstanding leaders in modern Western history. We can learn about these effects from speeches that are considered classic addresses of leaders, such as Abraham Lincoln's Gettysburg Address, Martin Luther King's 'I have a dream' or John Kennedy's 'I am a Berliner'.

However, the entire symbolic effect cannot be ascribed only to the content of the words. To be fully understood the symbolic effect has to be seen in the context of events. It appears that leaders (or their advisors) have a way of understanding the context into which the captivating symbolic words are interwoven. In this they resemble talented theatrical directors, who think in terms of the whole picture. They think of the scenery, the timing, the type of audience, the placement of the actors, the words and the sounds as a weave designed to arouse emotions by its very existence.[33] Lincoln delivered the Gettysburg Address at the height of the Civil War, immediately after the battle of Gettysburg, when the northern army succeeded for the first time in repulsing the advance of the southern army commanded by General Lee. The address was delivered at a moment when the mourning over the loss of many soldiers was mixed with the triumph over the glorious victory. The battle site was the stage and its results were the backdrop. At this moment Lincoln chose to emphasize the elevated moral aims of the war (not the operative objectives). The keywords in his speech were 'People were born equal', and the sentence most often repeated as a reminder to public servants throughout the world: 'Government of the people, by the people, for the people, shall not perish from the earth.' The main social themes in Lincoln's words inspired the listeners with a sense of the purpose, the cause. This effect is cardinal in motivational processes, especially in situations when people are expected to undertake the least instinctive action of all – to risk their lives.

Analysis of Martin Luther King's influential 'I have a dream' speech shows that he understood very well the power of symbolism. He commenced his address by referring to those who had composed the emancipation proclamation during the Civil War, went on to describe the true situation of the blacks in America, and proceeded to list his dreams, some of which were phrased in personal terms. 'I dream that my four small children will not be judged by the color of their skin but by the content of their character.' The emphasis on children is perceived as innocent and 'outside the political game' – 'I dream that in Alabama black boys and girls will hold hands with white boys and girls like brothers and sisters.' Later in the speech he said, 'all children are God's children.' He ended the speech declaring his firm belief that the dream would come true.

John Kennedy's speech of June 1962 in the divided city of Berlin near the wall that separated east from west, demonstrates clearly the symbolic thinking of a leader who knew how to touch people's feelings by evoking symbols. This speech also illustrates the non-verbal aspects that theatre directors (like great leaders) arrange so well in order to influence the audience. Kennedy made use of the 'natural scenery' and pointed to the wall as a physical illustration of separation – not between east and west but between freedom and tyranny. 'What country needs a wall within which to protect its citizens?' said Kennedy. The crowd of Berliners reached the peak of enthusiasm when Kennedy likened Berlin to a battlefront and the citizens to freedom fighters. He ended this part with a well-planned symbolic act. 'Ich bin ein Berliner' (I am a Berliner), thus arousing feelings of identity by conveying the message: I am one of you and we are fighting for freedom, nothing less. By this rhetorical gesture (and the fact that it was spoken in German), he transformed the citizen of Berlin who lived a dreary everyday life in the shadow of the wall and hostility into a soldier in the heroic battle for the exalted principles of freedom.

To explain this influence we need to understand the audience, which will help us to discern what symbols capture the people's emotions and involvement. This psychological process has been the subject of considerable research and numerous explanations, particularly by scholars who engaged in unravelling the riddle of the self. One of the major distinctions is between the private self and the collective self.

By definition, the collective self is a social category.[34] For example, it is clear that in a religious society the social self that develops will be distinct from non-religious societies. This conceptualization can cast light on deeper levels if we take the example of the Lubavitcher community mentioned in Chapter 3. In this community the self of the members is distinguished not only by external signs such as dress and manners, but by their way of thinking about basic subjects such as family, life and death and, as described, leadership. According to this explanation it will now be easier to understand why the Lubavitcher rabbi, the undisputed charismatic and venerated leader of his community, was not mere flesh and blood. People were (and still are) drawn to him because his social attraction was the hub of social identification processes.[35]

An identity game that is often played in school classrooms demonstrates the complexity of the self-concept, especially in social contexts. Identity tags bearing words such as brother, partner, religious (Christian, Jewish, Muslim), humanist, nationality (African-American, American, Hispanic-American) and so forth are scattered round the corners of the room. These tags represent various self-perceptions. Obviously one person can contain many of these identities. He may be American, Protestant, married, a father, a humanist and so forth. The players are required to make forced choices. In each round of the game they have to decide which is the primary component of their identity. Some people, when faced with the need to decide, will go straight for the religious person label, which means that they feel that this is their dominant identity. Others see themselves primarily as humanists, and so forth.

The leadership scholar Boas Shamir and his associates[36] claim that the symbolic effect of leaders lies in the emphasis of a particular identity over others. This may explain the symbolic influence of John Kennedy in the example mentioned earlier. Kennedy's words at the Berlin Wall emphasized the universal identity category of freedom fighter. The symbolic effect occurs because of people's inherent desire to see themselves in a positive light. Hence they will respond and undertake actions that provide opportunities for self-enhancement.[37] Reicher and Hopkins see leaders like King, Lincoln and Kennedy as 'entrepreneurs of identity', a phrase that aptly expresses the symbolic influence that enhances the followers' sense of self-worth.[38]

In an analysis of Reverend Jesse Jackson's address at a Democratic Party convention in Atlanta, Georgia in 1988, the researchers Shamir, Arthur and House[39] reveal the psychological foundations underlying the effect of his speech and present a conceptual frame for analysis of the influence of charismatic leaders' speeches. This address was chosen for illustrative analysis because, according to the reports in the important US newspapers, it entered the pantheon of great and moving speeches. *The New York Times* reported on 20 July 1988 that supporters and rivals alike stood and applauded Jackson with tears streaming from their eyes. 'I could hardly speak,' said a white delegate from Mississippi, wiping his tears and hugging a black delegate from Mississippi. Another delegate said, 'When a man like Jesse Jackson speaks to you, you feel that you can achieve something.'

The palpable emotional effect of the speech was created by the following psychological foundations, which may be seen in all the great speeches of charismatic leaders. The first is the much discussed need for a social identity. In his speech, Jackson likened America to a quilt with 'many patches, many pieces, many colors, and many sizes, all woven and held together by a common thread'. And like Martin Luther King, who interwove the collective dreams with personal talk of his four children, Jackson did not settle for the familiar image of a quilt but transformed it into genuine hope through his personal story. 'We were a very poor family from South Carolina,' he told the audience, 'the children snuggled under a blanket, but it wasn't enough, we were still cold. Mother cut pieces of cloth from old clothes, pieces of wool, and put them over the blanket, but that didn't help. With practiced hands she sewed all these pieces into a patchwork quilt and covered us with it.... America, too, is a collection of patches,' Jackson said to the excited audience, and pointed separately to each ethnic group sitting in the auditorium. 'If we know how to join together properly, this collection will become a patchwork quilt that will keep us all warm.' The immediate effect of this image was palpable and the audience responded with tears and enthusiastic handclapping. But beyond the visible response, at the more philosophical level, at the basis of this effect lies the assumption concerning human nature. That is, humans have an inherent need to be worthy. Speeches such as those discussed here touch this level of need and enable people to make themselves worthy in their own eyes and in the eyes of their significant others.

What then is the frame of reference that provides the themes of 'a worthy person'? In terms of contents, it is related to the idea of a community of memory, namely the important symbols in the historical memory of a given collective. In terms of psychology it concerns a need that has been discussed extensively in the psychological literature – the need for consistency.[40]

As described, Martin Luther King began his historic address by referring to 'people in whose symbolic shadow we stand', namely Abraham Lincoln and the history of struggles for equality. Jesse Jackson started his speech by stating that John Kennedy, Franklin Roosevelt and Martin Luther King 'would be proud to be in this meeting hall'.[41] These speeches connect the listeners to an illustrious ongoing heritage of great ideas and worthy people who embodied them and themselves became part of an ongoing noble heritage.

The emphasis on the theme of success, as expressed by Martin Luther King and his personal success as an educated black in America, Jesse Jackson's story of how his family overcame dreadful hardships or Lincoln's success in overcoming difficulties, strengthens components of shared identity reflected in their stories and speeches. But beyond this it also strengthens another aspect that has been studied a great deal in social psychology – belief in one's own ability, or *self-efficacy* as it is known in the professional literature. The numerous studies on the sources of self-efficacy have shown that its major source is the actual experience of success. When a person experiences success in any sphere, whether in mathematics or in sport, in leadership or in overcoming crises, their belief in their own capabilities in that sphere becomes strengthened.[42] Jesse Jackson's description of how he overcame severe hardships as a child in a poor family, his personal success and his mother's success in making a patchwork quilt, transmitted the following two messages: (1) we have the components of a common identity and, no less important, (2) we have the strength to succeed. (Years later, Barack Obama was to end all his speeches calling for change with the words: 'Yes, we can'.) Hope combined with belief in one's ability to fulfil it is what military people tend to call a power multiplier.

When it comes to leadership in everyday life and the influence of officers, managers or parents, the methods and processes that generate influence or identification are largely behavioural rather than rhetorical or metaphorical, as in the case of distant leaders. It is common knowledge that personal example is the most important form of influence in junior command. Soldiers see their commander's daily behaviour as an example to them.[43] Similarly, children are influenced by their parents in the socialization process.[44] The principle is that daily behaviours transmit messages, and in this sense behaviours are sources of symbolic influence. Take, for instance, the following anecdote. The employees in a certain organization complained to the CEO that he ascribed great importance to development and ignored other things such as production management, marketing and human resources. 'Never,' said the manager to the workers' representatives after thorough examination, 'never in my speeches, staff newsletters or any review have I expressed preference for R&D (research and development) issues or R&D workers.' 'True,' said the complaining employees, 'but everyone knows that you devote most of your time to meetings with R&D workers in your office or visits to the research and development branch.' Here we see that the value of the manager's time is not purely technical, as many people think; his time also has symbolic value. More than words and documents, it communicates to the employees the order of preference and the importance attributed to the occupations within the organization.[45]

Undoubtedly, daily behaviours and decisions in organizations have symbolic meaning. The appointment of a certain person to a coveted role for which there are many candidates is usually perceived as a technical bureaucratic act, but the symbolic significance of such decisions is no less important. The choice of a particular candidate conveys messages concerning the kind of people who are promoted and the behaviours that are acceptable. Likewise, cash bonuses, appreciation letters and similar gestures are not simply rewards in the narrow sense. They transmit powerful messages concerning the required behaviours in the organization. Every act of this kind has symbolic meaning, and managers who think in terms of leadership are well aware of it.[46]

To take an example from another sphere, innumerable reports on psychotherapy patients show clearly the influence of parents' daily behaviour on their children's self-concept, expectations and behaviours. What influences the children is not verbal declarations of love and caring but the parents' attention, their hugs, their constant interest. These things, or their absence, are the decisive influence.[47]

With respect to the academic discussion summarized in Chapter 2, it is now possible to formulate some theoretical principles in a more focused and organized manner. First, as regards the distinction between close and distant leaders, when the leader is more distant from the followers (which is mostly the case with political leaders), theories and models dealing with psychodynamic and attributive levels of identity formation are more relevant to the understanding of processes of influence in this space. With regard to the dynamics between followers and close leaders, behavioural models are a better source for the analysis and understanding of processes of influence. Second, different collectives have different symbols. Understanding of this diversity is a key to understanding the influence of leaders, because they are simultaneously culture heroes and representatives of social categories.

Looking at leaders both as cause and effect in a distinct and thoroughly analysed cultural context can cast light on the questions as to who is likely to be accepted as a leader and how far the leader's influence will extend over time. The discussion on these issues is not as yet satisfactory, partly because of the reason stated – that one particular discipline or angle cannot address an area which by its nature can only be understood through multidisciplinary views. However, the analysis presented thus far can point to certain aspects derived from the major propositions hitherto presented. In the concluding chapter I will examine some aspects (mainly pragmatic) that emerge from these propositions.

NOTES

1. Evans, R. (interviewer) (1980), *The Making of Social Psychology: Discussions with Creative Contributors*, New York: Gardner.
2. Collier, Gary, Henry L. Minton and Graham Reynolds (1991), *Currents of Thought in American Social Psychology*, New York: Oxford University Press, p. 122.
3. Spencer, Herbert (1876), *Principles of Sociology*, New York: Appleton.
4. Lampert, Ada (1995), *Evolutzia shel ahava [Evolution of Love]*, Publication of Open University [Hebrew].
5. Buss, David M. (1994), *The Evolution of Desire: Strategies of Human Mating*, New York: Basic Books.
6. Wilson, Edward O. (1978), *On Human Nature*, Cambridge, MA: Harvard University Press.
7. Skinner, Frederic (1974), *About Behaviorism*, New York: Vintage.
8. Benedict, Ruth (1934), *Patterns of Culture*, Boston: Houghton Mifflin.
9. Mead, Margaret ([1930] 2009), *Coming of Age in Samoa: A Psychological Study of Primitive Youth for Western Civilizations*, New York: HarperCollins.
10. Heifetz, Ronald H. (1994), *Leadership Without Easy Answers*, Cambridge, MA: Harvard University.
11. Asch, Solomon E. (1953), *Social Psychology*, Englewood Cliffs, NJ: Prentice Hall.
12. Milgram, Stanley (1974), *Obedience to Authority: An Experimental View*, New York: Harper & Row.

13. Arendt, Hannah (1963), *Eichmann in Jerusalem: A Report on the Banality of Evil*, New York: Viking Press.
14. Browning, Christopher (1992), *Ordinary Men: Reserve Police Battalion 101 and the Final Solution in Poland*, New York: HarperCollins.
15. Goffman, Erving (1959), *The Presentation of Self in Everyday Life*, New York: Doubleday.
16. Zimbardo, Philip (2007), *The Lucifer Effect: Understanding How Good People Turn Evil*, New York: Random House.
17. There are some leadership scholars who see *expectations* as a key concept in explaining the leadership phenomenon. This concept has diverse expressions and uses, but in general it refers to expectations that exist in a social context and therefore the analysis of leadership can only be understood within this understanding. See, for example, the work of the Australian researcher Michael Hogg: Hogg, Michael (2001), 'A social identity theory of leadership', *Personality and Social Psychology Review*, **5** (3), 184–200.
18. There are some who say that mass psychology cannot be discussed in the terms of individual or group psychology. The mass is not a collection of individuals or groups, and the concepts related to norms, conformity, obedience and so forth that were developed in social psychology are inadequate and perhaps irrelevant. See: Le Bon, Gustave (1952), *The Crowd: A Study of the Popular Mind*, London: Ernest Benn; Tarde, Gabriel (1903), *The Laws of Imitation*, New York: Henry Holt and Co.
19. Freud, Sigmund (1961), *Civilization and its Discontents* [trans. and ed. by James Strachey], New York: W.W. Norton.
20. Aberbach, David (1995), 'Charisma and attachment theory: A crossdisciplinary interpretation', *International Journal of Psychoanalysis*, **76**, 845–55.
21. Popper, Micha (2001), *Hypnotic Leadership: Leaders, Followers and the Loss of Self*, Westport, CT: Praeger.
22. Mead, George H. (1934), *Mind, Self and Society*, Chicago: University of Chicago Press.
23. Charon, Joel M. (1979), *Symbolic Interactionism: An Introduction, an Interpretation, an Integration*, Englewood Cliffs, NJ: Prentice-Hall.
24. A comprehensive survey of the thinking on various aspects of the human ability to create and relate to symbols, from the creation of language to objects, appears in Joel Charon's book (see note 23).
25. Blumer, Herbert (1986), *Symbolic Interactionism*, Berkeley: University of California Press; Stryker, Sheldon (1980), *Symbolic Interactionism: A Social Structural Version*, Menlo Park, CA: Benjamin Cummings.
26. Bandura, Albert (1982), 'Human agency in social cognitive theory', *American Psychologist*, **44** (9), 1175–84.
27. Festinger, Leon (1954), 'A theory of social comparison processes', *Human Relations*, **7** (2), 117–40.
28. Goffman, Erving (1959), *Presentation of Self in Everyday Life*, New York: Doubleday.
29. Markus, Hazel and Shinobu Kitayama (1991), 'Culture and the self. Implications for cognition emotion and motivation', *Psychological Review*, **98** (2), 224–53.
30. Hofstede, Geert and Jan Hofstede (2005), *Culture and Organizations: The Software of the Mind*, New York: McGraw-Hill.
31. Markus, Hazel and Elissa Wurf (1987), 'The dynamic self-concept: A social-psychological perspective', *Annual Review of Psychology*, **38**, 299–337.
32. Ramsden, John (2002), *Man of the Century: Winston Churchill and his Legend since 1945*, London: HarperCollins.
33. Gardner, William and Bruce Avolio (1998), 'The charismatic relationship: A dramaturgical perspective', *Academy of Management Review*, **23** (1), 32–58.
34. Hogg (2001).
35. Tajfel, H. and J.C. Turner (1979), 'An integrative theory of inter-group conflict', in W.G. Austin and S. Worchel (eds), *The Social Psychology of Intergroup Relations*, Monterey, CA: Brooks/Cole, pp. 33–47.
36. Shamir, Boas, Robert J. House and Michael B. Arthur (1993), 'The motivational effects of charismatic leadership: A self-concept-based theory', *Organizational Science*, **4** (4), 577–93.
37. Beauregard, Keith and David Dunning (1998), 'Turning up the contrast: Self-enhancement

motives prompt egocentric contrast effects in social judgments', *Journal of Personality and Social Psychology*, **74** (3), 606–21.

38. Reicher, Stephen D. and Nick Hopkins (2003), 'On the science of the art of leadership', in D. Van Knippenberg and M.A. Hogg (eds), *Leadership and Power: Identity Processes in Groups and Organizations*, London: Sage, pp. 65–78.

39. Shamir, Boas, Michael B. Arthur and Robert J. House (1994), 'The rhetoric of charismatic leadership: A theoretical extension, a case study and implications for research', *Leadership Quarterly*, **5** (1), 25.

40. Shamir et al. (1993).

41. Shamir et al. (1994).

42. Bandura, Albert (1977), 'Self-efficacy: Toward a unifying theory of behavioral change', *Psychological Review*, **84**, 191–215.

43. Popper, Micha (1996), 'Leadership in military combat units and business organizations: A comparative psychological analysis', *Journal of Managerial Psychology*, **11** (1), 15–25.

44. Popper, Micha and Ofra Mayseless (2003), 'Back to basics: Applying a parenting perspective to transformational leadership', *Leadership Quarterly*, **14** (1), 41–65.

45. Popper, Micha (1994), *Al Menahalim Kemanhigim [On Managers as Leaders]*, Tel Aviv: Ramot Publishing House, Tel Aviv University [Hebrew].

46. Popper (1994).

47. Yalom, Irvin D. (1980), *Existential Psychotherapy*, New York: Basic Books.

Conclusion

All that is necessary for the triumph of evil is for good men to do nothing.
(Edmund Burke)

One of the 'everlasting' debates in academia concerns the issue of basic research versus applied research. The purpose of basic research is to expand the boundaries of knowledge regardless of the extent of its applicability, whereas applied research is conducted in order to generate *knowledge for action*, as defined by Chris Argyris,[1] a Harvard scholar who has extensively studied this issue of the goals of research. In the natural sciences the debate over the goals of research is less intense because, as many examples have shown, knowledge engendered by basic research in the natural sciences can develop at some stage into applied knowledge (in medicine for example).

However, when it comes to psychological topics the debate is not only over the aims but also over the research methods and design. For example, the area known as 'decision-making', a major field of research in psychology, is often studied in laboratory conditions in an attempt to maintain strict research procedures that meet the scientific requirement of maximum control over the research variables. Researchers like Argyris resist this approach, arguing that no laboratory conditions can provide real understanding of processes such as decision-making or leadership, which in reality always happen in different and unique ways. The true research laboratory, they assert, is the things that happen in reality.

Therefore, those who share this position argue that it is futile to predict decisions that are made in laboratory simulations, and the better way is to analyse and study decisions made in real life. According to this approach the important issue is not prediction, but rather the extraction of knowledge that can serve as an input to knowledge for action.[2] It appears, then, that the debate is highly complicated and touches on substantive issues of the level of generalization in constructing and examining theories.

My intention in beginning this conclusion with a reference to the above debate is not to discuss questions of research methodologies or research aims but to share with the reader my feelings on reaching this point. While leafing through the pages of the manuscript in order to commit to paper a clear and focused conclusion, my thoughts kept returning to this debate in connection with something that I remarked on in the Introduction. I began the book by

114

saying that I did not intend to write another book that would show once again that leadership is a complex multifaceted phenomenon like love, for instance. My aim, as I stated explicitly, was to advance in *clarifying* the phenomenon. I believed that looking at leadership as a psychological phenomenon from the perspective of the followers could help to clarify it further. Now, on rereading the text, it seems to me that some aspects of the discussion on leadership may still remain abstruse. Therefore, I wish to ensure that at least some major points (as I see them) will be expressed more clearly in the context of knowledge for action. The conclusion will be devoted to these points, mainly with regard to three aspects:

1. *Political leadership* – an area in which many people are sometimes emotionally involved on a daily basis in observing the leaders' behaviour through the media. Furthermore, people's concepts, images and intuitive theories regarding leadership reach expression in the paramount act of voting in the elections. By this act, the people (in democratic countries) determine who will be their leaders.
2. *Leadership in organizations* – in the course of his/her life everyone has lived in some kind of organizational setting, from the family with its own structure of authority, to small or large work places. *Leadership in everyday life*, a term that appears often in this book, is manifested largely in organizational contexts. Hence I will elaborate on some practical insights relating to the leader's actions and influence in light of the basic mechanisms that are fundamental in the act of organizing, which differs from the more technical and static term, organization.[3]
3. *Research on leadership* – bearing in mind that this book contains a considerable amount of criticism of leadership theories and research, it seemed to me that I could not finish the book without devoting some attention to the question of creation of relevant knowledge on leadership. In other words, I thought it fit to emphasize a few recommendations that may have significance for research in light of the analysis presented in the book.

SOME ASPECTS OF KNOWLEDGE FOR ACTION IN THE SPHERE OF POLITICAL LEADERSHIP

Gary Hart, a handsome senator from Colorado, was a leading candidate in the USA presidential elections of 1988. The polls predicted certain success for him. He had all the required qualities: good looks, eloquence, education, an impressive political record. But his candidacy collapsed all at once because of a photograph showing him on the deck of a yacht with a young lover. It is doubtful that an event of this kind would affect the chances of a presidential candidate in France. Evidence that can destroy the career of a brilliant politician in one society may be greeted in another society with a shake of the head or a tolerant grin. Incidents like these, which are numerous, exemplify at a most simplistic level the principle that it is necessary to understand the symbols that are important to certain societies. With respect to followers' attraction to a leader, especially a political leader, understanding of the context is particularly important. Perhaps not by chance, it was a sociologist (Max Weber) who discovered this and identified the *charisma of office*, a sociological concept that separates the concept of charisma from the leader's actual personality.

According to Weber, authority has charisma that can be understood and interpreted in a sociocultural context. A salient example of this is the position of chief of staff in Israeli society; the commander of the armed forces enjoys prestige that is unparalleled in the Western world. The reason for this is that security is a central issue in Israel; hence the office of the person who is seen as responsible for protecting the people and their country carries enormous prestige. From this elevated office the charisma is projected to the role bearer himself. There have been many cases of chiefs of staff who took up a political career after retiring from the military. This syndrome is familiar. As chiefs of staff they had huge electoral value when in uniform, and were constantly courted by political parties who knew very well that their public status would be enhanced in the elections if they could present to the public a former chief of staff. However, another syndrome may be observed here; the charisma of these former chiefs of staff faded with the passage of time out of uniform, when their personality was exposed separately from their charismatic role. The same principle applies to other societies and other roles that have charismatic value derived from the sociocultural context. Vaclav Havel received credit points during the 'Velvet Revolution' in Czechoslovakia, perhaps because he was also a playwright who represented to many people the spirit of the country that was the cultural cradle of Central Europe. Michael Bloomberg, Mayor of New York, based his election campaign on the fact that he was a successful businessman – a prestigious image in American society.[4] A political leader needs to understand the cultural climate and, as mentioned more than once in this book, a leader who is outstanding in a certain place or role will not necessarily excel in another place or another culture.

The cultural context argument has been discussed in this book so much that the reader might easily arrive at the conclusion that the leadership phenomenon has no universal base (apart from the biological instinctive base that is stimulated in certain situations, particularly situations of threat and anxiety), and that in its psychological senses it is entirely contextual. This conclusion would be too far-fetched, so I decided to elaborate on the distinction between universal and cultural contexts in terms of knowledge for action.

If I were to ask the readers to stop at this point and think of all the people whom they see and admire as leaders and try to summarize in one sentence their feelings towards those leaders, I believe it would almost certainly be summed up in the words 'I feel that he/she is someone I can rely upon.'

The basic feelings towards leaders are universal. The intercultural differences are not in the basic feeling but in what the American leadership scholar Edwin Hollander called 'credit', meaning attributes that build trust in the leader.[5] This is an apt metaphor, taken from the world of banking; just as a bank needs signs to prove that it can trust the client, so do the followers need signs from their leader. Leaders, according to Hollander's metaphor, are not a static stimulus but rather build credit with the followers. The more credit they accumulate, the more the followers will be ready to comply with them.

The credit metaphor illustrates further the differences between leaders in organizations and distant leaders (especially political leaders) in the means of influence available to them. The former build their credit through their daily behaviour, setting a personal example, serving as role models, paying constant attention to the followers' development, the tasks they assign and their ability to reward the followers psychologically or otherwise.

In the case of distant leaders the credit-building processes have a different dynamic, based more on rhetoric referring to symbols with emotional value, as we saw in the analysis of the speeches of Abraham Lincoln, Martin Luther King, Winston Churchill, Jesse Jackson and others. Moreover, the credit of a political leader can be built very quickly. Barack Obama's sweeping speech at the Democratic Party Convention in 2004 reveals swift adjustment based on rhetoric. It enabled an unknown young man to take his place on the racetrack to national leadership in a way that could not be ignored. In contrast, the credit of leaders in everyday life is not built on symbolic rhetoric, however captivating it may be. Teachers, army officers, parents and managers build trust among the people whom they influence through countless behaviours, actions and decisions displayed over a long period.

These differences are perhaps more perceptible when it comes to *loss of credit*. Political leaders can lose credit very quickly, even if it appears stable and was accumulated over a long period. An example of this is the speech delivered by Levy Eshkol, Israel's premier and defence minister on the eve of the Six Day War. The Israeli public, overwhelmed by apocalyptic fear in the days preceding the war, waited anxiously to hear their leader talking to the nation over the radio. And when the many thousands of radios were turned on, instead of a reassuring and confident message they heard stuttering, incoherent speech. Thus, despite the appreciation that Levy Eshkol had received during his years of leadership in many roles, including that of prime minister, the credit he had accumulated collapsed all at once. The public pressed for his resignation from the Defence Ministry, and the government had no choice but to replace him with Moshe Dayan, who had considerable credit as a success-ful chief of staff. Loss of credit due to stammering is less likely to occur in the case of leaders in everyday life.

Similarly, it is advisable to relate to the situational and cultural contexts as frames that permit the existence of processes, particularly various means of building credit for the leader. Whether it is a matter of differences between types of organizations or of collectives with different cultures, the concept of credit calls for explanation of the means of influence in the given context. This requires deep diagnostic understanding.

Another metaphor, which was described in Chapters 3 and 4 in connection with the symbolic influence of leaders, is that of the theatre. This metaphor permits deeper scrutiny in order to obtain knowledge for action concerning the impact of the universal component compared with the local cultural compo-nent. Looking at leadership in terms of the theatre may provide important practical psychological insights relating to the influence of distant leaders. For example, if we analyse deeply the thinking and functioning of great theatre directors we will find that their manner of thinking resembles that of managers of election campaigns. Both arrange a pre-planned one-off meeting with the audience, a meeting that is designed to make an impression, influence the audience and move them, all within a short time.[6] To create this kind of effect profound psychological wisdom is required. As described with regard to the great rhetorical scenes like those of Martin Luther King and Jesse Jackson (see Chapter 4), it is not just a question of understanding the themes and the symbols that can get through to a certain audience; it concerns the entire audiovisual presentation, from the scenery (e.g., the Berlin Wall that provided the background for Kennedy's famous speech or the auditorium on Mount Scopus overlooking the Judean Desert that served as the background for Yitzhak Rabin's most famous speech after the Six Day War) to the body language, gestures and emphases. The director thinks of all the relevant aspects that might influence the audience, but we should not assume that it is simply a matter of randomly putting together a set of components that all carry equal weight. At the end of the day, say some eminent directors, successful direction can bring out the best in the actors, scenery can create impressive effects, but none of these can save a story that does not appeal to the audience. Hence the choice of a story is the most important decision that the director has to make. As we saw in the case of Mahatma Gandhi, in the end the message, the narrative, the story that the leader presents, these are the basis of the 'show'. To understand this we can take the analogy of canonization of literary works. Just as the story chosen reflects the culture and the local historical and sociological context, so do the messages of leaders and their narrative.

This form of analysis was exemplified in Chapters 3 and 4 in the examina-tion of two aspects: (1) concepts suited to the period, and (2) social contagion (as demonstrated in relation to the case of Lincoln). The cases that were analysed clarify another point that is worth mentioning.

The criteria of the leader's exact reflection in the followers' eyes are not derived only from pragmatic evaluations (e.g., efficiency in budget management or treatment of problems of poverty and social gaps), as many believe, but also from deeper spheres that are expressive and symbolic, some of them perhaps rooted in the generational and intergenerational memory of the collective (as discussed in Chapters 3 and 4). True, such aspects are more visible in the case of political leadership, when judgments and inferences regarding leaders are clearly and unequivocally manifested in the act of election. However, they do also exist in other forms of leadership that are not necessarily political. In such cases they are simply less visible at first sight and cannot be inferred from a single act of the followers.

A FEW REMARKS ABOUT LEADERSHIP IN ORGANIZATIONS

Management and Leadership

The abundant literature on organizations contains a large measure of ambiguity with regard to the difference between *management* and *leadership*. Many people use these terms interchangeably in the belief that good managers are good leaders and vice versa. This confusion is evident not only in the literature but also in training programmes offered by various institutes such as schools of business management, which provide training in subjects like marketing, budgeting, operations management and planning.

The distinction between management and leadership is important, and a significant contribution to the clarification of this distinction was made by the Canadian scholar Henry Mintzberg.[7] Departing from the conventional research approaches of the 1970s, Mintzberg adopted the approach that one can learn about the work of the manager from observation of his or her work. Mintzberg, and other scholars following him, began to examine basic questions concerning the work of managers, such as what actions they perform, which actions are repeated methodically, how much time they devote to various activities, why there are differences in managers' investment of time and effort, and what distinguishes between successful managers and those who are less successful.

The methodology of these studies was anthropological in essence, consisting of observation of managers in their daily work, participation in discussions, documentation, examining business diaries and so forth. These studies rebutted many myths that existed in management literature, such as the myth that the manager's work is always preceded by methodical planning, that the manager relies completely on data and facts. They also exposed many activities of the manager that were not mentioned in the literature, such as the managers' wasting a lot of time on activities such as retirement parties, funerals, weddings and receptions. They constructed a *descriptive empirical model* of the manager's work in which every manager has ten roles organized in three clusters: (1) decisional, which includes the following four roles: handling disturbances, allocating resources, conducting negotiations and initiating new projects; (2) informational, including three roles: disseminating information, monitoring information and spokesmanship, and (3) interpersonal, including: representation (mainly towards the outside), liaison and *leadership*.

Thus, a manager does many things, most of them of a technical-organizational nature. He or she engages in allocating resources, distributing tasks, solving organizational problems, holding progress report meetings, spokesmanship and PR work. Briefly, he or she is overloaded (according to all the managers' reports) and yet has to deal with many unexpected matters that crop up in his or her busy schedule. Leadership, according to these studies, is just one of the manager's roles and it concerns influencing people (i.e., what was described as 'touching people's hearts and minds'). Thus, an individual may excel in all the roles of the manager except for the leadership role, just as someone else may excel in the ability to influence people and yet be weak in the other roles of the manager. John Kotter[8] showed the difference between leadership and management in distinguishing between routine conditions and situations of change. He argued that routine requires management while change requires a great deal of leadership: choosing a direction and harnessing people to it.

This basic distinction has significance that is not sufficiently discussed, namely that the inherent need for leadership differs according to the objectives of the organization, its culture and its nature. In some organizations a considerable amount of leadership is required, whereas in others optimal management of routine is the main thing. It may be said (contrary to common belief) that 'too much leadership' can even harm the functioning of such organizations.

How can we evaluate the potential importance that should be attributed to leadership in a given organization? Mintzberg's work supplies a highly efficient conceptual frame that can serve as a scale for measuring the basic dynamics relevant to such an analysis. According to Mintzberg, organizations are simply *work coordination mechanisms*. Examination of the manner of functioning of organizations reveals five such mechanisms, as follows:

Mutual adjustment – a simple mechanism that coordinates what is done during the work, such as may be found in a small local grocery where the staff can perform all the tasks. By nature this kind of mechanism is relevant to a small organization in which the people are all in contact with each other, but when the organization grows and the small grocery becomes a large supermarket with dozens of employees, the mutual adjustment mechanism is not suitable. To achieve coordination in this case a manager is appointed, whose major role is to coordinate the work and supervise its execution. This is *direct supervision*.

However in the case of large organizations with thousands of employees, such as automobile manufacturers, the two coordination mechanisms of mutual adjustment and direct supervision are clearly insufficient. In order to arrive at coordination among thousands of people and their actions, a process is initiated to structure their activities; this is *standardization of the process*. The manufacture of the vehicle is divided into thousands of simple work units. As we saw in Charlie Chaplin's famous film *Modern Times*, every worker performs a few simple actions (e.g., tightening a number of screws) and thus the vehicle is the sum of all the standard actions of thousands of people working at different stations. A large part of the industry functioned in this manner until the introduction of robotics, which was especially relevant to organizations characterized by standardization of processes.

Still, there are organizations such as universities, research institutes and hi-tech industries in which the work cannot be standardized because the process is complex and requires extensive knowledge. In these organizations the coordination mechanism is *standardization of skills*. For example, in open-heart surgery, an extremely complex procedure, the work is coordinated through the specialization of all the participants. One anaesthetizes the patient, another connects the heart-lung machine, another sutures the bypasses and so forth. The orchestration of the entire complex procedure is based on the skills and training of the individuals as experts, and on the team working in harmony.

Finally, there are organizations that are not responsible for all the parts of the procedure but only for the ultimate output. An example of this is the functioning of a building contractor or construction company. In many cases they hire ad hoc subcontractors who provide parts of the product. Thus, the skeleton is constructed by one group, the electricity installed by another, the roof is built by a third and so on. The sum total of all these components is the building or the apartment to be handed over to its purchaser. The coordination mechanism is one of *work outputs*. Unlike the other mechanisms described, the contractor is not involved in the specific processes of producing each component. They establish a framework, mainly of costs and time, and inspect the end result (the finished skeleton, the electricity installed, etc.).

In structural terms, we can liken an organization to a configuration constructed of five Lego blocks, when the importance and centrality of each one is determined by the coordination mechanism needed for performing the tasks of the organization. The Lego blocks are the management, which is responsible for the strategy; the mid-level management (production managers, marketing managers, head of finance department, etc.) is responsible for the performance of ongoing tasks; the operational core is responsible for performing the core tasks of the organization (e.g., production workers in industry, researchers in universities or medical staff in hospitals). Finally, there are two more Lego blocks that are not in the 'mainstream' (in terms of the organization's structural design) of the managerial operational axis. One of these, termed by Mintzberg *technostructure*, is a body of experts (e.g., engineers in the case of hi-tech or mechanical industries) that provides professional services relevant to the core projects of the organization. The other one is the support staff, which provide general services that are not necessarily related to the core projects, for example legal counselling.

A look at the meaning of these concepts may help to explain the logic of the functioning of organizational systems and may also clarify issues of leadership in organizations in the context discussed in this book. In an organization characterized by standardization of work processes, the senior management and mid-level management are the more significant Lego blocks. The employees who perform standard tasks that require relatively cheap and simple training can be easily and quickly replaced, while in sophisticated systems that require a high level of expertise, the doctors in hospitals, researchers in universities and so forth who comprise the operational core possess knowledge and skills acquired in prolonged and expensive training. In such organizations the mid-level management and staff units are small in number and less significant. In fact these organizations are based on the operational core and the strategic management level.

Thus, organizations based on standardization of output can maintain secondary organizations that operate on the basis of outsourcing – a practice that has been growing in recent years. However, we cannot understand the manners of organizational functioning if our analyses rely merely on efficiency-oriented considerations. In order to understand how and why organizations operate in certain ways, we also have to take into account cultural aspects and, as discussed throughout this book, leadership is an intrinsic part of this view.

This approach links together various levels of analysis that appear in the book: from the level of national culture, through the organizational level, to the subject of leadership as it emerges from the analysis at the other levels. For example, Japan, Germany, Korea and China all have huge manufacturing industries. Given that this is not based solely on the existence of cheap labour (apart from China, the other examples are not based on cheap labour), we may assume that the national culture plays some part in this result. Strict obedience, work by the book, following instructions to the letter, showing respect to the manager and suchlike behaviours create a convenient cultural basis for industries of the kind that Mintzberg calls machine bureaucracy – organizational structures based on standardization of processes in which the mid-level management and the technostructure are mainly occupied with the ongoing management of standard processes. In such organizations it is only the senior management that deals with such matters as setting directions and forming visions. Therefore, it may be said with some degree of generalization that in the industries that represent most totally the machine bureaucracy model most of the managers deal more with administration and less with leadership in its classic senses. Furthermore, we may say that the managers' main influence in these organizations stems from their professionalism in technical matters and their understanding of the organization's procedures.

On the other hand, in countries typified by cultural characteristics such as a small extent of power distance (in Hofstede's terms), less obedience to authority, more intimacy and familial behaviour, along with individualism and achievement orientation, there is more likelihood of maintaining organizations that are based on standardization of skills, namely more R&D organizations and less organizations of a machine bureaucracy nature.[9] As stated, organizations of this kind are characterized by the presence of an operational core (e.g., researchers, technology developers) based on forms of work that are the reverse of standardization of processes. In such organizations initiative, creativity and collaboration in teamwork are the most important things. Therefore, as Kotter[10] remarked, these organizations are focused less on the daily routines and more on creating and dealing with change – the essence of the work of leaders. Furthermore, organizations of this kind require a special kind of leadership that emphasizes *individualized consideration* and *intellectual stimulation*.[11]

Thus, the centrality of the leadership function in general and of leadership styles in particular is not detached from the organizational context (in the sense of the configurations presented by Mintzberg) and the organizational context cannot be viewed as unrelated to the context of the national culture.

This analysis is congruent with some classical psychological distinctions that are discussed in the book, the simplest and most comprehensive of which is the one propounded by Mischel,[12] who distinguishes between strong psychological situations, characterized by a sense of organization, order and certainty, and weak psychological situations, characterized by a low sense of certainty and order. Clearly, cultures characterized by low tolerance of uncertainty (in Hofstede's terms, a great need for order and organization) will have a tendency for forms of organization that express this inclination. In Mischel's terms they will be less inclined to adopt manners of work and types of industries that are prone to weak psychological situations.

It seems therefore that a contextual perspective, from the level of the dominant characteristics of a collective (e.g., national) culture to its reflections at the organizational level, can illustrate more clearly the difference between leadership and management, and also reveal the leadership prototypes that are more attractive or are likely to be more influential.

DEVELOPMENT OF LEADERSHIP IN ORGANIZATIONS

As described in Chapter 3, during the 1980s there was a huge movement of enhancement of the leadership function in organizations. The dominant manifestation of this was the growing number of books on leadership in organizations, along with the increased occupation with leadership development.[13] Universities changed the titles of management programmes to leadership programmes and many bodies bearing the name 'leadership development' were established. Since organizations, and notably American organizations, invest huge sums in the development of managers and leaders[14] one may well wonder whether 'leadership development' is just another expression of cultural bias or simply a passing fashion. In other words the question is this: what in the leadership development process is generic, crossing borders, cultures and contexts, and what is local and perhaps dependent on time and cultural fashion? The following anecdote from the field of medicine demonstrates a generic aspect of professional development. Two doctors, one older and more experienced, and the other a young man who had graduated with honours, examined (in my presence) a computerized graph seeking to reach a conclusion regarding a patient's condition. After they had studied the graph for a while, it turned out that the older doctor saw many more aspects and complexities than the young one, whom I had regarded as possessing more updated and technological knowledge. My question as to how that came about resulted in some interesting phenomena. First, the older doctor was surprised by the actual question, and it took him some time to find an answer to the question, which he said he had never considered. Second, in reconstructing the process and attempting to explain it, he had difficulty formulating a theoretical principle. His explanation was based on examples and illustrations. Third, when we all finally managed to formulate a few principles it appeared that the experienced doctor thought differently than the young doctor. He visualized rapidly (without being aware of the speed) many graphs that he had seen, while the young doctor examined symptoms according to the formal rules that he had learned at medical school. In other words the older doctor, learning from experience, had accumulated *tacit knowledge*, meaning knowledge that is not acquired in a classroom but over years of experience. As remarked by Polanyi, a pioneer of research on tacit knowledge, 'We (the experienced) know more than we can describe.'[15]

The leader's work involves a large measure of tacit knowledge. That is to say, a considerable part of the knowledge included in leaders' processes and means of influence is tacit knowledge acquired from experiences that began in their early childhood, within the family and with friends, in sports teams, summer camps, class committees or student councils. Thus, the universal component in leadership development is development of the ability to explore and identify this tacit knowledge. This is defined by some scholars as reflectivity or introspection.[16] Whatever the name, it refers to a process of self-learning based on experience in a certain area, a quality that transcends cultural and contextual boundaries.

The obvious meaning of this perception is that the platform for leadership development is much broader than direct dealing with the leader's work in his or her formal role as a manager or commander – a bias that is reflected in most leadership development programmes. A survey of the contents of these programmes, and also some evaluation studies,[17] reveal that most of the endeavour to develop leaders in organizations is done through *feedback methodologies*.

Feedback on aspects that are considered characteristic of leaders, such as motivating people, is provided by a variety of sources on diverse platforms. It may be given by followers, colleagues and higher ranks during performance of the role. Mentors from the organization or people from the outside, such as consultants, may provide feedback. It can also be given in simulation programmes constructed specifically for leadership development and in conditions similar to those of the organization (like the business games conducted in some schools of management, or war games in military academies) or in difficult field conditions (e.g., outdoor training programmes) where the participants are supposed to manifest their leadership skills by surmounting difficulties set before them. There are also programmes focusing on specifically psychological aspects of the leader's work, such as 'sensitivity training', based on the assumption that leadership means dealing with people, so leadership training is simply sensitivity training for interpersonal processes. The assumption is that the leader is a person with self-awareness who understands the people around him or her, and this awareness is the basis for his or her ability to motivate people. In all these programmes the focus is on developing leadership in the present, understanding the leader's actions in *real time*, whether in actuality or in simulation.

The argument presented here is different, and the gist of it (on which I expanded in Chapter 3) is that looking at leadership development in terms of the here and now, or of feedback focused on action or behaviour according to a normative leadership model, is reductive. Leadership develops in broad contexts that do not appear under the title 'leadership'. Its development begins in the early stages of life. Let us return for a moment to the study cited in Chapter 3, comparing army officers who were parents with others who were not. It was found that those with longer experience of parenting revealed more highly developed components of transformational leadership. True, not every parent wants to be, or technically or psychologically can be, a leader in an organization, but leaders in organizations often report that past experiences such as parenting helped them a great deal in developing their leadership.

The leadership scholar Warren Bennis, in a well-known book that examines the development of leaders in different spheres in organizations,[18] comments on the abundance of courses and incentives for leaders' development. The evidence describing leaders' development reveals processes, observations and insights acquired from outside the organizational world, beginning with the family setting, via travels in the world, to encounters that seemingly have no connection with the actual work although deeper analysis reveals the existence of some governing order behind this.[19]

The claim, then, in the context of leadership development is that the essence of learning on leadership is related to the generic ability to extract knowledge for action from the variegated experiences that the learner associates with his or her leadership. Most of these experiences do not occur in the actual time and place of the individual's functioning in the role or the simulation. In this perspective, leadership development, especially in organizations, is simply the development of exploratory abilities of this kind.

Another point worth emphasizing is that in addition to experience and introspection (which is undoubtedly an important way of learning about leadership), there is another learning process that is important for leaders (of which we saw some examples in Chapters 2 and 3), namely *learning by imitation* (termed in the literature as 'vicarious learning'), meaning observation and internalization of the behaviours of figures who are reported by leaders to be admired. Contrary to conventional belief, the learner in this case is not always aware of the process while it is happening, and the knowledge is often 'extricated' afterwards in various investigatory processes.[20] This learning is based on the principle defined by the American psychologist Bandura as *social learning*.[21] Studies conducted on the development of leaders in organizations have shown that leaders' reflection on their development yielded insights regarding their social learning from figures whom they had met in the past. Kotter, for example, describes managers' reports testifying that their leadership was influenced in particular by authority figures whom they had met in their first assignments at the beginning of their careers.[22] Senior officers in the Israel Defense Forces stated in retrospect that their commanders at the beginning of their military service had considerable influence on their perception of their leadership.[23] Similar findings have been reported by researchers from diverse countries.[24] The conclusion is clear. The development of leaders at all levels and in all spheres, from philosophical outlooks, approaches in principle, to specific behaviours, begins in the early stages and occurs through various channels (which are usually not called leadership development). This brief discussion indicates the important distinction that while the learning and exploration process is generic, the contents of the learning, the people, the processes and the actions chosen as objects for imitation are all context bound.

A FEW REMARKS ON LEADERSHIP RESEARCH

It is a well-known fact that the more limited the research variables, the easier they are to define and measure, and to examine statistically the correlations between them. For example, the correlations between perceptual stimuli of light and the subjects' reaction time to these stimuli can be measured and controlled much more precisely than the development of a transformational leader's world view or the followers' perception of a leader's charisma.

Leadership studies can also be classified according to this general rule: the more specific the variables, the more measurable they are, and the results show generalized findings that are usually not connected with a contextual discussion. For example, there are many studies on correlations between leadership styles as measured by various questionnaires, and dependent variables such as leaders' satisfaction with specific tasks or success in task performance.[25] The broader the variables included in the research, say, for example, in comparative studies of leaders in different countries, the more disputable they are with regard to generalizability.[26] This claim reflects a familiar debate in the social sciences, particularly in psychology.[27]

It is not my intention here to discuss methodological issues in leadership research, which are complex in the nature of things, but rather to present briefly some aspects concerning fundamental approaches to a research strategy for investigating the leadership phenomenon that may help to create knowledge for action.

First, as I mentioned in the Introduction, the gestalt principle (the whole is greater than the sum of the parts) is crucial for understanding the nature of leadership. For this reason the attempts made in psychological research literature to divide the leadership phenomenon into specific variables with optimal measurability not only failed to expand the understanding of its psychological essence but rather, I argue, decreased this potential understanding and in fact formulated leadership as a phenomenon that is essentially behavioural. For instance the major instrument for measuring transformational leadership, the Multifactor Leadership Questionnaire (MLQ), displays a set of behaviours that are supposed to reflect the phenomenon. This is analogous to the claim that personality is what personality tests measure. Everyone knows that personality is a quality much more complex than a personality test, however statistically valid. Nevertheless personality tests can be a useful tool for selection to specific roles in organizations. Thus, the prevalent research deals with certain parts of leadership; for example, studies on the effectiveness of various leadership styles on task performance usually appear under the general heading 'leadership'. This manner of presentation helps to blur the phenomenon rather than clarify it. To rectify this the researcher should indicate clearly the parts to be investigated within the whole when choosing the title of the study. As I have shown in the book, some of the biases concerning leadership stem from the absence of a multidisciplinary view in leadership research. There is a theoretical and empirical failure in this area, manifested in the absence of adequate distinctions between political leaders, leaders in organizations, close leaders, distant leaders and other categories.

One of the more obvious inferences to be drawn from the discussion in this book is the need to examine the followers because they are the cornerstones in the structure of the leadership phenomenon. To recall James Meindl's words on leadership, 'Followers, not the leader and not researchers, define it.'[28] There has been growing awareness of this,[29] but the awareness is not focused clearly enough for empirical research.

The book accentuates the need to study the followers more deeply in two respects: examination of social contagion processes and comparative research on followers. Deeper understanding of social contagion processes may help to explain more clearly than before the secret of followers' attraction to a leader, and also clarify the role of interpersonal, group and intergroup processes in this means of influence. As mentioned, there has been some research in these directions, but that is just the beginning. Precisely in this space new knowledge has been created rapidly, knowledge that is relevant to leadership and also strengthens the multidisciplinary perspective. For example, social networks, which develop and change, among other things due to technological development, can contribute enormously to the understanding of social contagion processes. These processes were previously perceived as more relevant to leadership in everyday life, but they are now also relevant to political leadership. The example of Barack Obama's election campaign and his deportment at 'town meetings' on the Web illustrates the potential contained in social contagion processes in a manner hitherto unknown.

The points elucidated in the book regarding the significance of identities, collective memories and other symbolic variables clarify that comparative research has special value. In fact it is a critical research strategy. Symbolization processes are important for the construction of leadership images; therefore, understanding the sources of the symbols beyond the specific personality of the leader is highly important with regard to distant leaders, and especially political leaders.

The importance of theoretical frames of reference such as *community of memory*, short-term and long-term *collective memories* for understanding the growth and influence of leaders is demonstrated in the book to a lesser extent. These research fields need to be expanded. Moreover, since part of the discussion and research on leadership is based on psychosociological models, which dedicate considerable space to concepts such as schemas, prototypes, norms and values, comparative research is a way to test the generalizability of the various models. This concerns both the empirical and the theoretical aspects of the discussion on leadership. Comparative studies on followers can focus a discussion on the contextual meaning of leadership much more precisely than the comparative studies that focused in the past on leaders.

In this context I wish to draw attention to the following methodological issue. Most empirical research deals with the *testing of theories*, testing specific hypotheses derived from familiar theories. A much smaller part of the research work on leadership is devoted to *constructing theories*, namely, examining a phenomenon without hypothesizing its functioning and the rule governing it, a manner of observation that may be likened to the work of zoologists, who observe the lives of animals, try to characterize their lives by meticulous documentation and only afterwards attempt to formulate models. This manner of observation does not direct the view to specific variables. Analogous to photography, it attempts to broaden the lens as far as possible. Decisions concerning narrowing and focusing are made later, on the editor's table. This distinction is very important in leadership research, particularly in comparative studies. In this area there is obviously room and need for expansion of the attempts to construct theories in a more gestalt-like manner than we see in most of the literature.

Finally, with regard to research on leaders themselves, I wish to raise a point that has a broader psychological base if we relate also to the psychology of the followers. As stated earlier, most of the leadership research deals with the leader's influence over his or her people and includes aspects such as leadership styles, the leader's psychological skills and analysis of leader–follower interactions.[30] One of the least discussed questions at the level of research is: what are the sources of motivation to lead? Objectively, being a leader entails overload at every level of leadership. Company commanders have to get up before their soldiers and go to bed after the last of them. Most managers do not finish their day's work when they leave the office; their work stays in their minds not just for many hours a day but sometimes at weekends and on holidays. Contrary to what many people think, political leaders do not always enjoy the 'pleasures of government'. Many leaders gave up part of their income in order to reach the leadership position. Moreover, not only do they work hard but they are also vulnerable to cruel exposure of their private lives. Some are actually exposed to harassment and limitations that are not found in most occupations. And yet there are people who want this status, who struggle determinedly for it.

Thus, the sources of motivation to lead are complex, sometimes hidden, and also diverse. It is important to understand them for research purposes because these sources, it appears, are not only part of the family dynamic – an aspect to which the literature has ascribed almost exclusive weight,[31] but they also originate in social contexts. Research in this field may generate knowledge that will contribute to the understanding of motivation to lead and also of the link between the social context and this motivation.

The assumption underlying the suggested research approaches is that leadership is not a phenomenon whose nature comes to light with a sudden discovery à la Eureka. It requires a consistent ongoing process in which systematic comparison of the numerous theories constructed yields an overall picture from which it is possible to formulate a law explaining the similarities and differences in the leadership phenomenon, with followership as the foundation stone of this analysis.

One last remark concerning a point that was mentioned in Chapters 2, 3 and 4, but needs to be emphasized again here at the end of the book, after all the propositions, examples and explanations. As we now know, there are many people who deal with development of leaders, but the reviews and analyses presented in this book may perhaps suggest that there is room to think of *follower development.* Since the followers both elect the political leaders and comply with them in all the organizational and social systems, it is within their (the followers') power to improve the quality of the leaders both in choosing them and in determining the limits of compliance with them. From this point of view, the claim that a leader is 'a person who has followers' is not purely technical. The more we learn about followership, and the more the followers understand the sources and principles governing their relations with leaders, the more their choices of and response to leaders will be based on knowledge and understanding. The tendency to see leaders as larger than life will decrease, as will the tendency to ascribe to leaders the full responsibility for every stupid or wicked act. And concomitantly the followers' sense of responsibility for creating their leadership – determining its subjects, boundaries and directions – will increase.

NOTES

1. Argyris, Chris (1993), *Knowledge for Action*, San Francisco: Jossey-Bass.
2. Discussions on the nature of knowledge for action and ways of creating it appear in the works of the following scholars: Argyris, Chris (1980), *Inner Contradictions of Rigorous Research*, New York: Academic Press; Argyris, Chris, Robert Putnam and Diana McLain Smith (1985), *Action Science*, San Francisco, CA: Jossey-Bass; Schon, Donald (2000), *Reflective Practitioner: How Professionals Think in Action*, New York: Basic Books.
3. Karl Weick distinguishes between organization and organizing. While the former has a static connotation the latter implies activity. The term organizing is not related to any particular

organizational structure but is relevant at every level and in every context; see Weick, Karl E. (1969), *The Social Psychology of Organizing*, New York: McGraw-Hill.

4. For a discussion (and illustrative research) on the prestige of occupations as reflecting the importance of certain values in a society, see the doctoral dissertation of Moshe Lissak: Lissak, Moshe (1961), 'Magamot Bivkhirat Miktzoa Bikerev Noar Ironi Biyisrael', ['Trends in choice of occupations among urban youth in Israel'], doctoral dissertation, Hebrew University, Jerusalem. See also Hall, John and Caradog Jones (1950), 'Social grading of occupations', *British Journal of Sociology*, **1** (1), 31–55.

5. Hollander, Edwin P. (1993), 'Legitimacy, power and influence: A perspective on relational features of leadership', in M.M. Chemers and R. Aymon (eds), *Leadership Theory and Research: Perspectives and Directions*, San Diego, CA: Academic Press; Hollander, Edwin P. (1978), *Leadership Dynamics*, New York: Free Press.

6. Gardner, William and Bruce Avolio (1998), 'The charismatic relationship: A dramaturgical perspective', *Academy of Management Review*, **23** (1), 32–58.

7. Mintzberg, Henry (1973), *The Nature of Managerial Work*, New York: Harper & Row; Mintzberg, Henry (1975), 'The manager's job: Folklore and facts', *Harvard Business Review*, **53** (4), 53–65; Mintzberg, Henry (1979), *The Structuring of Organizations: A Synthesis of the Research*, Englewood Cliffs, NJ: Prentice-Hall.

8. Kotter, John P. (1988), *The Leadership Factor*, New York: The Free Press; Kotter, John P. (1990), 'What leaders really do', *Harvard Business Review*, **68** (3), 103–11.

9. Israel is an example of a country in which (according to Hofstede's criteria) there is relatively high tolerance of lack of clarity, less power distance and a large measure of individuality existing in a small family-like society. Hence it is rich in inventive industries but less successful in service industries and manufacturing industries based on standardization of processes. For examples and data supporting this argument, see Senor and Singer's book: Senor, Dan and Saul Singer (2009), *Start-Up Nation: The Story of Israel's Economic Miracle*, New York: Hachette Book Group.

10. Kotter (1988).

11. Bass, Bernard M. (1985), *Leadership and Performance beyond Expectations*, New York: Free Press.

12. Mischel, Walter (1973), 'Toward a cognitive social learning conceptualization of personality', *Psychological Review*, **80** (4), 252–83.

13. Bennis, Warren and Burt Nanus (1985), *Leaders: The Strategies for Taking Charge*, New York: HarperCollins.

14. McCall, Morgan W., Jr., Michael M. Lombardo and Ann Morrison (1988), *The Lessons of Experience*, Lexington, MA: Lexington Books.

15. Polanyi, Michael (1966), *The Tacit Dimension*, London: Routledge & Kegan Paul.

16. Schon (2000).

17. In a survey of the research literature on leadership, Bernard Bass also surveyed evaluation studies of leadership development programmes. This survey is presented on pages 1051–112 of his book: Bass, Bernard M. (2008), *The Bass Handbook of Leadership*, 4th edition, New York: Free Press.

18. Bennis, Warren (2003), *On Becoming a Leader*, New York: Basic Books.

19. Gibbons, Tracy C. (1986), 'Revisiting the question of born vs. made: Toward a theory of development of transformational leaders', unpublished doctoral dissertation, Santa Barbara, CA: Fielding Institute.

20. Amit, Karin, M. Popper, R. Gal, T. Mamane-Levy and A. Lisak (2009a), 'Leadership shaping experiences: A comparative study of leaders and non-leaders', *Leadership and Organizational Development Journal*, **30** (4), 302–18.

21. Bandura, Albert (1982), 'Human agency in social cognitive theory', *American Psychologist*, **44** (9), 1175–84.

22. Kotter (1988).

23. Popper, Micha (1994), *Al Manahelim Kemanhigim* [*On Managers as Leaders*], Tel Aviv: Ramot Publishing House, Tel Aviv University [Hebrew].

24. Avolio, Bruce (2005), *Leadership Development in Balance: Made/Born*, Mahwah, NJ: Lawrence Erlbaum.

25. Bass (2008).
26. Den Hartog, Deanne N., R.J. House, P.J. Hanges, S.A. Ruiz-Quintanilla and P.W. Dorfman (1999), 'Culture specific and cross-culturally generalizable implicit leadership theories: Are alternatives of charismatic/transformational leadership universally endorsed?', *Leadership Quarterly*, **10** (2), 219–57.
27. Bruner, Jerome (1986), *Actual Minds, Possible Worlds*, Cambridge, MA: Harvard University Press.
28. Meindl, James R. (1995), 'The romance of leadership as follower-centric theory: A social constructionist approach', *Leadership Quarterly*, **6** (3), 329–41.
29. Shamir, Boas, Rajnandini Pillai, Michelle C. Bligh and Mary Uhl-Bien (2007), *Follower-Centered Perspectives on Leadership*, Greenwich, CT: Information Publishing.
30. Bass (2008).
31. Kets de Vries, Manfred (1988), 'Prisoners of leadership', *Human Relations*, **41** (31), 261–80.

References

Aberbach, David (1995), 'Charisma and attachment theory: A crossdisciplinary interpretation', *International Journal of Psychoanalysis*, **76** (4), 845–55.

Adams, John Stacey (1965), 'Inequity in social exchange', in L. Berkowitz (ed.), *Advances in Experimental Social Psychology*, vol. 2, pp. 267–99.

Ainsworth, Mary D., M.C. Blehar, E. Waters and S. Wall (1978), *Patterns of Attachment: A Psychological Study of the Strange Situation*, Hillsdale, NJ: Earlbaum.

Amit, Karin, A. Lisak, M. Popper and R. Gal (2007), 'Motivation to lead – research on the motives for undertaking leadership roles', *Military Psychology*, **19** (3), 137–60.

Amit, Karin, M. Popper, R. Gal, T. Mamane-Levy and A. Lisak (2009a), 'Leadership shaping experiences: A comparative study of leaders and non-leaders', *Leadership and Organizational Development Journal*, **30** (4), 302–18.

Amit, Karin, M. Popper, R. Gal, T. Mamane-Levy and A. Lisak (2009b), 'Leaders and non-leaders: A comparative study of some major developmental aspects', *Journal of the North American Management Society*, **4** (2), 2–19.

Arendt, Hannah (1963), *Eichmann in Jerusalem: A Report on the Banality of Evil*, New York: Viking Press.

Argyris, Chris (1980), *Inner Contradictions of Rigorous Research*, New York: Academic Press.

Argyris, Chris (1993), *Knowledge for Action*, San Francisco: Jossey-Bass.

Argyris, Chris, Robert Putnam and Diana McLain Smith (1985), *Action Science*, San Francisco, CA: Jossey-Bass.

Asch, Solomon E. (1953), *Social Psychology*, Englewood Cliffs, NJ: Prentice Hall.

Avolio, Bruce J. (2005), *Leadership Development in Balance: Made/Born*, Mahwah, NJ: Lawrence Erlbaum.

Avolio, Bruce J., Bernard M. Bass and Dong I. Jung (1996), 'Construct validation of the Multifactor Leadership Questionnaire, MLQ-Form 5X', CLS Report 96-1, Center for Leadership Studies, Binghamton University, State University of New York.

Bandura, Albert (1977), 'Self-efficacy: Toward a unifying theory of behavioral change', *Psychological Review*, **84**, 191–215.

Bandura, Albert (1982), 'Human agency in social cognitive theory', *American Psychologist*, **44** (9), 1175–84.

Bandura, Albert (ed.) (1995), *Self-efficacy in Changing Societies*, New York: Cambridge University Press.

Basler, Ray (ed.) (1953–55), *The Collected Works of Abraham Lincoln*, 9 vols, New Brunswick: Rutgers University Press, pp. 145–6.

Bass, Bernard M. (1985), *Leadership and Performance Beyond Expectations*, New York: Free Press.

Bass, Bernard M. (2008), *The Bass Handbook of Leadership*, 4th edition, New York: Free Press.

Bass, Bernard M. and Bruce J. Avolio (1990), 'The implications of transactional and transformational leadership for individual, team, and organizational development', in R.W. Woodman and W.A. Passmore (eds), *Research in Organizational Change and Development*, Greenwich, CT: JAI Press.

Beauregard, Keith and David Dunning (1998), 'Turning up the contrast: Self-enhancement motives prompt egocentric contrast effects in social judgments', *Journal of Personality and Social Psychology*, **74** (3), 606–21.

Benedict, Ruth (1934), *Patterns of Culture*, Boston: Houghton Mifflin.

Bennis, Warren (1997), *Managing People is like Herding Cats*, Provo, UT: Executive Excellent Publishing, p. 22.

Bennis, Warren (2003), *On Becoming a Leader*, New York: Basic Books.

Bennis, Warren and Burt Nanus (1985), *Leaders: The Strategies for Taking Charge*, New York: HarperCollins.

Best, Geoffrey (2001), *Churchill: A Study in Greatness*, London and New York: Hambledon & London.

Blumer, Herbert (1986), *Symbolic Interactionism*, Berkeley: University of California Press.

Bowlby, John (1969), *Attachment and Loss: 1, Attachment*, New York: Basic Books.

Bowlby, John (1973), *Attachment and Loss: 2, Separation*, New York: Basic Books.

Bowlby, John (1988), *A Secure Base: Clinical Applications of Attachment Theory*, London: Routledge.

Browning, Christopher (1992), *Ordinary Men: Reserve Police Battalion 101 and the Final Solution in Poland*, New York: HarperCollins.

Bruner, Jerome (1986), *Actual Minds, Possible Worlds*, Cambridge, MA: Harvard University Press.

Bryman, Alan, M. Stephens and C. Campo (1996), 'The importance of context: Qualitative research and the study of leadership', *Leadership Quarterly*, **7** (3), 353–71.

Burns, James MacGregor ([1956] 2002), *Roosevelt: The Lion and the Fox*, New York: Mariner.

Burns, James MacGregor ([1970] 2002), *Roosevelt: Soldier of Freedom 1940–1945*, New York: Harcourt, p. 9.

Burns, James MacGregor (1978), *Leadership*, New York: Harper & Row.

Buss, David M. (1994), *The Evolution of Desire: Strategies of Human Mating*, New York: Basic Books.

Carlyle, Thomas ([1841] 1907), *On Heroes, Hero-Worship and the Heroic in History*, Boston: Houghton Mifflin.

Chadha, Yogesh (1997), *Gandhi: A Life*, New York: John Wiley & Sons.

Charon, Joel M. (1979), *Symbolic Interactionism: An Introduction, an Interpretation, an Integration*, Englewood Cliffs, NJ: Prentice Hall.

Chittenden, Lucius Eugene (1909), *Lincoln and the Sleeping Sentinel: The True Story*, New York: Harper and Brothers.

Collier, Gary, Henry L. Minton and Graham Reynolds (1991), *Currents of Thought in American Social Psychology*, New York, Oxford: Oxford University Press.

Collins, James C. and Jerry I. Porras (1997), *Built To Last*, New York: HarperCollins.

Conger, Jay A. and R.N. Kanungo (1987), 'Toward a behavioral theory of charismatic leadership in organizational settings', *Academy of Management Review*, **12** (4), 637–47.

Cooley, Charles H. (1964), *Human Nature and the Social Order*, New York: Schocken.

Davidovitz, Rivka, M. Mikulincer, P. Shaver, R. Iszak and M. Popper (2007), 'Leaders as attachment figures', *Journal of Personality and Social Psychology*, **93** (4), 632–50.

Day, David V. (2000), 'Leadership development: A review in context', *Leadership Quarterly*, **11** (4), 581–613.

Day, David V., Stephen J. Zaccaro and Stanley M. Halpin (eds) (2004), *Leader Development for Transforming Organizations: Growing Leaders for Tomorrow*, Mahwah, NJ: Erlbaum.

DellaPergola, Shulamit (2002), 'Leadership and fatherhood', MA thesis submitted to University of Haifa, Department of Psychology [Hebrew].

Den Hartog, Deanne N., R.J. House, P.J. Hanges, S.A. Ruiz-Quintanilla and P.W. Dorfman (1999), 'Culture specific and cross-culturally generalizable implicit leadership theories: Are alternatives of charismatic/transformational leadership universally endorsed?', *Leadership Quarterly*, **10** (2), 219–57.

Dorfman, Peter W. (1996), 'International and cross-cultural leadership research', in Betty J. Punnett and O. Shenkar (eds), *Handbook for International Management Research*, Oxford: Blackwell, pp. 267–349.

Durkheim, Emile (1973), 'The dualism of human nature and its social conditions', in Robert N. Bellah (ed.), *Emile Durkheim on Morality and Society*, Chicago: University of Chicago Press.

Ellis, Joseph J. (2004), *His Excellency George Washington*, New York: Random House.

Emmons, Nuel (1988), *Manson in His Own Words*, New York: Grove Press.

Erikson, Eric (1959), *Identity and the Life Cycle*, Bloomington, IN: Indiana University Press.

Etzioni, Amitai (1975), *A Comparative Analysis of Complex Organizations*, New York: Free Press.

Evans, R. (interviewer) (1980), *The Making of Social Psychology: Discussion with Creative Contributors*, New York: Gardner.

Fest, Joachim (1974), *Hitler*, New York: Harcourt Brace.

Festinger, Leon (1954), 'A theory of social comparison processes', *Human Relations*, **7** (2), 117–40.

Fiedler, Fred E. (1964), 'A contingency model of leadership effectiveness', in L. Berkowitz (ed.), *Advances in Experimental Social Psychology*, New York: Academic Press.

Fiedler, Fred E. (1967), *A Theory of Leadership Effectiveness*, New York: McGraw-Hill.

Fine, Gary A. (2001), *Difficult Reputations: Collective Memories of the Evil, Inept and Controversial*, Chicago: University of Chicago Press.

Frankl, Viktor (1959), *Man's Search for Meaning*, Boston: Beacon Press.

Freud, Sigmund (1920), *A General Introduction to Psychoanalysis*, American edition, New York: Garden City Press, pp. 363–5.

Freud, Sigmund (1939), *Moses and Monotheism*, London: Hogarth Press, standard edition of the *Complete Psychological Works of Sigmund Freud*, vol. XVIII, pp. 109–10.

Freud, Sigmund (1961), *Civilization and its Discontents* [trans. and ed. James Strachey], New York: W.W. Norton.

Gandhi, Mahatma (1957), *An Autobiography: The Story of My Experiments with Truth* [trans. Mahadev H. Desai], Boston, MA: Beacon Press.

Gardner, William and Bruce Avolio (1998), 'The charismatic relationship: A dramaturgical perspective', *Academy of Management Review*, **23** (1), 32–58.

Gelber, Yoav (2008), *Historia, Zikaron Ve ta'amula* [*History, Memory and Propaganda*], Tel Aviv: Am Oved (Ofakim) [Hebrew].

George, Alexander L. and Juliette L. George (1956), *Woodrow Wilson and Colonel House: A Personality Study*, New York: Macmillan.

Gerth, H. and C. Wright Mills (eds) (1946a), *From Max Weber: Essays in Sociology*, New York: Oxford University Press.

Gerth, H. and C. Wright Mills (eds) (1946b), 'The sociology of charismatic authority', in *From Max Weber: Essays in Sociology*, New York: Oxford University Press.

Gibbons, Tracy C. (1986), 'Revisiting the question of born vs. made: Toward a theory of development of transformational leaders', unpublished doctoral dissertation, Santa Barbara, CA: Fielding Institute.

Goffman, Erving (1959), *The Presentation of Self in Everyday Life*, Garden City, New York: Doubleday.

Golan, Avirama (1988), *Al Da'at Atzman* [*Of Their Own Accord*], Tel Aviv: Am Oved (Ofakim) [Hebrew].

Goldstein, Yosef (2007), *Rabin – Biographiya* [*Rabin – A Biography*], Tel Aviv: Schocken Publishing [Hebrew].

Goleman, Daniel J. (1989), 'What is negative about positive illusions? When benefits for the individual harm the collective', *Journal of Social and Clinical Psychology*, **8**, 191.

Goodwin, Doris K. (1995), 'Franklin Roosevelt 1933–1945', in R.A. Wilson (ed.), *Character Above All: Ten Presidents from FDR to George Bush*, New York: Simon & Schuster.

Gullan, Harold I. (2004), *First Fathers: The Men Who Inspired our Presidents*, Hoboken, NJ: John Wiley & Sons.

Halbwachs, Maurice ([1926] 1950), *The Collective Memory* [trans. F.J. and V.Y. Ditter], London: Harper Colophon Books.

Hall, John and Caradog Jones (1950), 'Social grading of occupations', in *British Journal of Sociology*, **1** (1), 31–55.

Halpern, James and Ilsa Halpern (1983), *Projections: Our World of Imaginary Relationships*, New York: Putnam Publications.

Hazan, Cindy and Philip Shaver (1987), 'Romantic love conceptualized as an attachment process', *Journal of Personality and Social Psychology*, **52** (3), 511–24.

Heider, Fritz (1944), 'Social perception and phenomenal causality', *Psychological Review*, **51** (6), 358–74.

Heifetz, Ronald H. (1994), *Leadership Without Easy Answers*, Cambridge, MA: Harvard University.

Hersey, Paul and Kenneth Blanchard (1969), 'Life cycle theory of leadership', *Training and Developmental Journal*, **23** (5), 26–34.

Hertzler, J.O. (1940), 'Crises and dictatorships', *American Sociological Review*, **5** (2), 157–69.

Hill, Melvyn A. (1984), 'The law of the father: Leadership and symbolic authority in psychoanalysis', in B. Kellerman (ed.), *Leadership: Multidisciplinary Perspectives*, Englewood Cliffs, NJ: Prentice Hall.

Hofstede, Geert (2001), *Culture's Consequences: Comparing Values, Behaviors, Institutions, and Organizations Across Nations*, Thousand Oaks, CA: Sage Publications, pp. 388–9.

Hofstede, Geert and Jan Hofstede (2005), *Culture and Organizations: The Software of the Mind*, New York: McGraw-Hill.

Hogg, Michael (2001), 'A social identity theory of leadership', *Personality and Social Psychology Review*, **5** (3), 184–200.

Hollander, Edwin P. (1978), *Leadership Dynamics*, New York: Free Press.

Hollander, Edwin P. (1993), 'Legitimacy, power and influence: A perspective on relational features of leadership', in M.M. Chemers and R. Aymon (eds), *Leadership Theory and Research: Perspectives and Directions*, San Diego, CA: Academic Press.

Houghton, David P. (2009), *Political Psychology*, New York: Routledge, p. 163.

House, Robert J. and Jane M. Howell (1992), 'Personality and charismatic leadership', *Leadership Quarterly*, **3** (2), 81–108.

Huntington, Samuel P. (1998), *The Clash of Civilizations and the Remaking of the World*, New York: Simon & Schuster.

Huntington, Samuel P. (2004), *Who Are We? The Challenges to America's National Identity*, New York: Simon & Schuster.

Illouz, Eva (2007), *Cold Intimacies: The Making of Emotional Capitalism*, Cambridge, UK: Polity Press.

Jones, Edward E. and Victor A. Harris (1967), 'The attribution of attitudes', *Journal of Experimental Social Psychology*, **3** (1), 1–24.

Jones, Stephen C. (1973), 'Self and interpersonal evaluations: Esteem theories versus consistency theories', *Psychological Bulletin*, **79** (3), 185–99.

Jung, Carl Gustav (1986), *Analytical Psychology*, London: Routledge.

Keegan, John (1987), *The Mask of Command*, New York: Jonathan Cape Ltd.

Kellerman, Barbara (2004), *Bad Leadership: What it Is, How it Happens, Why it Matters*, Boston: Harvard Business School Press.

Kelley, Robert E. (1992), *The Power of Followership*, New York: Currency/Doubleday.

Kershaw, Ian (1998), *Hitler: 1889–1936 Hubris*, New York: W.W. Norton.

Kershaw, Ian (2001), *Hitler: 1936–1945 Nemesis*, New York: W.W. Norton.

Kershaw, Ian (2008), *Fateful Choices: Ten Decisions That Changed the World*, New York: Penguin Books.

Kets de Vries, Manfred (1988), 'Prisoners of leadership', *Human Relations*, **41** (31), 261–80.

Kets de Vries, Manfred (1995), *Life and Death in the Executive Fast Lane*, San Francisco: Jossey-Bass.

Kets de Vries, Manfred and Elisabet Engellau (2004), *Are Leaders Born or Are They Made? The Case of Alexander the Great*, London: Karnacs.

Kilborne, Benjamin and L.L. Langness (1987), *Culture and Human Nature: Theoretical Papers of Melford E. Spiro*, Chicago: University of Chicago Press.

Klein, Katherine and Robert House (1995), 'On fire: Charismatic leadership and levels of analysis', *Leadership Quarterly*, **6** (2), 183–98.

Kluckhohn, Florence (1950), 'Dominant and substitute profiles of cultural orientations. Their significance for the analysis of social stratification', *Social Forces*, **28** (4), 376–93.

Kohlberg, Lawrence (1971), *From Is to Ought: How to Commit the Naturalistic Fallacy and Get Away With It in the Study of Moral Development*, New York: Academic Press.

Kosinski, Jerzy (1972), *Being There*, New York: Bantam Books.

Kotter, John P. (1988), *The Leadership Factor*, New York: Free Press.

Kotter, John P. (1990), 'What leaders really do', *Harvard Business Review*, **68** (3), 103–11.

Lampert, Ada (1995), '*Evolutzia shel ahava* [*Evolution of Love*], Publication of Open University [Hebrew].

Le Bon, Gustav (1952), *The Crowd: A Study of the Popular Mind*, London: Ernest Benn.

Lewin, Kurt (1947), 'Frontiers in group dynamics: Concept, method, and reality in social science', *Human Relations*, **1** (4), 5–42.

Lewin, Kurt, Ron Lippitt and Ronald White (1938), 'An experimental approach to the study of autocracy and democracy', *Sociometry*, **1**, 292–300.

Liddel-Hart, Basil H. (1991), *Strategy*, 2nd edition, New York: Plume Books.

Lifton, Robert Jay (1986), *Medical Killing and the Psychology of Genocide*, New York: Basic Books Inc.

Lindholm, Charles (1988), 'Lovers and leaders', *Social Science Information*, **16**, 227–46.

Lipman-Blumen, Jean (2007), 'Toxic leaders and the fundamental vulnerability of being alive', in Boas Shamir, R. Pillai, M.C. Bligh and M. Uhl-Bien (eds), *Follower-Centered Perspectives on Leadership*, Greenwich, CT: Information Age Publishing, p. 4.

Lippman, Walter (1913), *A Preface to Politics*, New York: Mitchell Kennerly.

Lipshitz, Raanan (1991), '"Either a medal or a corporal". The effects of successes and failure on the evaluation of the decision making and the decision makers', *Organizational Behavior and Human Decision Processes*, **44** (3), 380–95.

Lipshitz, Raanan, Victor Friedman and Micha Popper (2007), *Demystifying Organizational Learning*, Thousand Oaks, CA: Sage Publications, p. 187.

Lissak, Moshe (1961), 'Magamot Bivkhirat Miktzoa Bikerev Noar Ironi Biyisrael' ['Trends in choice of occupations among urban youth in Israel'], doctoral dissertation, Hebrew University, Jerusalem.

Locke, John ([1690] 1952), *The Second Treatise of Government*, Indianapolis: Bolls-Merril.

Lord, Robert G., R.J. Foti and C.L. Devader (1984), 'A test of leadership cate-gorization theory: Internal structure, information processing, and leader-ship perception', *Organizational Behavior and Human Performance*, **34** (3), 343–78.

Lorenz, Konrad (1977), *Behind the Mirror: A Search for Natural History of Human Knowledge* [trans. Ronald Taylor], London: Methuen.

Maariv, 14 March (1997), 'I am Charles Manson', interview with Manson, weekend supplement [Hebrew].

Machiavelli, Nicolo (1985), *The Prince*, Chicago: University of Chicago Press.

Mannheim, Karl (1952), 'The problem of generations', in *Essays on the Sociology of Knowledge*, New York: Routledge and Kegan Paul, pp. 276–322.

Markus, Hazel and Shinobu Kitayama (1991), 'Culture and self. Implications for cognition, emotion and motivation', *Psychological Review*, **98** (2), 224–53.

Markus, Hazel and Elissa Wurf (1987), 'The dynamic self-concept: A social-psychological perspective', *Annual Review of Psychology*, **38**, 299–337.

Martin, Joanne, M.S. Feldman, M.J. Hatch and S.B. Sitkin (1983), 'The uniqueness paradox in organizational stories', *Administrative Science Quarterly*, **28** (3), 438–53.

Maslow, Abraham (1970), *Motivation and Personality*, New York: Harper & Row.

Mayo, Margarita and Juan Carlos Pastor (2007), 'Leadership embedded in social networks: Looking at inter-follower processes', in Boas Shamir, R. Pillai, M.C. Bligh and M. Uhl-Bien (eds) (2007), *Follower-Centered Perspectives on Leadership*, Greenwich, CT: Information Publishing, pp. 93–114.

Mayseless, Ofra, R. Sharabany and A. Sagi (1997), 'Attachment concerns of others as manifested in parental, spousal and friendship relationships', *Personal Relationships*, **4**, 255–69.

Mazlish, Bruce (1984), 'History, psychology and leadership', in Barbara Kellerman (ed.), *Leadership: Multidisciplinary Perspectives*, Englewood Cliffs, NJ: Prentice Hall.

McCall, Morgan W., Jr., Michael M. Lombardo and Ann Morrison (1988), *The Lessons of Experience*, Lexington, MA: Lexington Books.

McCullough, David (1995), 'Harry Truman 1945–1953', in R.A. Wilson (ed.), *Character Above All: Ten Presidents from FDR to George Bush*, New York: Simon & Schuster, p. 39.

Mead, George H. (1934), *Mind, Self and Society*, Chicago: University of Chicago Press.

Mead, Margaret ([1930] 2009), *Coming of Age in Samoa: A Psychological*

Study of Primitive Youth for Western Civilizations, New York: Harper and Collins.

Meindl, James R. (1990), 'On leadership: An alternative to conventional wisdom', *Research in Organizational Behavior*, **12**, 159–203.

Meindl, James R. (1995), 'The romance of leadership as follower-centric theory: A social constructionist approach', *Leadership Quarterly*, **6** (3), 329–41.

Milgram, Stanley (1974), *Obedience to Authority: An Experimental Approach*, New York: Harper & Row.

Mintzberg, Henry (1973), *The Nature of Managerial Work*, New York: Harper & Row.

Mintzberg, Henry (1975), 'The manager's job: Folklore and facts', *Harvard Business Review*, **53** (4), 53–65.

Mintzberg, Henry (1979), *The Structuring of Organizations: A Synthesis of the Research*, Englewood Cliffs, NJ: Prentice Hall.

Mischel, Walter (1973), 'Toward a cognitive social learning conceptualization of personality', *Psychological Review*, **80** (4), 252–83.

Misztal, Barbara A. (2003), *Theories of Social Remembering*, Philadelphia: Open University Press.

Omer, Haim and Nechi Allon (1997), *Ma'aseh Hasipur Hatipuli* [*The Therapeutic Story*], Tel Aviv: Modan [Hebrew].

Newman, Rachel (2001), 'The day the world changed, I did too', *Newsweek*, 1 October, 9.

Parry, Ken (1998), 'Grounded theory and social process: A new direction for leadership research', *Leadership Quarterly*, **9** (1), 85–105.

Parsons, Talcott (1947), *The Theory of Social and Economic Organizations by Max Weber*, New York: Free Press.

Pastor, Juan-Carlos, James R. Meindl and M.C. Mayo (2002), 'A network effects model of charisma attributions', *Academy of Management Journal*, **45** (2), 410–20.

Peters, Tom and Robert Waterman (1982), *In Search of Excellence: Lessons from America's Best-Run Companies*, New York: Harper Business.

Pillai, Rajnandini (1996), 'Crisis and the emergence of charismatic leadership in groups: An experimental investigation', *Journal of Applied Social Psychology*, **26** (6), 543–62.

Plato (1973), *The Collected Dialogues of Plato*, Princeton, NJ: Princeton University Press.

Polanyi, Michael (1966), *The Tacit Dimension*, London: Routledge & Kegan Paul.

Popkin, Samuel (1993), 'Decision making in presidential primaries', in Shanto Iyengar and William McGuire (eds), *Explorations in Political Psychology*, Durham, NC: Duke University Press.

Popper, Micha (1994), *Al Menahalim Kemanhigim* [*On Managers as Leaders*], Tel Aviv University: Ramot Publishing House [Hebrew].

Popper, Micha (1996), 'Leadership in military combat units and business organizations: A comparative psychological analysis', *Journal of Managerial Psychology*, **11** (1), 15–25.

Popper, Micha (1998), 'The Israeli Defense Forces as a socializing agent', in Daniel Bar-Tal, D. Jacobson and A. Klieman (eds), *Concerned with Security: Learning from the Experience of Israeli Society*, Stamford, CT: JAI Press, pp. 167–80.

Popper, Micha (1999), 'The sources of motivation of personalized and socialized charismatic leaders', *Psychoanalysis and Contemporary Thought*, **22** (2), 231–46.

Popper, Micha (2001), *Hypnotic Leadership: Leaders, Followers and the Loss of Self*, Westport, CT: Praeger.

Popper, Micha (2002), 'Narcissism and attachment patterns of personalized and socialized charismatic leaders', *Journal of Social and Personal Relations*, **19** (6), 796-808.

Popper, Micha (2004), 'Leadership as relationship', *Journal for the Theory of Social Behaviour*, **34** (2), 107–25.

Popper, Micha (2005), *Leaders Who Transform Society: What Drives Them and Why We Are Attracted*, Westport, CT: Praeger.

Popper, Micha and Salman Khatib (2001), 'Intercultural differences and leadership styles of Druze and Jewish school principals', *Journal of Educational Administration*, **39** (3), 221–32.

Popper, Micha and Ofra Mayseless (2003), 'Back to basics: Applying a parenting perspective to transformational leadership', *Leadership Quarterly*, **14** (1), 41–65.

Popper, Micha, Karin Amit, Reuven Gal, Moran Sinai and Alon Lisak (2004), 'The capacity to lead: Major psychological differences between "leaders" and "non leaders"', *Military Psychology*, **16** (4), 245–63.

Ramsden, John (2002), *Man of the Century: Winston Churchill and his Legend Since 1945*, London: HarperCollins.

Reeves, Richard (1995), 'John F. Kennedy', in R.A. Wilson (ed.), *Character Above All: Ten Presidents from FDR to George Bush*, New York: Simon & Schuster.

Reicher, Stephen D. and Nick Hopkins (2003), 'On the science of the art of leadership', in D. Van Knippenberg and M.A. Hogg (eds), *Leadership and Power: Identity Processes in Groups and Organizations*, London: Sage, pp. 65–78.

Remini, Robert V. (1999), *The Battle of New Orleans*, New York: Penguin Books.

Rholes, Steven W. and Jeffrey A. Simpson (eds) (2004), *Adult Attachment: Theory, Research, and Clinical Implications*, New York: Guilford Press.

Riggio, Ronald E., Ira Chaleff and Jean Lipman-Blumen (2008), *The Art of Followership*, San Francisco, CA: Jossey-Bass.

Ronen, Avihu (1992), 'Hamanhig Vihakhevra' (Leader and society), in Micha Popper and Avihu Ronen (eds), *Al Hamanhigut [On Leadership]*, Tel Aviv: Ministry of Defense Publications, p. 38 [Hebrew].

Roosevelt, Theodore (1913), *Lincoln Day Speech*, Progressive Service Documents, New York: Progressive National Committee.

Rosnow, Ralph L. and Gary A. Fine (1976), *Rumor and Gossip: The Social Psychology of Hearsay*, New York: Elsevier.

Ross, Lee D., Teresa M. Amabile and Julia L. Steinmetz (1977), 'Social roles, social controls and biases in social perception processes', *Journal of Personality and Social Psychology*, **35** (7), 485–94.

Rossiter, Clinton (1961), *Introduction to the Federalist Papers*, New York: Mentor, p. xiv.

Rousseau, Jean-Jacques ([1762] 1968), *The Social Contract* [trans. Maurice Cranston], Middlesex, UK: Penguin Classics.

Rycroft, Charles (1995), *A Critical Dictionary of Psychoanalysis*, London: Penguin.

Salo, M., M. Popper and A. Goldberg (2007), 'Pertinent research questions on group leadership', in A.J. Huhtinen and J. Rantapelkonen (eds), *Fundamental Questions of Military Studies*, Finland: Naval Academy.

Schechter, Rivka (1990), *Hashorashim Hateologiim shel Hareich Hashlishi (The Theological Roots of the Third Reich)*, Tel Aviv: Ministry of Defense Publishing House [Hebrew].

Schein, Edgar (1985), *Organizational Culture and Leadership*, San Francisco, CA: Jossey-Bass.

Schlesinger, Arthur Meier, Jr. (1958), *The Coming of the New Deal*, Boston: Houghton Mifflin, pp. 1–2.

Schneider, Benjamin (1987), 'The people make the place', *Personnel Psychology*, **40** (3), 437–53.

Schon, Donald (2000), *Reflective Practitioner: How Professionals Think in Action*, New York: Basic Books.

Schwartz, Barry (1986), *The Battle for Human Nature. Science, Morality and Modern Life*, New York: Norton.

Schwartz, Barry (1987), *George Washington: The Making of an American Symbol*, New York and London: Free Press/Collier Macmillan.

Schwartz, Barry (2000), *Abraham Lincoln and the Forge of National Memory*, Chicago: The University of Chicago Press.

Segal, Robert (2004), *Myth, A Very Short Introduction*, Oxford: Oxford University Press.

Senor, Dan and Saul Singer (2009), *Start-Up Nation: The Story of Israel's Economic Miracle*, New York: Hachette Book Group.

Shamir, Boas (1995), 'Social distance and charisma. Theoretical notes and explanatory study', *Leadership Quarterly*, **6** (1), 19–48.

Shamir, Boas (2007), 'From passive recipients to active co-producers: Followers' role in the leadership process', in B. Shamir, R. Pillai, M.C. Bligh and M. Uhl-Bien (eds), *Follower-Centered Perspectives on Leadership*, Greenwich, CT: Information Publishing, pp. ix–xxxix.

Shamir, Boas and Galit Eilam (2005), '"What's your story?" A life-stories approach to authentic leadership development', *The Leadership Quarterly*, **16** (3), 395–417.

Shamir, Boas, Michael B. Arthur and Robert J. House (1994), 'The rhetoric of charismatic leadership: A theoretical extension, a case study and implications for research', *Leadership Quarterly*, **5** (1), 25.

Shamir, Boas, Hava Dayan-Horesh and Dalia Adler (2005), 'Leading by biography: Towards a life-story approach to the study of leadership', *Leadership*, **1** (1), 13–29.

Shamir, Boas, Robert J. House and Michael B. Arthur (1993), 'The motivational effects of charismatic leadership: A self-concept-based theory', *Organizational Science*, **4** (4), 577–93.

Shamir, Boas, Rajnandini Pillai, Michelle C. Bligh and Mary Uhl-Bien (2007), *Follower-Centered Perspectives on Leadership*, Greenwich, CT: Information Publishing.

Shapira, Anita (1997a), *Yehudim Hadashim, Yehudim Yeshanim [New Jews, Old Jews]*, Tel Aviv: Sifriat Ofakim and Am Oved [Hebrew].

Shapira, Anita (1997b), 'Historiography and memory: The case of Latrun in 1948', in *Yehudim Hadashim, Yehudim Yeshanim [New Jews, Old Jews]*, Tel Aviv: Sifriat Ofakim and Am Oved, pp. 46–87 [Hebrew].

Shapira, Anita (1997c), 'The mysteries of biography', in *Yehudim Hadashim, Yehudim Yeshanim [New Jews, Old Jews]*, Tel Aviv: Sifriat Ofakim and Am Oved [Hebrew].

Shapira, Anita (1997d), 'Hamitus shel hayehudi hehadash' (The myth of the new Jew), in *Yehudim Hadashim, Yehudim Yeshanim (New Jews, Old Jews)*, pp. 155–74.

Sher, Moran (2008), 'Keshe'orot habama nidlakim (When the stage lights go on): On leadership and acting', MA thesis submitted to University of Haifa, Department of Psychology [Hebrew].

Shils, Edward (1975), 'Ritual and crisis', in *Center and Periphery: Essays in Macrosociology*, Chicago: University of Chicago Press.

Shils, Edward A. and Morris Janowitz (1948), 'Cohesion and disintegration in the Wermacht in World War II', *Public Opinion Quarterly*, **12** (2), 280–315.

Skinner, Frederic (1974), *About Behaviorism*, New York: Vintage.

Sklar, Kathryn K. (1988), 'Organized womanhood: Archival sources on women and progressive reform', *Journal of American History*, **75** (1), 176–83.

Smith, Jeffrey A. and Roseanne J. Foti (1998), 'A pattern approach to the study of leader emergence', *Leadership Quarterly*, **9** (2), 147–60.

Spencer, Herbert (1876), *Principles of Sociology*, New York: Appleton.

Spiro, Melford E. (1954), 'Is the family universal?', *American Anthropologist*, **56** (5), 839–46.

Spiro, Melford E. (1956), *Kibbutz: Venture in Utopia*, Cambridge, MA: Harvard University Press.

Stalker, S. (7 February 1909), 'Tolstoy holds Lincoln world's greatest hero', New York: *The World*.

Storr, Anthony (1972), *The Dynamics of Creation*, London: Secker and Warburg.

Stryker, Sheldon (1980), *Symbolic Interactionism: A Social Structural Version*, Menlo Park, CA: Benjamin Cummings.

Tajfel, H. and J.C. Turner (1979), 'An integrative theory of inter-group conflict', in W.G. Austin and S. Worchel (eds), *The Social Psychology of Intergroup Relations*, Monterey, CA: Brooks/Cole, pp. 33–47.

Tarde, Gabriel (1903), *The Laws of Imitation*, New York: Henry Holt and Co.

Terman, Lewis Madison ([1904] 1974), 'A preliminary study of the psychology of leadership', in Ralph M. Stogdill, *Handbook of Leadership Research: A Survey of Theory and Research*, Riverside, NJ: Free Press.

Tollgerdt-Andersson, Ingrid (1996), 'Attitudes, values and demands on leadership. A cultural comparison among some European countries', in P. Joynt and M. Warner (eds), *Managing Across Cultures: Issues and Perspectives*, London: Thomson, pp. 166–78.

Triandis, Harry C. (1973), 'Culture, training, cognitive complexity and interpersonal attitudes', in D.S. Hoopes (ed.), *Readings in Intercultural Communication*, Pittsburgh, PA: Regional Council for International Education, pp. 55–68.

Tuchman, Barbara (1984), *The March of Folly: From Troy to Vietnam*, New York: Knopf.

Vardi, Yoav, Yoash Wiener and Micha Popper (1989), 'The value content of organizational mission as a factor of the commitment of members', *Psychological Reports*, **65** (1), 27–38.

Volkan, Vamik (1980), 'Narcissistic personality organization and "reparative" leadership', *International Journal of Group Psychotherapy*, **30** (2), 131–52.

Volkan, Vamik D. (2004), *Blind Trust: Large Groups and Their Leaders in Times of Crisis and Terror*, Charlottesville, VA: Pitchstone Publications.

Volkan, Vamik D. and Norman Itzkowitz (1984), *The Immortal Ataturk – A Psychobiography*, Chicago: University of Chicago Press.

Volkan, Vamik, Gabriele Ast and William Greer (2002), *The Third Reich in the*

Unconscious: Transgenerational Transmission and its Consequences, New York: Brunner-Routledge.

Washington, George (17 September 1796), *Farewell Address*.

Weber, Max ([1924] 1947), *The Theory of Social and Economic Organization* [trans. Talcott Parsons], New York: Free Press.

Weber, Max (1946), *From Max Weber: Essays in Sociology*, in H. Gerth and C. Wright Mills (eds), New York: Oxford University Press.

Weick, Karl E. (1969), *The Social Psychology of Organizing*, New York: McGraw-Hill.

Weick, Karl E. (1995), *Sensemaking in Organizations*, Thousand Oaks, CA: Sage Publications.

Westlake, Martin (ed.) (2000), *Leaders of Transition*, London: Macmillan Press.

Willner, Ann R. (1984), *The Spellbinders: Charismatic Political Leadership*, New Haven, CT: Yale University Press.

Wilson, Edward O. (1978), *On Human Nature*, Cambridge, MA: Harvard University Press.

Wilson, Woodrow (1917), *Compilation of the Messages and Papers of Presidents*, 20 vols, prepared under the direction of the Joint Committee of Printing of the House and Senate, New York: Bureau of National Literature, **17**, 7868–70.

Yalom, Irvin D. (1980), *Existential Psychotherapy*, New York: Basic Books.

Zakay, Eliav and Amir Scheinfeld (1993), *Mifakdei Gidudim Mitztayanim Bitzahal* [*Outstanding Battalion Commanders in the IDF*), Research Report, School of Leadership Development, Israel Defense Forces (IDF) [Hebrew].

Zerubavel, Yael (1995), *Recovered Roots*, Chicago: University of Chicago Press.

Zimbardo, Philip (2007), *The Lucifer Effect: Understanding How Good People Turn Evil*, New York: Random House.

Index